William Henry Beckett

The English Reformation of the Sixteenth Century

William Henry Beckett

The English Reformation of the Sixteenth Century

ISBN/EAN: 9783744704496

Printed in Europe, USA, Canada, Australia, Japan

Cover: Foto ©Lupo / pixelio.de

More available books at **www.hansebooks.com**

ARCHBISHOP CRANMER.
(From the portrait at Lambeth Palace.)

The Church History Series
VII

THE ENGLISH REFORMATION

OF THE SIXTEENTH CENTURY

WITH CHAPTERS ON MONASTIC ENGLAND, AND THE
WYCLIFFITE REFORMATION

*Illustrated by Maps, showing where the principal English Monastic
Institutions were situated, over what districts Lollardy spread, and
where the Martyrs were burnt in the persecution under Mary
Tudor; and also by portraits of Cranmer, Wycliffe,
Erasmus, Wolsey, Tindale, More, Latimer,
Coverdale and Mary Tudor.*

BY

W. H. BECKETT

London
THE RELIGIOUS TRACT SOCIETY
56, PATERNOSTER ROW; 65, ST. PAUL'S CHURCHYARD
AND 164, PICCADILLY
1890

'The Reformation was not the work either of a year or of a generation. The foundation was laid both in the good and in the evil qualities of our nature. Love of truth, reverence for sacred things, a sense of personal responsibility, a desire for the possession of full spiritual privileges co-operated with the pride of human reason, the natural impatience of restraint, and the envy and hatred inspired among the nobles by a rich and powerful hierarchy, to make the world weary of the papal domination, and desirous of reform in things spiritual and ecclesiastical.'—BISHOP HAROLD BROWNE.

INTRODUCTION.

When on the 29th day of April, in the year 1509, the young Prince Henry Tudor, at the age of eighteen, succeeded to the throne left vacant by the death of his father, Henry VII., the country of which he became monarch was already in a transition state. 'Old things were passing away, and the faith and the life of ten centuries were dissolving like a dream. Chivalry was dying, the abbey and the castle were soon together to crumble into ruins, and all the forms, desires, beliefs, convictions of the old world were passing away, never to return.' Had Henry VIII. never reigned, there would have been a history of religious reform in England. The notorious divorce question did but confirm and hasten tendencies which were already at work. A long series of historical facts exercised an obvious influence in producing the critical events which took place in the reign of Henry VIII. Spiritual, intellectual, political forces were at work, of which the Reformation was the resultant.

For full a hundred and fifty years before the great changes of the sixteenth century, Wycliffe's teaching and that of his followers was influencing the hearts of men. Humble Lollards, who laboured they knew not for what, save to accomplish the necessities of their spiritual life, in spite of persecution, spread their opinions far and wide, awakening in the hearts of thousands who never joined their fellowship desire to see the creed of the Church made simpler and more in harmony with the Bible. To this influence, and in no small degree, was due the widespread sympathy that welcomed Tindale's Testament, and the rapid succession of translations of the Scripture that followed its publication.

Wholly distinct from spiritual aims and religious thought was the rise and development of the intellectual movement known as the Renaissance; yet its influence was great in aiding the onward course of the Reformation. A keen spirit of inquiry, excited by the invention of printing, the discovery of the then 'new world' of America, and the general revival of art and classical learning, had grown up, which fearlessly criticised what had hitherto been taken on trust. Influenced by the revival of learning, Colet, founder of St. Paul's School, Wolsey in his foundation of Cardinal College, More and Erasmus by their writings, aimed at reformation by plans for the education of both clergy and laity.

In matters moral and religious this spirit of inquiry was further intensified by the conduct of the Church in its undisguised worldliness, by its opposition to the circulation of the Scripture it professed to honour, and by its harassing persecution of the Lollard followers of Wycliffe. There was a revival of spiritual aspirations in the hearts of men, a growing conviction that religion was wider than 'the Church' as then known, and an increasing consciousness that the needs of the spiritual life of man were not to be met in the observances and ceremonies which the Church demanded. From German Protestantism more than the English Reformers came the spiritual teaching that helped to bring deliverance to England. In the brave, true, outspoken utterances of Martin Luther many of our nation found spiritual enlightenment and liberty.

Others there were—indeed, the vast majority of Englishmen—who felt that the supremacy claimed by the Bishop of Rome in all the ecclesiastical affairs of the English nation was injurious to the interests of the State. Again and again had such claims been resisted, and the question raised, Who should rule, the king or the pope? In the interests of national freedom the answer was given; and in both spiritual and national strength England has grown stronger and greater by the answer she gave.

Such were the forces, the history of which we purpose to sketch, that prepared the way for the long and intricate struggle which occupied the reign of Henry and his three successors, and which are far from spent even now. The impulse of the English Reformation came from within, and not from without. It came from the people, especially from those who dwelt in the cities and towns of the midland and eastern counties. All the Acts of Parliament passed to promote reform would have been of no avail had not a large number of the people seen how great was the need. Rightly thought of, the Reformation will be regarded as a process, and as one not yet exhausted, rather than an event to be assigned to any special date in the calendar. Long before the years of Henry VIII. there were Reformers, poets, and statesmen, philosophers and theologians, as brave indeed and as noble in life as any to whom the title is popularly ascribed. And since the eventful century that began with the reign of Henry and ended with that of Elizabeth there have been raised up those who have been true reformers in the onward movement of religious life and work in England.

The supply of material for a history of the English Reformation, both in contemporary sources and subsequent, is super-abounding on many points, and disappointingly deficient on others. In an Appendix will be found a list of authorities, which it is believed is fairly representative of the diverse views of the complex events passed under review in the following pages, and which may be useful to readers seeking further information. To illustrate the position of the principal abbeys, priories, and other monastic institutions existing at the time of the dissolution of the monasteries, the map on pages xiv and xv has been specially prepared, showing their situation and the various orders to which they belonged. The intimate connection between Lollardy and the spiritual awakening of the sixteenth century, a continuity ignored by some authorities and denied by others, is exhibited in the maps on pages 97, 258, and 259, which, so far as the writer is aware, are the first of their kind, showing that the area of country in which Lollardy prevailed was that in which the Marian persecutions were fiercest.

Respect for facts, whether in regard to the Protestant martyrs of Mary's reign or the Romanist martyrs of her successor, has been the aim in the endeavour to summarize the causes and the events of the great Ecclesiastical Revolution of the English nation.

CONTENTS.

	PAGE
INTRODUCTION	V

PART I.—MONASTIC ENGLAND.

CHAPTER
I.—DESTRUCTION OF MONASTERIES 3
II.—ATTEMPTS AT REFORMATION 8
III.—ADVANCE IN MONASTIC REFORM 17
IV.—THE INSTITUTION OF THE FRIARS, A FURTHER ADVANCE IN REFORM 21
V.—BISHOPS AND PAROCHIAL CLERGY 31

PART II.—THE WYCLIFFIAN REFORMATION.

VI.—THE SPIRITUAL AWAKENING 43
VII.—THE GREAT PLAGUE AND ITS CONSEQUENCES . . 47
VIII.—THE ENGLAND OF WYCLIFFE'S DAYS . . . 52
IX.—JOHN WYCLIFFE 62
X.—THE EARLY FOLLOWERS OF WYCLIFFE, OR LOLLARDS . 78
XI.—LOLLARD LITERATURE 87
XII.—THE LATER LOLLARDS 93

PART III.—THE GREAT REFORMATION OF THE SIXTEENTH CENTURY.

XIII.—OXFORD REFORMERS 101
XIV.—COTEMPORARIES AT CAMBRIDGE 119
XV.—THE REFORMATION PARLIAMENT AND CONVOCATION, 1529-1536 136
XVI.—REFORM OF DOCTRINE 148
XVII.—EARLY REFORMATION LITERATURE 157
XVIII.—THE PROTECTORATE, 1547-1553 177
XIX.—REFORMATION LITURGIES AND MANUALS OF SPIRITUAL INSTRUCTION, 1534-1553 195
XX.—REFORMATION PREACHERS 207

CONTENTS.

CHAPTER	PAGE
XXI.—The Dark Days of Mary	217
XXII.—The Triumph of Spanish Policy, 1555-1558	231
XXIII.—The Elizabethan Compromise	263
XXIV.—Doctrines of the English Reformation	284
XXV.—'The Romanist Martyrs'	291
Chronological Summary	296

APPENDIX I.

List of Abbeys, Priories, and Friaries of England . . 300

APPENDIX II.

Dates Relative to the Translations and Use of the Bible in England 304

APPENDIX III.

Reformation Formularies of Faith 305

APPENDIX IV.

Works for Reference on the History of Religious Reform in England 306

Index 309

LIST OF ILLUSTRATIONS.

	PAGE
ARCHBISHOP CRANMER.	*Frontispiece*
JOHN WYCLIFFE	63
ERASMUS	105
SIR THOMAS MORE	112
CARDINAL WOLSEY	115
WILLIAM TINDALE	123
HUGH LATIMER	128
MILES COVERDALE	160
EDWARD THE SIXTH	176
MARY TUDOR	216

MAPS.

MAP OF MONASTIC ENGLAND	xiv, xv
MAP OF ENGLAND, SHOWING THE COUNTIES OVER WHICH THE INFLUENCE OF LOLLARDRY EXTENDED	97
MAP OF THE DIOCESES OF ENGLAND AND WALES IN THE TIME OF MARY TUDOR, SHOWING THE AREA OF THE PERSECUTIONS, THE PLACES WHERE MARTYRS SUFFERED, AND THE NUMBER OF SUFFERERS	258, 259

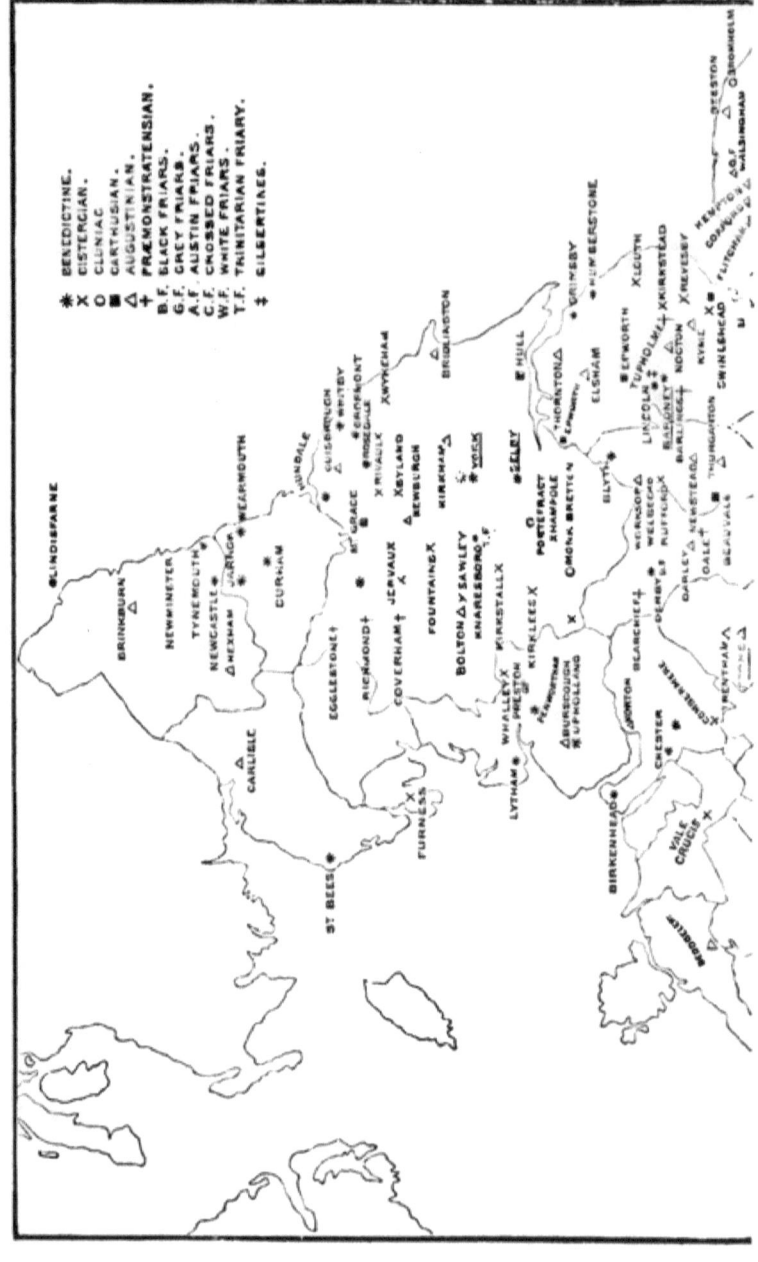

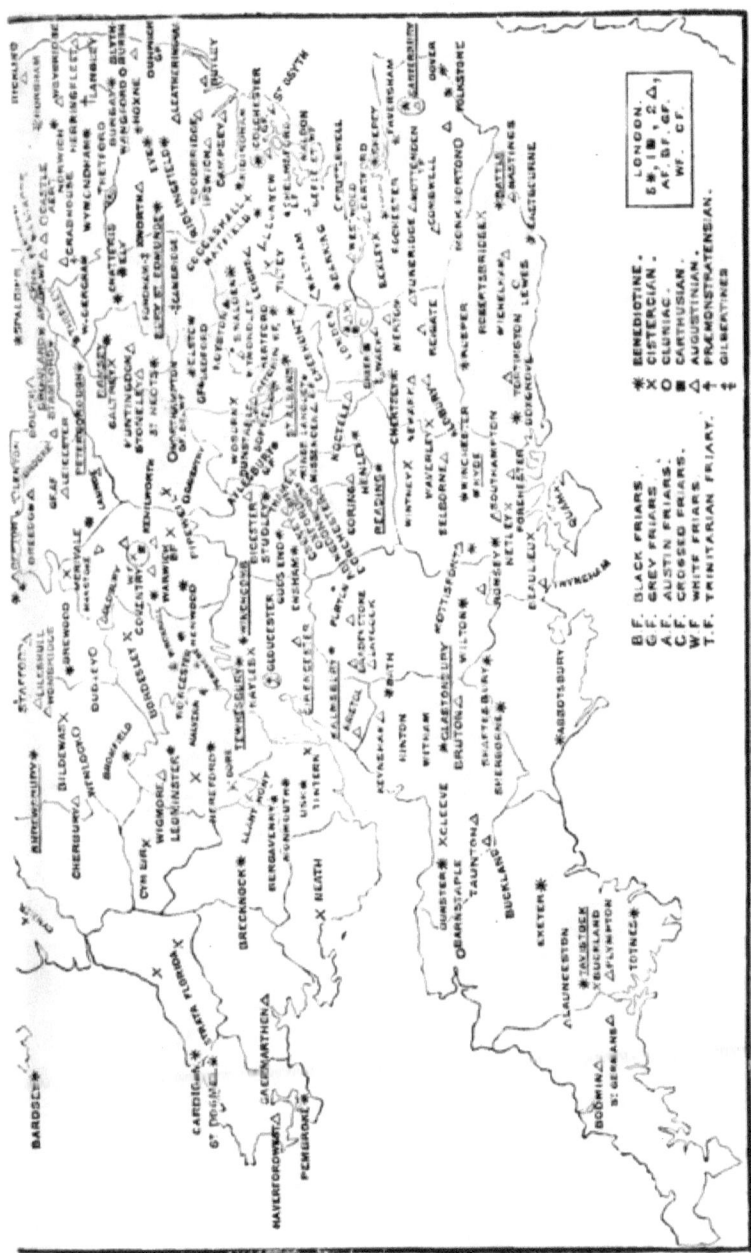

MAP OF MONASTIC ENGLAND.

Showing the principal Abbeys, Priories, Nunneries, and Friaries. Names underlined were Mitred Abbeys, their abbots having seats in Parliament.

Part I.
MONASTIC ENGLAND.

PART I.

MONASTIC ENGLAND.

CHAPTER I.

DESTRUCTION OF MONASTERIES.

When we look upon the grey, weather-beaten ruins of Fountains, or Bolton, or Tynemouth, or Tintern, or Glastonbury, conflicting thoughts possess the mind, as we think of the times in which such glorious edifices were reared and of the circumstances of their final and complete overthrow. There is the sense of regret and loss at the wholesale destruction of the treasures of art and works of mediæval piety, and of valuable libraries, not scattered, but ruthlessly destroyed. Our surprise is there was not a general outcry throughout the kingdom. We think of the princely hospitality shown by the monasteries and the abundant alms reported to have been distributed; yet in many counties hardly a murmur was heard. How is it that feelings so familiar and natural to us were then so completely overruled? We find the answer in concurrent causes.

1. The lack in those days of what is an unprecedented characteristic of these—the love of what is old, beautiful, and venerable. Historical or antiquarian tenderness is 'God's compensation to the world for its advancing years.' *Causes of their destruction.*

2. The animosity existing between the monks and clergy. Bishops and parochial clergy were not likely to plead the cause of the monks, at whose hands they had suffered much, and whose constant ambition had been to exempt themselves from episcopal jurisdiction and to appropriate parochial benefices.

3. The rapacity of the nobles and gentry, eager to

enlarge their estates by purchasing at easy prices lands which their forefathers had granted away. Rising statesmen and flattering courtiers also approved and received a share in the scramble. Most of our nobility who date their honours from Tudor times are indebted to the plunder of the abbeys for their rich estates.

4. Above all was the general conviction on the part of the nation that the mission of monasticism was fulfilled. There is no resisting the evidence that the monastic system worked its own ruin in abuses and enormities that occasioned an overwhelming necessity for its suppression. The violence and injustice with which the overthrow was accomplished are as characteristic of the roughness of the times as they are of the prejudices of the times against everything monkish. In proportion as the dangers and necessities of the Reformation struggle are realized, much of the regret now so often expressed concerning the dismantled monasteries is changed into gratitude for the religious and national freedom then secured to our country. What John Knox is accredited with having said of the ruined monasteries of Scotland might be said of those of England—that the best way to keep the rooks from returning was to pull down their nests. Mr. Froude well observes, 'Never were any institutions brought to a more deserved judgment than the monastic orders of England.'

The evil end of monasticism in England need not, ought not, to make us unmindful of the earlier influence of monastic communities upon English civilization. In seeking their own interests the monks advanced the interests of society in general. The monkish ecclesiastics were patrons of architecture. We owe to them some of the most exquisite and graceful architectural forms which combined taste and skill ever achieved. Few are the parishes in our country which have not some expression of monastic thought and munificence in fragments of stately buildings, in abbey, church, or minster. In the early days, monks by their own labour changed sterile wastes into fertile and productive lands. To the last the abbey lands were the best cultivated in England, and furnished an example of good husbandry which imparted a stimulus to the agricultural interests of the country.

The good work of the monks in the past.

Monks were the chroniclers of their times, to whose often graphic representations of passing life the historians of succeeding generations are so greatly indebted. Among such chroniclers were the patient, good-humoured William of Malmesbury, the pedantic Matthew of Paris, a monk of St. Albans, and another monk of the same abbey—the ill-tempered Thomas of Walsingham, who repaid Wycliffe's estimate of the monks by calling him 'an angel of darkness.' The service of the later monks to literature is often greatly exaggerated. Here and there amongst them may have been an abbot or prior of scholarly tastes and aspirations, but least of all among the 'lovers of the cloisters' was the revival of letters welcomed. For some time before their overthrow no name of eminence in service either to Church or State had appeared amongst them. Constantly we hear of monasterial munificence. Open house was kept for all travellers, with accommodation and provision according to their degree in rank. The charity of the monks to the poor was often liberal to prodigality, but in its indiscriminate character was the occasion of increasing mendicancy with its train of vices; it was a charity which fed the clamorous with no thought of their improvement as fellow beings. The popular supposition that no 'Poor Law' was required prior to the suppression of monasteries is contrary to historic fact. The problem of social pauperism had long been a State question of great difficulty.

For many generations before the Reformation the mission of monasticism had been fulfilled. The monasteries had practically ceased to be the abodes of God-fearing, evil-shunning men, bound by vows of celibacy, poverty, and obedience. *Deterioration of monastic life.* The inmates of the monasteries had become a great religious aristocracy, which at last had little or nothing in common with the people. Dr. Jessopp, in his *Coming of the Friars*, thus disposes of the popular idea that the mission of the monks was one of ministry to others: 'The idea of men and women, weary of the hard struggle with sin and fleeing from the wrath to come, joining together to give themselves up to the higher life, out of the reach of temptation and safe from the witcheries of mammon, was a grand idea, and not unfrequently it had been carried out grandly. But the monk was nothing and did nothing for the townsman: he fled away to his solitude; the rapture of silent adoration was his joy and exceeding great reward; his nights and days might be spent in prayer and praise, sometimes in study and research, sometimes in battling with the powers of darkness and ignorance, sometimes in throwing himself heart and soul into art, which it was easy to persuade himself he was doing only for the glory of God: but all this must go on far away from the busy haunts of men, certainly not within earshot of the multitude. Moreover, the monk was by birth, education, and sympathy one with the upper classes. What were the rabble to him? In return, the rich burgher hated him cordially, as a supercilious aristocrat and pharisee, with the guile and greed of the scribe and lawyer superadded.'[1]

If in our contemplation of the ruins of an ancient monastery our thoughts go back to the twelfth century, *Founding monasteries a fashion of the twelfth century.* it is to a time when the country was becoming rapidly studded with monasteries, priories, and other religious houses. Founding monasteries, endowing them with the property of parochial benefices, was as much the fashion then as founding grammar schools was in the sixteenth century. In the twelfth century the busy sound of axe and hammer was heard in many of the waste places of England. Multitudes of men dressed in doublet and hose, as masons, carpenters, and press-gangs of labourers, were toiling in raising the vast piles of buildings which make up a religious house—cloisters, dormitories, chapels, hospitals, granaries, barns, storehouses. We gain some faint idea of the amazing stir and industry which the erection of monasterial buildings implied by following, in our modern farms and pasture lands, the traces which even now may be seen of their possessions three hundred years ago. It was the time when the architects of the great Yorkshire abbeys, of the magnificent choir of Canterbury, and of some of the noble spires and towers of the ecclesiastical buildings of our land, were carrying forward buildings which for excellence of construction and beauty of design have never been surpassed. Mon-

---

[1] Page 7.

astic houses in considerable number existed before the Norman Conquest, but during the three hundred years between that epoch and the end of Edward III.'s long reign about twelve hundred of these institutions were founded. One hundred and fifteen were built during the nineteen troubled years of Stephen's reign, and to these were added a hundred and thirteen during the reign of Henry II.

Yet it must not be forgotten that at the same time these noble buildings, 'palaces of stone,' were being reared all below the class of barons, merchants, and traders were living in wattled cottages of but one storey, and with smoke-holes instead of chimneys,—hovels of such a kind that Henry II. could order that the houses of heretics should be carried outside the town and burned. To those 'who delved, and ditched, and dunged the earth, ate bread of corn and bran, worts fleshless'—*i.e.* vegetables, but no meat—the times were about as hard as they well could be. The statute book declared that he *or she* who laboured at the plough or other service of husbandry till they were twelve years old should not be permitted ever to leave that labour for another kind. They were serfs, bound to the estate upon which they were born, and regarded as much a part of it as the cattle of the field.

Condition of the peasantry.

CHAPTER II.

ATTEMPTS AT REFORMATION.

THE history of monasticism in this country is that of successive attempts at reform and of successive failure. Attractive to the imagination as a life of self-denial in retirement from the world for the culture of the spiritual life is to many, the experience of centuries has shown it to be an illusion. Service in the world, not selfish seclusion from its needs, sorrows, temptations, and business, is the true doctrine of the cross of Christ. The unsocial religion of monasticism, contrary to nature, contrary to the highest ideal of Christian perfection as seen in the life of Christ, was constantly breaking down. Great reformers arose, sincere and earnest, who, oppressed with sorrow at the sense of failure in the monastic system, devised fresh methods to correct and prevent the corruptions which excited their indignation and provoked the scorn of the world. In the four great monasterial orders we see the expression of such reforms. Gradually there dawned upon the minds of thoughtful observers the mistake of the system in its seclusion and isolation. In the institution of the order of Canons, of the religious military orders, and yet more conspicuously in the institution of the orders of the Friars, we see a further effort of reformation, in the recognition of active usefulness as a necessary sign of religious life.

Of the monasterial orders in the country, the Benedictines, founded by the renowned Benedict of Nursia in the fifth century, is alike the oldest and most prominent. To them we owe the revival of whatever remained of the ancient British Church that had passed through the fiery trial of the Diocletian persecution; for Augustine of Canterbury, with his forty companions, sent by the famous Pope Gregory, were Benedictine monks. The monasteries of Glastonbury and Abingdon, of Ely and Peterborough, of Crowland and St. Edmundsbury—in fact, all the English

The Benedictine.

monasteries prior to the time of the Norman Conquest—
were under the famous Benedictine rule, revised and
adapted to English life by Dunstan, the versatile and
energetic Archbishop of Canterbury, and real master of
the realm in the days of Eadmund. Characteristically
he gives prominence to bell-ringing in his rule. Benedict himself was a reformer of a degenerate system of
monasticism, based upon the merely meditative seclusion
of Eastern monachism. The rule which he instituted is set forth in an elaborate code of seventy-four chapters. The distinguishing feature of his system is that to the foundation rules of all monastic life, poverty, celibacy, obedience, he added WORK. At a time when, in a degree scarcely possible to realize in these days, toil of all kinds was regarded as the lot only of slaves and serfs, Benedict prescribed manual labour as part of a monk's duty. 'Idleness,' wrote the great monastic legislator of Western monachism, 'is an enemy of the soul.' *Orare est laborare* was the motto of the Benedictine order. Even the elderly and the sickly were to employ such time as their state permitted in copying the writings of the Fathers—the Scriptures, etc. All the work needful for the management of the monastery and for the wants of the brethren was to be taken in turn by the monks. The literary labour that subsequently became intimately associated with Benedictine editions of great books, the work of laborious scribes and editors, certainly was not contemplated by the founder of the order. The natural force of circumstances, however, made the monasteries the rallying-point of men of learning and studious habit. Obedience was another prominent feature of the Benedictine rule. Its law was absolute, but was tempered by the necessity on the part of 'the abbot to call the entire body of the brethren together to deliberate on any weighty matter, and not to decide it till he had heard the counsel of the very youngest.' Equality was recognised: no distinction of worldly rank or station was to be considered amongst the inmates of the monastery. Their food was limited to two meals a day, and always during meals there was reading aloud, when no conversation was permitted; communications for any-

Sidenotes: Benedict's 'rule.' Its characteristics. 1. Labour. 2. Obedience. Manner of life and dress of the Benedictines.

thing needed had to be made by signs. At first, the Benedictine monks had no distinctive dress; with the characteristic liberality of this founder's rule it was left to be determined according to climate and locality. In England their gown or cassock was black, with a cowl or hood of the same colour. Hence they became known as the Black Monks. The Benedictine rule allowed parents to dedicate young children to a monastic life—the parents at the same time giving a promise never to endow them with any property, though they might give to the monastery if they pleased. Such children were instructed in reading, writing, and religious learning, and especially in psalmody and music. The presence of this young life must have brought a gleam of joyousness, and at the same time a sort of homeliness, to some of the dwellers in monastic seclusion. Among the names of eminence connected with this order and prominent in the religious history of our own country are those of the illustrious Lanfranc, the trusted friend and counsellor of the Norman Conqueror, and the zealous representative of his Church and clergy; and of Anselm, his successor—one holy in life, profound as a theologian, great as a worker and teacher. Lanfranc himself was a reformer of monastic observance, and on account of the laxity of discipline and general morality which he found in England, revised and adapted the Benedictine rule especially for his own monks, an adaptation afterwards adopted in all the great Benedictine abbeys in England.

Children in the monastery.

Eminent Benedictines.

Where there is no single recognised authority, discipline cannot be effectively maintained. Though the Benedictine monks vowed obedience to the rule, there was no general executive to enforce submission. Each monastery was an independent institution under its own abbot. This independence was not found to work well. In many of the monasteries the restrictions were disregarded: monks abandoned their profession, or did worse—lived in riotousness and profligacy. Reform was again wanted, and it was not long before a reformer arose. In the celebrated abbey of Clugny, in Burgundy, was one who saw the evil, and proposed a remedy. Berno, its abbot, not only insisted on a vigorous

The Cluniac.

observance of the Benedictine rule by the monks under him, but likewise introduced stricter regulations as regards fasting and silence. Looked up to as a reformer and leader, he required every monastery following the Cluniac rule to be subject to the abbot of Clugny, and to receive its prior from his appointment. Such subordination tended to greater regularity of discipline, but eventually occasioned political suspicions that in the reign of Henry V. led to the suppression of all alien priories. The first and only monastery of the Cluniac order in England for nearly a hundred and fifty years was the stately priory at Lewes, in Sussex, founded by Gundrada, a step-daughter of William the Conqueror, and her husband, the Earl of Warren. William of Malmesbury says of it, 'None excelled it in the piety of its monks, in its hospitality to strangers, and in charity towards all.' The dress of the Cluniacs was the same as that worn by the Benedictines. They spent much of their time in meditation, and a great strictness was observed among them with regard to silence: to speak before prime (6 a.m.) was deemed a very serious offence; signs instead of words were their means of communication. In the *History of the Diocese of Chichester*, the Rev. W. R. W. Stephens refers to an official connected with the priory of Lewes called the 'circuitor,' whose duty was to perambulate the monastery 'in so religious and stately a manner as to inspire terror into the beholders.' During the services held at night in the dimly lighted church, when much light was not supposed to be required by those who could recite by heart the different offices, the circuitor was 'to go round the choir with a lanthorn in his hand, and if he detected any brother dozing, he was to hold the lanthorn so as to shine full in his face, and startle him from his nap; whereupon the offender had to beg pardon upon his knees, and then to take the lanthorn and continue the search himself for other offenders.' The Cluniacs, though a popular order abroad, were never numerous in this country; 'the alien priories' —priories affiliated to religious houses abroad—were always regarded with suspicion, and again and again suppressed.

Berno's attempt to reform.

Lewes Priory.

The circuitor.

Straitest of all the monastic sects known in England

was that of the Carthusians, so called from Chatreuse, a mountainous solitude near Grenoble, where, in 1084, was founded by Bruno the far-famed monastery of La Grande Chartreuse, still standing. Absolute solitude, and silence, and self-mortification were the rule of this order, copying and gardening the only occupation allowed. The Carthusians were the only order of Western monks who literally dwelt in cells. These cells were in reality tiny three-roomed cottages, containing what we may call a sitting-room, in which in the stern twelfth century the cloistered inmate was not allowed, even in winter, the luxury of a fire; a sleeping room, provided with a bed—

The Carthusian.

Carthusian cells.

> 'That wooden bed,
> Which shall their coffin be when dead,'—

a table, a bench, and a book-shelf; a third apartment was a stowaway place for anything to be put out of the way. One meal a day was all allowed; that the inmate received through a grating in the door, so contrived that neither he nor the person that handed in what was required could see each other. Meat was never a part of the fare; on Fridays and during Lent only bread, water, and salt were allowed. To each cell was attached a small garden, surrounded by high walls that could only be overlooked by the abbot. The only occasions on which the monks met were in the church services and on certain great festivals in the refectory. Add to these conditions of life that of a horsehair shirt worn next the skin, and need it be said that an order so austere in its regulations was never popular in England? No nunnery of this order was ever founded in this country, and only nine monasteries. Two of these were in Yorkshire, of which the ruins of one—Mount Grace Priory, near Northallerton—still remain, and in which the peculiar arrangement of the cells can be seen. The first was founded at Witham, in Somersetshire, in the reign of Henry II., and had for its prior the holy Hugo, afterwards Bishop of Lincoln, who never flattered, and often reproved, yet was always loved and trusted by the king whom Thomas of Canterbury could only defy. The most celebrated house of the Carthusian

Carthusian austerity.

order in England was the Chartreuse, in London, the site and name of which are still preserved in the familiar Charterhouse.

To the great orders of the Benedictines and the Cluniacs were added at the close of the eleventh century the Cistercians. The founder of this famous order was an Englishman, Stephen Harding, brought up from early childhood in the Benedictine monastery of Sherborne, and who afterwards became head of the monastery at Citeaux. In a time when pomp and luxury prevailed, and the vows of monkish life were openly transgressed, Stephen was the leader of a reformation in monastic life that effected a considerable change both on the Continent and in England. The early Cistercians were the Quakers of their day. In contrast with the costly apparel of Benedictine monks, who appeared in garments richly trimmed with fur, or in gay clothing of scarlet or green, the Cistercians' habit was of the coarsest kind, consisting principally of white canvas. Under the exercise of the dispensations granted by abbots according to their discretion, Benedictines and Cluniacs had so degenerated that not only did they eat meat every day in the week except Friday, but they ransacked earth and air for highly-flavoured dainties. Their huntsmen brought them venison and wild boars; their falconers the choicest birds. Peter the Venerable, the abbot of the famous monastery of Cluny, speaks of the monks 'whose cloister was the whole world, whose god was their belly.' Degenerate monks divided their meals into two kinds: those allowed by the rule of their order, and those which went beyond. By eating the prescribed fare, they lived according to the letter of their rule, and all that was taken beside, especially as it was never blessed, was considered of no account, or as benevolently allowed in consideration of certain benefactions, to be laid out in relaxations for the monks on certain days. The Cistercians, in protest against such evasions, returned to the frugal fare prescribed by Benedict, and limited themselves during a great part of the year to one meal a day. At a time when the popular teaching was that nothing could be too rich or costly for Divine service the Cistercians were advocates of studied plainness. In their buildings and in their worship there was a Quaker-like

Cistercian.

Cistercians the Quakers of their day.

simplicity, compared with the splendour of the services of other monastic churches, where the altars gleamed with gold and gems, and ecclesiastics in splendid vestments ministered. The English monk forbad 'in the house of God . . . anything should be found which savoured of pride or excess.' All elaborate ornament was proscribed. The windows were to be plain, stained glass being forbidden. No pictures, or images, or jewelled crosses were allowed. The crosses were of wood, the candlesticks of iron. The vestments were of plain linen. Even in chanting the most rigid simplicity of style was to be observed. In their buildings only one tower, a central one, was permitted, and that was to be very low. Unnecessary pinnacles and turrets were prohibited. The spirit of rigid self-denial manifested itself in the choice of the sites of their monasteries. 'The more dismal, the more savage, the more hopeless a spot appeared, the more did it please this rigid order.'

To this order belonged the great St. Bernard of Clairvaux, whose marvellous eloquence kindled the enthusiasm for the second great crusade, and whose warm, passionate devotion still moves the hearts of thousands in the hymns, 'Jesus, the very thought of Thee,' 'Jesus, Thou joy of loving hearts,' 'O Jesus, King most wonderful!' portions of the poem, 'Jesus, dulcis memoria,' generally ascribed to St. Bernard as 'the father of mediæval hymnody.' From the connection of St. Bernard with the Cistercians they have sometimes been called Bernardine monks.

St. Bernard of Clairvaux.

In England, Waverley Abbey, in Surrey, the name of which Sir Walter Scott has made familiar to every reader of English literature, was the first foundation (A.D. 1128) of the Cistercian order. Three years later Tintern Abbey was founded. Other stately buildings followed in rapid succession. The magnificent ruins of Furness Abbey, and of the equally renowned Fountains Abbey, and, if less beautiful, yet more perfect in preservation, of Kirkstall, situated within sight and sound of busy Leeds, show the skill in architecture, as well as the great wealth, to which the order of the Cistercians soon attained. All their monasteries were arranged after the same plan, with only such variations as the circumstances of locality

Cistercian abbeys.

necessitated, and all were dedicated to the Virgin Mary.

The hard-working and self-denying Cistercians were familiarly known as White Monks, because their dress was a long coat, or cassock, over which they wore a black cloak when they went outside their monastery. Away from the common haunts of men, in wild and barren districts of country and in lonely valleys, they toiled, and under their guidance and direction scenes of barrenness were changed into those of beauty. They loved Nature rather than books, and their triumphs were over rocks and woods rather than in scholastic disputations. No names of eminence as scholars are connected with their famous abbeys, but the adjacent lands afford plain proofs of the immense work done in the patient building of hedges, embanking rivers, draining swamps, and making roads. Something akin to the spirit of the most renowned of their order, the Nature-loving St. Bernard, is seen in their work, for he had said : 'Believe me, you will find more lessons in woods than in books. Trees and stones will teach you what you cannot learn from masters. You have need not so much of reading as of prayer; and thus may God open our hearts to understand His law and His commandments.' *[margin: Characteristics of the Cistercians.]*

Of the religious influence of the Cistercian movement the late Professor J. R. Green wrote : 'At the close of Henry's reign, and throughout the reign of Stephen, England was stirred by the first of those great religious movements which it was to experience afterwards in the preaching of the Friars, the Lollardism of Wycliffe, the Reformation, the Puritan enthusiasm, and the mission work of the Wesleys. Everywhere, in town and country, men banded themselves together for prayer, hermits flocked to the woods, noble and churl welcomed the austere Cistercians. . . . A new spirit of devotion woke the slumbers of the religious houses, and penetrated alike to the home of the noble and the trader.'[1] *[margin: Religious influence of the Cistercian movement.]*

Long before the sixteenth century the reforming spirit of the Cistercians had spent itself. Wealth became the

[1] *History of the English People*, vol. i., p. 156.

parent of luxury and the root of idleness; and between the enthusiastic devotion and ascetic lives which distinguish the earlier monks of Fountains and those of even a hundred years later there was a descent as great as that of the Benedictines and Cluniacs, which called forth the Cistercian reform.

CHAPTER III.

ADVANCE IN MONASTIC REFORM: THE AUGUSTINIANS, OR AUSTIN CANONS.

WHOLLY distinct from the monks, and under discipline less rigid, were the Regular Canons, who claimed Augustine of Hippo as their founder, but were not known as a distinct order till the eleventh century. The members of this order were regular clergy, holding a middle position between monks and secular Canons. They lived together, as a community of parish priests might do, under monastic rules, and observed the seven canonical hours. The first house of their order in England was founded at Colchester about the year 1105. From the colour of their dress they were commonly called Black Austin Canons, they generally wearing a long black cassock, with a white rochet, or short surplice, over it, and over that a black cloak or hood. The monks always shaved, but these Canons wore their hair and beards, and caps on their head. To this order belonged Bolton Priory, secluded among the woods on the banks of the Wharfe, and Walsingham Abbey, in Norfolk, famed for its shrine of the Virgin Mary, to which pilgrims resorted in large numbers. *Black Austin Canons.*

Offshoots of this order were the Præmonstratensians, or White Canons, deriving their name from Præmonastre, where they were founded by a German named Norbert, in 1211. They were simply a stricter order of the Austin Canons, standing towards them much as the Cluniacs did to the Benedictines. They were further distinguished from the Austin Canons by wearing white robes instead of black; hence they were called White Canons. They never rose to great influence in England, numbering only thirty-five houses; of these Welbeck Abbey, in Nottingham, was the chief. The Gilbertines were a purely English order, which took its rise (1148) at Sempringham, in Lincolnshire, and was named after its founder, *Præmonstratensians, or White Canons.* *Gilbertines.*

Gilbert, a priest. This order was a curious combination of the Austin and Cistercian rule, the Canons following the former, the nuns and the lay-brethren the latter. The convents for the men and women adjoined, and the inmates worshipped in the same church, separated by a longitudinal wall. The number of Gilbertine houses in England was twenty-five. Of the Bonhommes,

Bonhommes. a name of uncertain origin, there were only two or three houses in this country. They were a branch of the Augustinian order. Excepting the Austin Canons, none of these orders in England gained great distinction or rendered eminent services.

During the time of the crusades the three celebrated orders of the Knights Templars, the Knights Hospitallers, and the Teutonic Knights arose. In these

The religious military orders. great and renowned military orders, bound by religious obligations, devoted to the interests of the cross, and to the rescue and care of those who suffered in its defence, we see an advance upon the selfish life of the monks, who renounced the duties, the charities, the sympathies of life for the supposed better culture of the spiritual life. The call to the

The crusades a call from monastic selfishness. crusades broke in upon the selfishness of monasticism. Politically and ecclesiastically the crusades were a disastrous failure; but they roused men to open conflict against the evils which affected the honour of the Saviour of mankind. To attempt the rescue of the Holy Land from the hand of the infidel it was thought would advance the glory of God, and be an accumulation of merit to all who shared in the enterprise. Kings, princes, wealthy men, and men of low degree, turned toward the East, and felt that they were as truly in the service of the Lord as the priest who recited his daily mass or the monk who cared only for his own spiritual welfare in solitude, labour, and silence.

To relieve the hungry, weary, homeless, and sick of their own faith, whom religious desire had brought to a

Knights Hospitallers of St. John of Jerusalem. far off land, was the original vocation of the Hospitallers, known also as Knights of St. John of Jerusalem. Grateful travellers spread their fame throughout Europe, and sent offerings to sustain so gracious an endeavour and work. As the organization increased in numbers and power, members being desirous of taking a more active part against the attacks of the Mohammedans, permission for them to become a military order was given by the Patriarch of Jerusalem and confirmed by Pope Pascal II. in 1113. Upon this many of the crusaders joined them. They were exempt from all ecclesiastical jurisdiction; and in a short time their wealth increased enormously from landed property in all parts of Europe. They were divided into three classes—nobility, clergy, and serving brothers; their religious houses into priories, bailiwicks, and commanderies, or preceptories. The commanderies, of which there were no less than fifty-three in England, were smaller houses, where candidates were received and trained. The first introduction of the Knights Hospitallers into England was in the year 1101. Their chief priory was in Clerkenwell, described at that time as 'nigh London.' The knights wore a black robe, having a white linen cross of eight points fastened on the left side, also a red military cloak. They took the usual monastic vows of chastity, obedience, and poverty.

The famous order of the Templars was introduced into England some years after the Hospitallers. Its earliest members banded themselves together for the express purpose of giving armed protection to the numerous pilgrims journeying in the Holy Land. In this order the great St. Bernard took an active interest, and under his direction its rules were framed. In the Knights of the Temple the endeavour was made, according to the ideas of the twelfth century, to combine the qualities of the Christian and of the soldier. Members of the order were either bound for life or for a fixed period. Married men were admitted. Like Augustinian Canons, they were to attend daily services; but to soldiers wearied with military duties leave of absence was granted on certain conditions. The Templars soon rivalled in wealth and power the Hospitallers. The similarity of their duties rendered it impossible at times to prevent collision, and during the intervals between the crusades generous emulation frequently gave way to a spirit of envy and detraction; for, as Fuller aptly says, 'Active men, like millstones in motion, if they have no other grist to grind, will set fire

Knights Templars.

to one another.' The danger to the State of military orders responsible to the pope only was also felt, and attempts were made for their suppression as early as the time of Henry III. Modern research has cleared the Templars from the charges on which, with much severity, their order was suppressed in the early years of the fourteenth century. Interesting memorials of the Knights of the Temple exist in the round churches built by them in imitation of the Church of the Holy Sepulchre at Jerusalem. Of these in this country four remain: *viz.* the Temple Church in London, rich in memorials of its ancient founders; the churches of St. Sepulchre's at Cambridge and Northampton; that at Little Maplestead, in Essex, is claimed for the Knights of St. John of Jerusalem.

<small>Military orders a danger to the State.</small>

<small>Round churches of the Templars.</small>

To the third great military order, the Teutonic Knights, no more than passing reference is here required. As its name intimates, this order was of German origin, and none but Germans of honourable birth were admitted as members. Like the two other military orders, the Teutonic order adopted the Augustine rule of life, and laid upon themselves the special obligations of tending sick and wounded pilgrims, and of fighting the enemies of Christendom at home or abroad. The distinguishing garb of the order consisted of a white mantle with a black cross.

<small>Teutonic Knights.</small>

With the popularity of the crusades there passed away the necessity of the service to which these religious military orders had devoted their lives, but not the spirit of enterprise they had helped to create, determined to war with evil, and, apart from monastic seclusion, to minister unto the needs of the sick and the poor.

CHAPTER IV.

THE INSTITUTION OF THE FRIARS, A FURTHER ADVANCE IN REFORM.

THE institution of the Friars was another departure from the isolation and seclusion of monastic life. The Friars, instead of withdrawing from men, were to seek out the poor, the sick, the outcast; to rebuke sin and exhort to repentance. According to their rule they were to labour for their food and clothing, taking only clothes and food in payment. If labour failed they might beg the necessaries of life. Such at least was their original rule; how soon modified every reader of history knows. Poverty, humility, and active benevolence in ministering to the spiritual and bodily needs of men—these were the general principles on which the mission of the Friars was founded.

No men could have been more opposite in temperament yet one in aim as reformers than Dominic Guzman of Osma, and Francis Bernardone of Assisi, the two great founders of the Friars. *Their founders.*

Dominic, born in the year 1170, a Spaniard of noble birth, was a man of letters and a priest. 'Fond to his own and dreadful to his foes,' is Dante's description of the great Dominican. In his self-imposed poverty he was once so distressed by the tears of a poor woman who wished to redeem her son from slavery that he offered himself to be sold in her son's place. His zeal against heretics has made him notorious in history as the founder of the remorseless Inquisition. In records of ecclesiastical inventions he is known as the inventor of the rosary. *Dominic.*

In striking contrast with the stern, mechanical temperament of Dominic is the gentle-souled, Nature-loving, impulsive, 'sweet St. Francis of Assisi,' his cotemporary, but twelve years his junior. Vividly in old pictures the contrasted founders are represented: Dominic with a cross and a bloodhound, *Francis of Assisi.*

Francis with a cross and a lamb; both loyal in heart to the Saviour of mankind, but one not knowing the spirit he was of, tenacious of purpose to destroy that which he took for evil; the other gentle and guileless, sacrificing everything for the good of others. The words, 'Sell all that thou hast, and give to the poor, then thou shalt have treasure in heaven,' were to Francis a Divine message, to be taken in their most literal sense. Poverty he wedded as his bride. At the age of about twenty-six he went forth to the mission of his life, barefooted, in a coarse garment of grey serge, drawn round his waist with a piece of common cord. His followers were at first few in number. When sanctioned by Innocent III., in 1208, the new order numbered only eleven members. Such was the origin of the great Franciscan order, which soon surpassed every other, both in numbers and importance, and which, together with its great rival order of the Dominicans, constituted for a long period the chief stay and support of the Church of Rome.

The dominant ideas of the two orders are seen in the character of their founders. The learned, zealous Dominic saw the need there was for more exact and intelligent teaching than could be had save in a few great cities. Rome was then in conflict with the Albigenses, whose opinions and tenets anticipated in a remarkable manner those of the Lutheran Reformation. Dominic saw how powerless the clergy were to contend with their rivals, whose zeal, life, and beliefs were making many converts. Heresy and schism were to him the great perils that beset the Church, and zealous systematic preaching with him was the method by which they were to be met. The Dominicans were therefore known as *Fratri Predicatori* — preaching brothers; while Francis, in his humility, styled his community *Fratri Minori*—Minorites, or lesser brothers, as the youngest and humblest of religious fraternities.

The Dominicans preaching brothers and heresy hunters.

The Franciscans missioners of active benevolence.

Of Francis' strivings after holiness, his simplicity of character, his sublime self-surrender to Christ, there can be but one opinion. In his nature there was a depth of love which made him passionately fond of all living things. Of birds and of animals he spoke as his friends, his kinsmen, his fellow-worshippers of the bountiful Creator, the love of whom he was ever asserting to the poorest, the meanest, the most repulsive of human kind. He taught by example and precept that activity in winning souls to God and in going forth to work for the benefit of those for whom Christ died was the true religious life. When Christians were more intent upon slaying Mohammedans than converting them Francis made his way into the army of the sultan of Egypt as a preacher of repentance. To one of his own order he wrote, 'There is only one mark by which I can know whether thou art a servant of God; namely, if thou compassionately bringest back wandering brethren to God, and never ceasest to love those who grievously err.'

In the magic charm of St. Francis' influence, that everywhere gained him multitudes of disciples, there are not lacking proofs of practical wisdom and shrewd discernment. He recognised the possibility of acceptable service to God in the ordinary every-day work of life, and founded in 1221 the order of Tertiaries, expressly for those who could only live in the world, and who could not join his order to the full. The members, who might be married persons, retained their social position while coming under a simple rule of faith and prayer to abstain from worldly dissipation and costly attire. In the Franciscan Tertiaries we see reproduced the idea of the religious military orders applied to the ordinary circumstances of life. *Franciscan Tertiaries.*

The founder of the renowned Franciscan order died at the early age of forty-four, in the year 1226, surviving his great compeer, Dominic, by five years.

Great was the stir the coming of the Friars excited in England. A band of the Dominicans, thirteen in number, landed at Dover in the year of their great leader's death, 1221. Their first settlement was in Oxford, where they addressed themselves especially to the Jews residing there; their next in London, where the lord mayor gave them two whole streets, in the part still known as Blackfriars, the name by which in this country the Dominicans became known, from the black cloak and hood which they wore. Franciscan Friars soon followed the Dominican. In the year 1224 a company of nine landed penniless at Dover. Of *Friars in England.*

this mission band four were Englishmen, four Italians, and one a Frenchman—Lawrence of Beauvais—an intimate and favoured friend of the founder of the order. From Dover the party, barefooted and clad in their grey or brown serge gowns, with a girdle of rope round their waists, made their way to Canterbury. There they divided company: four set out for London, the rest, remaining at Canterbury, lived on the chance charity of the inhabitants. Their fare was the meanest: meal, sometimes wheaten, at others only barley, eaten with onions and thick black beer. But they gained in estimation every day. The London party for a fortnight were hospitably entertained by the Dominicans. Then, in humble quarters in Cornhill, the Franciscans commenced their mission of preaching, visiting, and attending the sick. Thence they removed to a place near the Shambles, in Newgate, called Stinking Lane, known and celebrated henceforth as Greyfriars.

Wherever the early Franciscans went they made choice of the poorest and most neglected quarters for their settlements. Their earnest spirit of self-sacrificing love won them a welcome, though signs of ill-will and jealousy were not lacking on the part of the parochial clergy and monks. Some of the London party, proceeding on their way to Oxford, having lost their road at night, compelled by rain and stormy weather, sought shelter at a grange of the monks of Abingdon. They were mistaken from their dress and foreign accent for jugglers, and as such were admitted for the amusement of the inmates. Upon the discovery being made that they were not jugglers, but Friars, the charity of the monks was exhausted, and the belated travellers were thrust out into the darkness and wet of a stormy night.

Rapidly the number of Friars increased in England. The novelty of their self-sacrifice, their enthusiasm, their spiritual earnestness, their constant endeavour to alleviate every form of human misery, won the confidence and affection of the people. The poor welcomed the Friars into their homes as ministers of religion not too proud to sit down under the thatched roof and share with them their plain fare. The suffering and the miserable, even the fever-stricken and the loathsome leper, found

The mission of the Franciscans to the poor and neglected.

in them friends to sympathise and help. Dressed in a long robe of coarsest cloth, bareheaded, barefooted, they appeared by day, and at night they lay without a pillow in dwelling as mean as the wattled hovels around. Self-sacrificing for the sake of Christ was the sum of their lives, and the only reward they asked, food and shelter. For a time they kept nobly true to the spirit of their rule, and their success was correspondingly great.

Within thirty years after their arrival the numbers of the Franciscans amounted to twelve hundred and forty-two. The Benedictine monk known as Matthew of Paris, an antagonist to both orders, bears this testimony to the fervour and devotion which marked their first appearance: 'They filled the land, dwelling in cities and in towns, in societies of tens and sevens, having no worldly goods of any kind. They went about barefooted, showing a pattern to all of the greatest humility. On Sundays and holy days they went forth from their dwellings and preached the gospel in parish churches. They ate and drank whatever was set before them by those to whom they ministered. Deep was their insight into heavenly things, for their spiritual vision was unclouded by attachment to this lower world with its carnal pleasures.'

A monk's testimony to the Friars.

The two orders borrowed from each other: the Franciscans followed the Dominicans in their pursuit of intellectual culture; the Dominicans were influenced by the example of the severity of self-sacrifice as seen in the Franciscans, which included even the surrender of their breviaries. Their only book was the cross, and their breviaries, said their founder, were to be in their 'heart of hearts.' But it was soon found that books were a necessity. 'The popularity of their preaching' led them, says Professor Green, ' to the deeper study of theology. Within a short time after their establishment in England we find as many as thirty readers, or lecturers, appointed at Hereford, Leicester, Bristol, and other places, and a regular succession of teachers provided at each university. The Oxford Dominicans lectured on theology in the nave of their new church, while philosophy was taught in the cloister. The first provincial of the Grey Friars built a school in their Oxford house, and persuaded Grosseteste to lecture there.'[1] Less than fifty years after the landing of the little company of penniless Franciscans, one of their order, Robert Kilwardby, had been appointed Archbishop of Canterbury, and Bonaventura, the general of the order, had refused the archbishopric of York.

By their learning, their eloquence, their resolute action, the Friars rose to eminence in the universities. The foremost scholars in Oxford were Friars, Roger Bacon, the Mirabilis, or Wonderful Doctor, whose name stands first in the great roll of the worthies of modern science; Alexander of Hales, the 'Irrefragable Doctor,' great among the scholastic divines of the thirteenth century; Duns Scotus, his pupil, who won by his dialectical ingenuity the title Doctor Subtilis: and William of Occam, the Invincible Doctor, founder of the Nominalists, and whose doctrine of evangelical poverty helped to mould the mind of England's greatest Reformer, John Wycliffe. These were all Franciscans. While the Dominicans gloried in Thomas Aquinas the Angelic and Albertus Magnus, the two most eminent theologians of the Middle Ages, as being of their number; and from their ranks there rose in the fifteenth century the great Savonarola.

Eminence of the Friars in the universities.

So many imitators of Francis and Dominic arose, each founding a fresh order of mendicants, that it was found necessary to put a stop to their further increase. Accordingly, at the second Council of Lyons, in 1274, it was decreed that the number of recognised orders should be reduced to four; viz. the Dominicans, the Franciscans, the Carmelites, and the Austin Friars. The Carmelites, still a widespread order, claimed to have Elijah as their founder. Hence their name. Not satisfied with such honour, the assertion was added that the Virgin Mary joined their order, and gave them a precious vestment called a scapulary. This gave rise to another name, by which they are known, Friars of our Lady of Mount Carmel. More commonly, from the cloak and hood they wore, they were called White Friars, a name which still survives in the part of London adjoining Fleet, where in 1241 they settled. Readers of Sir Walter Scott's *Fortunes of Nigel* will

Increase in the orders of Friars.

The Carmelites, or White Friars.

---

[1] Green, *History of the English People*, vol. i., p. 258.

remember his description of the Whitefriars sanctuary as existing in the time of James I. The Austin Friars, or Friars Eremites, were in the Broad Street ward of London. To Protestants the association of interest connected with their order is that of Martin Luther's spiritual conflict in the Augustinian convent at Erfurt. There were also the Crutched or Crossed Friars, who were distinguished by carrying an iron cross in their hand—changed to silver afterwards. Members of these and other orders, far too numerous to mention, made their way into every part of the country, especially frequenting the towns, and always living on the alms of the benevolent, and giving in return, it must be remembered, from their skill and information, help in times of sickness to thousands, and religious knowledge to those who in many parishes had only the uncertain knowledge conveyed by the celebration in Latin of the services and sacraments of their Church. *The Austin Friars.* *The Crutched or Crossed Friars.*

The popular favour of the Friars procured them the favour of the popes. They were exempted from all episcopal authority. They were free to go from parish to parish, preaching where they pleased, in church or amid the hurly-burly of fairs and markets. They were privileged to administer the sacraments, to receive confessions, to bury any who desired it in their churches and inclosures, and to accept legacies. Pope Boniface VIII. established these privileges with the natural and hoped-for result that the different orders vied with each other in lauding and magnifying the Papal power. To the parish clergy this intrusion upon their parochial rights became the occasion of bitter jealousy and much complaint, as they saw their customary fees go to the Friars, and found themselves supplanted in their spiritual work. *The privileges of the Friars.* *The Friars and the parochial clergy.*

It was in the nature of things that such a system should degenerate. The vow of poverty was the first to break down. Great was the change when from dwelling in the humblest abodes the Friars began to build stately habitations rivalling the old monasteries in magnificence. In vain had Francis done *Signs of degeneracy among the Friars. Vow of poverty broken.*

his utmost to prevent such violation of his fundamental rule. 'I command positively,' he said, 'all my brethren that they receive no money in any way, directly or indirectly; that they acquire no property, no house, no place, nothing whatever.' The popes connived at the evasion of the rule by declaring that the use only of the property should belong to the Friars, and that the property should be vested solely in the pontiff.

To the honour of the Franciscans there were those amongst them who indignantly rejected this evasion of their founder's injunction, as well as the society of their brethren who gave their assent. It is worthy of note that the Friars loyal to the principle of poverty for the most part became associated with the anti-Romanist sects, such as the Fraticelli, the Beghards, and the Apostolici.

In the abuse of their spiritual functions as confessors and preachers is seen a further sign of the decline of the Friars.

Abuse of their spiritual functions as confessors and preachers. The early Dominican and Franciscan were true evangelizers of the country. Romanizers, it is true, but teachers of nobler aims and holier lives than those of their age. Going two and two in their long robes of coarse cloth, bareheaded, barefooted, whatever the weather and however rough the way, Friars had gone ministering to the poorest, praying, preaching, and administering the sacraments as occasion suggested or required. Abounding, though, is contemporary testimony to what they became in the day when the fervour of their first zeal was spent, and the 'barefooted Friar' was ludicrously associated with an indolent, sensual, self-seeking life. In the abuse of their privilege to give absolution for all sins, they made the confessional a means simply to get money. It was to no purpose a faithful parish priest refused absolution to any black sheep of his flock—a Friar could give it; and where money was in prospect Chaucer's testimony is that the Friar was an easy confessor,—

> 'Full sweetly heard he confession,
> And pleasant was his absolution.'

The preaching of the Friars degenerated into the mere repetition of the legends of saints and the praising of their own peculiar order; the Dominicans preaching most frequently on the rosary, the Franciscans on the rope of St. Francis, and the Carmelites on the scapulary. The principle of living on the alms of the benevolent degenerated into a system being established under which a certain district was assigned to each friary, within which members were free to go the round. From door to door, according to their custom, going together, followed by a third man with a sack, the begging Friars went for gifts of corn, bacon, cheese, and logs of wood for their fire, in return for which prayers were as readily promised as they were speedily forgotten. Such is Chaucer's description of a begging friar of the Carmelite order, vividly sketched in his *Sompnour's Tale.* The Friars even added the trade of pedlars to their multifarious character as preachers, confessors, and attendants upon the sick, and as common hucksters went their round with knives and pins for sale. *[margin: Character of their preaching. Friar-pedlars.]*

Such was the descent, with certain brilliant exceptions, within little more than a century, from the saintly rise of the reforming order of the Friars. The early part of the thirteenth century saw their growth, the early part of the fourteenth saw them as corrupt as the older orders. Francis and Dominic, as truly as Benedict, Berno, and Bernard, failed in effecting any permanent reformation of the Church.

Against the corruptions of the Friars, Fitzralph, the energetic and eloquent Archbishop of Armagh, preached and wrote. He had been a fellow of Balliol College and vice-chancellor of the university at the time of Wycliffe's student-life there. There is evidence that Fitzralph's teaching largely influenced the mind of Wycliffe in his doctrine of *dominium*, which he had employed against the Friars and in favour of the endowed clergy. In London the Irish primate preached a course of sermons in English against the Franciscans, which so enraged them that they appealed to the pope, Clement VI., who well knew of what incalculable importance they were to the Papal court, and one of his last acts was to defend their privileges against their adversaries. *[margin: Opponents of the Friars— Fitzralph, Abp. of Armagh, A.D. 1347.]*

Another who withstood the teaching of the Friars was

Thomas Bradwardine, whose great work in defence of the Augustinian doctrines of grace was called forth by the doctrines taught by the Friars at the universities in his time. Bradwardine has a name and place in the history of the Church for his great learning and benevolence of character, and in the history of the Reformation of England as that of on whose divinity lectures at Oxford helped to mould the mind of Wycliffe.

Thomas Bradwardine, d. 1349.

CHAPTER V.

BISHOPS AND PAROCHIAL CLERGY.

IN the celebrated conflict of Henry II. with the great Archbishop Thomas of Canterbury we see an anticipation of the ecclesiastical struggle of the sixteenth century. The earlier Henry, as the later, claimed supremacy in his own realm. One of the greatest of England's legal reformers— Henry of Anjou—aimed at the consolidation of royal power by means of a centralized system of justice administered to all classes equally. *Henry II.'s conflict with the clergy regarding the civil and ecclesiastical courts.* The great difficulty in his way was the freedom claimed from the jurisdiction of the secular courts by all who had any right of appeal to the ecclesiastical courts. This right extended far beyond the priesthood: it was the claim of the whole of the professional and educated classes. Becket, who as chancellor had shown every inclination to sustain the authority of his sovereign, as soon as he became Archbishop *Thomas of Canterbury* of Canterbury veered round and became the resolute defender of the ecclesiastical courts. What was his motive? Was it ambition to rule by his ecclesiastical authority all secular power in the kingdom? or was the startling change from a life of regal splendour to that of an ascetic, who ate the coarsest food, wore sackcloth, and washed the feet of beggars, the result of a spiritual conversion? Or yet again, was it sympathy of race, as the only Englishman raised to highest power since the Conquest, that led him resolutely to resist strengthening the power of Norman rule? 'The defences which have lately been set up,' observes Canon Robertson, 'vary according to the views and position of their ingenious authors, who might perhaps be safely left to refute each other.' Had Becket thrown the same vigour into the reform of the Church as he did into the defence of the privileges and immunities of the clergy, his claims to honour would have been great. As it was, his resistance confirmed the abuses which for nearly four centuries more darken the history of the Church, of which he claimed to be the champion. His tragic death was the result of his violent vindication of the rights of the see of Canterbury over those of York, rather than of his quarrel with Henry. The firm, resolute spirit shown in life did not fail him in the near prospect of his violent end: refusing to hide or flee, unblenchingly he met his enemies. Rome turned the death of the murdered archbishop to account, canonized him as a saint and a martyr to the general privileges of the Church. Four hundred years after, the principles of the constitution which he had so stoutly resisted triumphed, and the gorgeous shrine of St. Thomas of Canterbury became a memory of the past.

During the period now under review not only was there conflict concerning civil and ecclesiastical legislation, but constant disputes between bishops and monks concerning the jurisdiction of the numerous monasteries. The right of supervision claimed by the bishops was resented by the monks. William the Conqueror, exercising his ecclesiastical supremacy in England, exempted the famous abbey at Battle from the authority of the diocesan bishop, and with that act of his began the multiplying of such exemptions—some by the purchased permission of the pope, others by mysterious charters from pope or king. When the bishop failed to maintain his right of visitation, he tenaciously clung to that of enthroning the abbot and giving the benediction which confirmed the appointment, thus preserving some recognition of episcopal authority.

Bishops and monasteries.

Another source of grievance to the bishops, and one that severely affected the parochial or 'secular' clergy, was the greed of the older and larger monasteries in the appropriation of tithe and land; sometimes under very doubtful claims, at others in order to sustain parish churches whose revenues had declined. It is a popular belief that the alienation from Church purposes of so large a portion of the tithes and glebe lands was the work of Henry VIII. So far is this from being the case that by the middle of the thirteenth century more than one-third of the benefices of England had suffered through such spoliation. The bishops were often powerless to do more than stipulate that a

The monasteries and Church benefices.

sufficient stipend should be allowed for a resident vicar, and a certain annual sum set aside for the relief of the poor. The records of disputes between the vicars and their monasteries about the proportions of tithes and offerings which they were to receive show that, in spite of their precautions, the parochial clergy were often scantily paid and the interests of the parishioners neglected.

The glimpses we get of the condition and character of the clergy in the twelfth century, and of the habits of life and prevailing sentiment in coun- *Condition and* try parishes, are of those groping in thick *character of* darkness, and of not a few longing for the *the parochial* dawn. Vivid pictures of the condition of *clergy.* the religious life of England at this period are sometimes drawn from the bitter satires and the violent attacks on monks and ecclesiastics called forth by the strife of Henry II. with the Church. Scorn of the crime and vice which disgraced the Church appears in the satirical poems ascribed to Walter Map, and in the writings of Nigellus, a monk of Christ Church, Canterbury, and a contemporary of Thomas Becket. 'The bishops ordained men indiscriminately, without titles, filling the country with men calling themselves clergy and claiming privileges, while mere vagabonds.' Church benefices *Irregularities* were publicly bought and sold, given away as *in clerical* a provision to children, or held in indefinite *appoint-* numbers by foreign ecclesiastics, who left their *ments.* duties to be discharged by poorly paid curates. That the satires of the ecclesiastical life of the Middle Ages had substantial foundation of truth is proved by the published registers and injunctions of the bishops. These reveal an amount of religious zeal that in some instances has been overlooked, and at the same time they confirm the evidence of the evils resulting from simony, non-residence, pluralities, and the almost undisguised immoralities of those professing to live under a rule of celibacy. Speaking generally, such was the condition of the ecclesiastical life of the twelfth century.

It is a popular belief that before the Reformation there was a greater reverence than after for holy things and places. The contrary, though, is the fact: *Desecration* mediæval churches were as much places of *of mediæval* merchandise and sport as of worship. At the *churches.*

end of the twelfth century it was necessary for the Archbishop of York to protest against turning churches into market-rooms, and churchyards into places for wrestling, archery, and dancing. In the beginning of the fourteenth century a market was regularly held in Ripon Minster. Churches were also places of carousal.

Church-ales. The festive gatherings known as 'church-ales,' to raise money required for church expenses, were held in the building as well as in connection with it. Strong ale was brewed by the churchwardens, and set for sale 'either in the church or some other place.' Dancing also was an institution which brought in money. 'Item of Nicholas Parkes of dancing money' occurs in the churchwardens' accounts of Great Dunmow, Essex, and the custom is elsewhere alluded to.

Miracle plays. Miracle plays, representing scriptural scenes, or the legends of saints, were regularly acted, and were a profitable source of income, the performers sometimes going the round of neighbouring villages. It was not until the Reformation changes that a statute was passed that 'the churchwardens shall suffer no plays, feasts, banquets, suppers, church-ales, drinkings, to be kept in the church, chapel, or churchyard.' A frequently quoted passage from the celebrated Diary of John Evelyn refers to the time when under the Stuart dynasty the nave of old St. Paul's was a rendezvous for business, for pleasure, for public gossiping. Such desecration was a return to the spirit of pre-Reformation times rather than

St. Paul's in pre-Reformation times. their result; for in the year 1385 the Bishop of London complained that in the cathedral men and women stood daily selling their goods and merchandise; that others, idlers and wantons, shot or hurled arrows, darts, and stones at the crows, pigeons, and other birds building their nests in the walls or niches of the church, while others played at ball, not only without, but within the church. Another instance of mediæval regard for the sanctities of a church is

A fight in a Derbyshire church. found in an account of a tithe dispute between a prior and parochial clergy in Derbyshire. The disputed tithe of lambs and wool were inclosed within the church, but the monks burst the door, and a free fight ensued between the two parties. Sheep and lambs were butchered under the horses' hoofs, or by the weapons of the combatants, within the walls of the church.

Amid the multiplied evils of an age of such spiritual degeneracy preaching in many parishes was utterly neglected, and in others heard only at very irregular intervals. Archbishop Peckham, whose published register is a proof of his zeal and energy, felt he could not require of his diocesan clergy more than four sermons a year. Here and there, though, were conscientious priests striving to teach men their duty, in whose parishes the preaching Friars had not all their own way. Interesting and suggestive information concerning the preaching of the parochial clergy is found in old English homilies, long lying in dusty bundles in university libraries and other collections, but now published by the Early English Text Society. Differing in their dialect according to the part of the country where they were preached, and differing also not a little in doctrine, these old homilies show that amid much superstition there were men in whose life and teaching shone the true light of saving faith. Some of the early English preachers did not hesitate to reproduce in thirteenth and fourteenth century dress the yet older homilies of Ælfric's times, in the same manner as now the 'skeletons' and 'outlines' of seventeenth century divines reappear in nineteenth century dress and style. Many of the old English homilies have, though, a distinct characteristic of their own, as called forth by the necessities of the times in which they were addressed to their hearers of five and six centuries ago. The sermons of Latimer are not more racy in style and direct in application than those of some of the early English preachers. In the bygone years, when lady-followers of fashion wore saffron-coloured dresses, powdered their faces with blaunchet (fine wheat flour), and thus robed and dusted set themselves to make conquests, one of the preachers thus warned his sex against their allurements: 'These women are the devil's mouse-traps; for when a man will bait his mouse-trap he binds thereupon the treacherous cheese, and roasteth it, so that it should smell sweetly, and so entice many a mouse into the trap. Even so do many of these women: they smear themselves with blaunchet,

Mediæval preachers.

'The devil's mouse-trap.'

that is the devil's soap; and clothe themselves with yellow clothes, that is the devil's covert; and afterwards they look in the mirror, that is the devil's hiding-place.' Then zealously adds the preacher, 'Now, dear men, for God's love keep yourselves from the devil's mouse-trap.'

Much in these homilies is based upon mediæval superstitions and legends, but there is the evidence of more familiar acquaintance with the Scriptures than is often accredited to the preachers of their days. Plain and practical teaching is given to the man who says, 'I am whole and sound, and strong and stalwart; I may yet live long, and repent in due time.' Here is an exhortation that must have appealed to the consciences of some: 'Dear brethren and sisters, if we make confession of one or of two sins, and yet follow one, God Almighty will not be well pleased. The priest may not shrive thee unless thou wilt entirely forsake thy sins. How may the physician heal thee whilst the iron sticketh in thy wound? Never. Neither canst thou be shriven sufficiently well to please Almighty God unless thou forsake all thy sins. Know well that one sin will mar all the goodness and the alms, and the amends that thou dost for the other.' In another passage connected with shrift and confession this occurs: 'Dear men, the priest is not able to forgive any man's sins, not even his own, but he is ordained between God Almighty and thee to instruct thee how thou shalt have forgiveness of thy sins from God.' Some fencing about 'the priest's power from St. Peter to bind and unbind' follows, but soon the preacher returns to his point: 'If thou sinnest he shall advise, on God's behalf, how thou shalt have Christ's friendship. Assuredly thou needest ask no more.' A higher idea of shrift as simply confession followed by absolution is thus set forth: 'What is shrift but to renounce the devil, be sorry for, repent, and bewail one's sins, and have in mind never more to commit those sins that he goeth to shrift for?' Preaching so direct and forcible must, though, have been the exception, or such men as Stephen Langton and Hugh Grosseteste would never have given the welcome they did to the Friar preachers, nor would Wycliffe have felt necessity laid upon him to send forth his 'Poor Priests.'

Exhortations to repentance.

A few among those of episcopal rank there were

whose time and energies were devoted to the moral and spiritual welfare of the Church, rather than to the discharge of official positions in the State. Among these few was Hugo of Lincoln, to whom reference has already been made as a monk of the Carthusian order, and as the trusted friend and reprover of Henry II. Unlike his cotemporary, the great Archbishop Thomas, he had little to do with the affairs of State. A steady upholder of what he believed to be right, he let neither royal nor ecclesiastical favour rule him. Deep religious feeling, combined with a bluffness of humour and kindliness of spirit, gave Hugo influence where others would have failed. Fearlessly he excommunicated the king's head-forester for an act of oppression towards the poor in connection with the game laws, and as fearlessly he refused to bestow a prebendary-ship as the king desired, saying, 'Prebendal stalls were for priests, not courtiers.' The superstitious spirit of the age, that was always on the look-out for miracles, was checked by the matter-of-fact words and ways of one who said that signs and wonders were for unbelievers, and not for the faithful. Women he treated with a respect that astonished his clergy. Hugo's consideration and pity for the suffering, especially for lepers, his kindliness towards little children, his fondness for animals and birds, live in many a curious legend concerning him. A pet swan, it is said, followed and guarded him like a dog. To the sons of Henry II., Richard and John, he was as faithful a friend as to their father. He never flattered, and the highest and the lowest alike felt he was a man to be trusted. In Lincolnshire, for some time after the Reformation, his feast-day, 17th November, was remembered. It had perhaps fresh interest given to it by the welcomed accession of Queen Elizabeth on that day, in the year 1558.

Hugo of Lincoln.

One of the noblest of the Reformers of pre-Reformation times was another bishop of the same diocese of Lincoln, Robert Grosseteste. Though not so original in character as Hugo, he had greater adminis-trative skill, and was the most learned Englishman of his time. As fearlessly as Thomas of Canterbury he resisted whatever seemed an infringement of the rights of the Church, but, unlike Becket's, Grosseteste's was a life

Robert Grosseteste.

of simplicity, purity, and indefatigable disinterestedness. For nineteen years (1235–53) the administration of his diocese, then the largest and most populous in the country, was characterized by a holy rigour. Seven abbots, four priors, and many unworthy priests, by his episcopal authority were removed in one year. Prohibitions of the clergy to 'haunt taverns, to play at dice, to engage in drinking bouts, to hire out their services for mass in noblemen's halls, among dogs and polecats, drunken flunkeys and ribald minstrels,' throw light on the Church, and at the same time upon the bishop's zeal for a reformed clergy. The importance he attached to their spiritual functions caused him to forbid their holding any secular office under the State. Such energy did not pass without opposition. In malignant passion attempt was made upon his life by poison. For six years (1239–45) Grosseteste was in open conflict with the dean and chapter of Lincoln, they claiming exemption from episcopal visitation; but the bishop's indomitable will prevailed. Innocent IV., upon Grosseteste's personal appeal to him at Lyons, decided almost all the points at issue in favour of the bishop, who, with courage renewed, lost no time in putting his power into execution. On another occasion (1250) he was not so successful. To his mortification, he found the gold of the monks prevailed with the pope more than the claims for monasterial reform. 'O money, money, what canst thou not do in the court of Rome?' was the disappointed prelate's exclamation. He found opportunity, however, in a vigorous sermon before the pope and his cardinals, to denounce the abuses of the Papal court.

Resolutely, impartially this noble prelate refused to admit to benefices all incompetent for office. Regardless of personal consequences, he braved the pope's displeasure by refusing to admit an Italian priest to a rich living in his diocese. For this a sentence of suspension was passed upon him, but with no other effect than that two years after, when Innocent desired for a boy nephew of his a canonry at Lincoln, again he was met by the determined, yet respectful, refusal of the English bishop. The pope, in his wrath at opposition to his wishes, exclaimed: 'Who is this old dotard who presumes to judge our acts? By St. Peter and St. Paul, if we were not restrained by our generosity, we would make him a warning to the world!'

Reference has elsewhere been made to the favour with which Grosseteste regarded the Friars in their early fervour, and to the encouragement he gave them. His reputation for learning was as great as his zeal for reform. The contrast in the estimate of this bold reformer of abuses at Rome and in England is significant. By his purity of character, his kindness, his consistent piety he won men's hearts, and by his learning their admiration, in spite of the opposition his reforms excited. In England for centuries he was regarded with veneration as 'Saint Robert of Lincoln,' and miracles were supposed to be wrought at his grave in Lincoln Cathedral. In Rome the news of his death in the autumn of 1253 was received with joy, and proposals afterwards made for his canonization were rejected. Rome's refusal to canonize this distinguished and honoured prelate is the truest testimony to his influence in leading the way for yet greater reforms

PRINCIPAL RELIGIOUS ORDERS IN ENGLAND IN PRE-REFORMATION TIMES.

I.
Monks.

Benedictines.
Cluniacs.
Cistercians.
Carthusians.

II.
Canons.

Austin, or Black Canons.
Præmonstratensians, or White Canons.
Gilbertines.

III.
Military Orders.

Knights Hospitallers of St. John.
Knights Templars.

IV.
Friars.

Franciscans, Minorites, or Grey Friars.
Dominicans, Jacobins, or Black Friars.
Augustinians, or Austin Friars, or Eremites.
Carmelites, or White Friars.
  Crutched, or Crossed Friars.
Maturines, or Trinitarian Friars.

Part II.
THE WYCLIFFIAN REFORMATION.

CHAPTER VI.

THE SPIRITUAL AWAKENING.

IN the time of the twelfth century, England was outwardly of one faith in religious belief. The only recognised dissentients were the Jews, and they were so few in number that at the beginning of Henry II.'s reign it was possible to maintain a law which forbad their burial anywhere save in one cemetery near London. The Papal Church was in possession of almost all the knowledge, an enormous proportion of the property, and the largest share of the political power in the country. In his strife with the Church Henry II. practically won the victory in preserving control over the choice of bishops, and in effectually resisting the power of an ecclesiastical assembly to decree laws in England which were not authorized by the king. But the power of the Church was seen in a manner never to be forgotten when the most powerful king in Europe, not as king of England, but as lord of the Angevin empire, of which the larger part was south of England, submitted barefooted, and with no other covering than his shirt, to be publicly flogged by priests and monks in Canterbury Cathedral amidst wondering onlookers.

[side note: The power of the Papal Church in the twelfth century.*]*

Beneath the surface of outward uniformity in religion there was beginning to work the leaven of a purer faith.[1] About the year 1165, Foliot, Bishop of London, one of the chief scholars of his time, and Roger, Bishop of Worcester, had brought under their notice a company of Germans, no more than thirty in number, by trade weavers, who had been discovered actively engaged in disseminating opinions that in the judgment of the bishops were heretical. Their success, according to current report, had been small:

[side note: Foreign Reformers in England.*]*

---

[1] In this chapter use has been made of an article pointing out some curious and little known facts, by the late Rev. T. Davids, in the *British Quarterly*, April, 1870.

they had made but one convert, a woman, who immediately recanted. The arrest of this band of German weavers was regarded as a matter of sufficient importance for the convening of a council of bishops at Oxford. Inquiries were made as to their faith. 'They answered they were Christians, and that they reverenced the teaching of the apostles.' They were found sound in the faith, excepting in their belief concerning the sacrament of baptism, the eucharist, and matrimony; these 'they answered perversely on.' Upon their refusing to retract their opinions, they were branded on the brow with a red-hot iron, 'their garments cut off as far as the waist, they were publicly beaten, and with loud lashings were driven out of the city, and because of the inclemency of the weather, since it was winter, no one offering them the least pity, they miserably perished.' The fact that shortly after, at the famous Assize of Clarendon, a law was made that all heretics were to be treated as outlaws, and their houses destroyed, suggests that this company of German preachers had influenced more than was at first supposed.

Council at Oxford.

In this company of Germans, condemned, branded, flogged, and driven out half-naked to perish in the cold, we see the beginning in this country of the long conflict against the system of the mediæval Church, that was not to cease till many of like heroic faith had suffered, if it were possible, a yet sadder fate. The precise doctrinal opinions held by these early forerunners of reform it is difficult to determine, as all the teaching branded by their antagonists as heretical was not equally deserving of condemnation. The charges which come down to us of their rejection of the sacraments and of marriage may be due in part to the more scriptural and simpler views which they held with regard to baptism and the Lord's Supper, and that they denied marriage to be a sacrament. The old chroniclers identify them with the Publicani, or Paulicians, of whose opinions the oppressed and persecuted Albigenses were substantially, if not wholly, the inheritors; or they may have belonged to the kindred sect known in Germany as Catharists. Scattered about Europe at this time were many sects, whose discontent with the spiritual life of the times found expression, some in extravagant forms of asceticism, others in mysticism, others in socialism. The spirit of reform was in the air, and its awakening influence was about to be felt in England.

During the reign of Richard I. some of the early followers of Peter Waldo came into England, and settled in Kent, where they were known as Waldenses. Persecution followed the Albigenses here as elsewhere. In London one was burnt alive in 1210, and others suffered in different parts of the country. Some ten or twelve years later, complaints appeared that heresy had infected some of the monastic orders of the day. *Heresy in the monasteries.* There were monks who had cast off 'the religious habit, and lived just like the laity.' In the reign of Henry III., in the year 1240, a Carthusian monk was put under arrest at Cambridge who seems to have held opinions which were substantially scriptural. Six years after, a writ was issued by the king, addressed to all the sheriffs of the kingdom, commanding them to arrest all Friars who had apostatized from their order, and to commit them to the king's prison. Foxe, the martyrologist, publishes a writ of that monarch's, under date of 23rd November, 1263, addressed to the Sheriff of Oxford, requiring him to suppress 'certain vagrant persons who call themselves Harloti,' who 'made their meetings, assemblies, and unlawful matches against the honesty of the Church and good manners.' In the reign of Edward I. a council was held in London, which formally condemned certain persons who held doctrines contrary to the Roman Church, especially on the subject of the Lord's Supper. *Councils in London and Winchelsea.* At Winchelsea a council was held in 1296, when bitter complaints were made by the clergy that 'a great part of the people had fallen off from the Articles of Faith which the Church was bound to hold.' In the beginning of the next century, conversions appear to have been numerous among the Friars, a succession of writs being issued for the apprehension of certain 'Friars who had apostatized from their order, and were wandering through the country clad as laymen.' *Conversions among the Friars.*

It is thus clear that though no sects and divisions of prominence had appeared in England outside the Papal Church before Wycliffe's time, there had been some awakening of the Reformation spirit, which the great

Oxford Reformer was destined to aid so heroically, and with such wonderful success. No improbable conjecture is it that others of the Continental sects besides the thirty German weavers came over to England, and that in unobtrusive manner they influenced the thought and belief of those around them. At all events, there is the evidence that among persons of humble degree in life, and amongst the monks and Friars, were those awakened in some degree to the errors of their time. Before long though the great leader of reform was to appear.

CHAPTER VII.

THE GREAT PLAGUE AND ITS CONSEQUENCES.

DURING the fourteenth century the terrible visitations of epidemic disease known as the Black Death made a lasting impress upon the social and religious life of England. Four times within the short space of thirty years the disease devastated the country. Like most epidemics, it was much more deadly at first than it was subsequently. It is only within recent years, through the researches of Professor Thorold Rogers and Mr. Seebohm, the far-reaching consequences of this succession of epidemics upon the national life have been at all realized. The terrible disease, starting from China, gradually overran nearly the whole of Europe. In England, it first entered the western counties in the summer of 1348. The mortality was enormous. Generally the stricken perished within a few hours; the strongest rarely survived the second or third day. [Enormous mortality.] In Bristol 'the living were hardly able to bury the dead,' and 'grass grew several inches high in the High Street and Broad Street.' 'In order if possible to arrest its progress,' says Mr. Rogers, 'all intercourse with the citizens of Bristol was prohibited by the authorities of the county of Gloucester. The precautions, however, were taken in vain: the plague extended to Oxford, and travelling slowly in the same measured way, reached London by the 1st of November.' Twice the meeting of Parliament was prorogued on its account; the second time *sine die*. After all the churchyards of London had been filled, a special burial place was purchased, in which more than 50,000 corpses were interred. In towns the courts of justice were closed. In the country cattle strayed about ownerless, 'harvests rotted on the ground, and fields were left untilled.' In Yorkshire the mortality was such that no fewer than one-half of the clergy perished. Throughout the eastern counties the disease increased alarmingly. Dr. Jessopp, from a careful study of court rolls and diocesan institution books, estimates that 'more than half the population of East Anglia was swept away by the Black Death.' Horror and sorrow were on every hand. In the wattled cottages of the villages and the filthy crowded hovels, in quaintly built manor-houses and stately monasteries—there were the suffering and the dying, while the churchyards reeked with the crowded, newly buried dead. In the November of 1349 the disease began to abate, and ceased about the following March. In 1361 and 1362 there was another outbreak; a third in 1369; a fourth in the years 1375 and 1376. By these repeated visitations it is estimated more than half the population of England perished.

In such an overwhelming series of calamities the superstitious and religious spirit of the age read the signs of Divine chastisement and the near approach of the end of all things. Such sentiments found expression in a small treatise, long erroneously ascribed to Wycliffe, *The Last Age of the Church*, and in the curious poem, called the *Pricke of Conscience*, by Richard Rolle, better known as Richard of Hampole, the hermit poet and preacher of Yorkshire. A fearful picture of the state of the world, and of the deaths of the conscience-stricken even in the experience of good men, and of the torments of condemned souls, is presented to the reader in his poem. Dr. Lechler ascribes the authorship of *The Last Age of the Church* to a Franciscan Friar of awakened spiritual sympathies. With pathos and solemnity, mingled with much superstition, the writer mourns the evils of his times, believing that the prophecies of Scripture, supplemented by those of the famous Abbot Joachim, pointed to the end of the fourteenth century as that of the final judgment. The times were those of spiritual awakening, when in their terror, as well as in their pain, their thoughts were of judgment to come.

Effects of the Great Plague upon the religious and social life of the people.

Another result, not accomplished at once, but eventually, was the emancipation of the serfs from the state of villeinage. The deaths of thousands upon thousands of the tillers of the soil put the landlords and employers of labour into great straits for labourers. The free labourers, the

Emancipation of the serfs.

'landless men,' wanderers in search of work, seeing their opportunity, struck for higher wages than they had had before. And the labour-tenants, the villeins, whose rent for the plot of land they held was paid in certain forms of service at certain seasons of the year, seeing the increased value of their labour, were less inclined to give as much as they had given before. The villeins, with the serfs, who had to labour all the year round, were regarded as much a part of the estate on which they lived as the cattle or trees. None of these classes had any voice in the political management of affairs; they were not allowed to carry arms, even to defend themselves. No consideration was there in those days for the rights of man in the law of supply and demand. To enforce the service of the labouring classes, the Parliament of 1349 decreed that any labourer who asked for more wages than he had before the depopulation occasioned by the Black Death was to be imprisoned.

Under a bitter sense of grievance, the wage-earning classes resisted, and being masters of the situation, refused to work except at double or treble wages. Sterner measures were resorted to, fixing not only the rate of wages, but the place of labour and the price of food. 'Fugitive labourers,' by whom, says Mr. Rogers, must be meant other than serfs, since these could always be reclaimed, were to be outlawed and branded with the letter F on the forehead. For more than twenty years this fourteenth century conflict of capital and labour went on. One of the few clerical advocates of the rights of the oppressed peasantry was the often misrepresented John Ball, a priest and popular preacher of the diocese of Norwich. He was excommunicated for his zeal, and persons were forbidden by Simon Langham, Archbishop of Canterbury, to listen to Ball's preaching. Of the anti-feudal bias of this 'crazy priest of Kent,' as the courtly Froissart calls him, there can be no doubt. The levelling spirit of his teaching is expressed in the old adage ascribed to him— *[margin: Conflict between capital and labour. John Ball.]*

> 'When Adam delved and Eve span,
> Who was then the gentleman?'

There was also a religious element in his teaching that

made him obnoxious to the ecclesiastics of his time. His utterances are described in a bill of excommunication by Simon de Sudbury, Langham's successor in the primacy of Canterbury, 'as scandals against the pope not fit for any pious ears to hear.'

Notwithstanding the murmurs of the peasant class at successive harsh and harassing Labour Acts, the burden of their grievances was increased by the imposition of the infamous poll-tax. This final act of oppression occasioned the outburst of long pent up wrath known as the Peasant Revolt. Thousands of serfs and villeins rose in rebellion. 'From Suffolk, where the most sturdy opposition had been offered to the first enactment of the Statute of Labourers; from Norfolk, where the ruffianism of Leg, the collector of the poll-tax, and his friends had been carried out in the same manner as in Kent; from Sussex, where the traditions of common action with Kent and Surrey still prevailed; from Hertfordshire, where the struggle had been specially violent between the abbey of St. Albans and the neighbouring town; from Cambridgeshire, which seemed to some extent to share the grievances of Herts; from Lincolnshire, where the oppressions of the king's officers had been specially severe; from Somersetshire, where the abbots of Glastonbury had struggled to keep down their serfs; from Yorkshire, where the men of Beverley had their own grievance against the convent of Meaux; Warwickshire and Staffordshire, which were suffering from the lawless inroads of the men of Chester—in short, from every part of the kingdom where oppression and violence reigned men came flocking to London to join the standard of Tyler.'

The Peasant Revolt.

The madness and excesses of the insurgents, the blood that was spilt, the fires that were kindled, and not least the terrible fate of the insurgents, form one of the saddest of the many sad scenes of the fourteenth century history. In Canterbury the archbishop's palace was attacked, in London the stately palace of John of Gaunt was burnt down, and the Archbishop of Canterbury, the energetic and vigorous Sudbury, and several other high officers of State, were beheaded as traitors to the interests of the people. The popular estimate of the monasteries is seen in the attacks made upon the great abbeys of St. Albans and of St. Edmundsbury—an estimate not without discrimination, for though encamped in Smithfield, the mob laid not a hand on the plate or money belonging to the Priory of St. Bartholomew the Great.

More through the delusive promises of pardon and the granting of charters of emancipation than any strategic action of the Government forces, the insurgent peasants were dispersed; but with their dispersion passed the panic of the ruling classes. *Suppression of the revolt.* The lords and employers of labour no more liked to lose the forced service of the serfs and villeins than the slaveholders of America liked to have slavery abolished. Instead of the promises of the king being confirmed, revenge was taken in the death of seven thousand of the unhappy peasantry, maddened into revolt by the wrongs of their class. At such terrible cost was emancipation from serfdom gained in England. The battle for freedom and independence, though seemingly lost, was yet gained. The feudal landlord had learned a lesson which henceforth led to the gradual abolition of serfdom and villeinage.

In the midst of this century, darkened by the most terrible plague which the world ever witnessed, and troubled by years of social unrest, culminating in open rebellion, followed by executions bloody and barbarous beyond all precedent, lived William Langland, in whose pages are portrayed all the darker and sterner aspects of the times, and Geoffrey Chaucer, who, with infinite grace, and skill, and humour, set forth in bright, unfading colours the social and ecclesiastical life in the midst of which lived and wrought England's boldest and greatest Reformer—JOHN WYCLIFFE.

CHAPTER VIII.

THE ENGLAND OF WYCLIFFE'S DAYS.

IN the troubled years of the second half of the fourteenth century there lived in London, in Cornhill, with his wife Kitte and his daughter Calote, a certain clerk in minor orders. To us he is known as William Langland, or Longland. He wore long robes and had a tonsured head. In spirit he was independent, in circumstances poor; too proud in spirit he was to bow to the gay lords and ladies, or to salute the law serjeants as he passed them in the street. His home at one time had been among the rural poor of the Malvern Hills. In London he was eking out a livelihood—in part by singing *placebos* and *diriges* for the souls of the dead, in part by writing legal documents for the lawyers at Westminster. With keen satire Langland regarded the selfishness and corruptions of the rich, with sadness he contemplated the condition of the poor, battling against oppression, legislation, hunger, and all the stern realities and hardships that tried them as gold is tried in the fire. Yet Langland was no revolutionary, no welcomer of Wat Tyler, when he marched into London at the head of a hundred thousand men, no admirer of John Ball, who hailed him as a fellow worker in the cause of popular liberty. Langland was a loyalist and an orthodox Catholic, whose voice, independent of that of the insurgents, and independent of that of the theological Wycliffe, was raised with such power in the cause of social and ecclesiastical reform that next to that of Wycliffe none was greater.

William Langland.

Langland's poem, *The Vision of William concerning Piers the Plowman*, is one of the greatest and most original of all our English poems. It is written in alliterative verse, and divided into twenty portions, each portion being called a passus. William, the dreamer, is described as tired out by wandering, sitting down by

Langland's poem, The Vision of William concerning Piers the Plowman.

the side of a stream among the Malvern Hills, and there as 'he lay and leaned and looked in the water' he slept, and as he slept he dreamed that he saw a 'fair field full of folk,' of poor and rich, ploughmen toiling hard in setting and sowing, anchorites and hermits, minstrels and jesters, 'bidders and beggars,' with wallets well crammed, pilgrims and palmers, some bound for the shrine of St. James, having leave to lie all their life after, others of our Lady of Walsingham. Friars of the different orders, a pardoner, ready to absolve any of breaking their vows, parsons and parish priests, bishops and also a king, Richard II., to whom an angel speaks words of advice. Beside the king, knights and lawyers, burgesses and bondmen, tradesmen, bakers, hewers, weavers, tailors, tinkers, and taverners, touting for custom, and labourers of all kinds, ditchers and delvers, are depicted in bold, picturesque language. In the midst of this description is introduced the story of the Belling of the Cat, the cat being none other than John of Gaunt, concerning whom rumours were current that he aspired to royal dignity, the rats representing the burgesses, the mice men of lower degree. These sketches form the graphically written prologue.

In the first passus a lady lovely of countenance, the personification of Holy Church, appears, tells the dreamer how great a treasure is Truth, that Faith without works is dead, and that the way to Heaven lies through Love. In the second passus, the dreamer inquires of Holy Church how he may know Falsehood. He is thereupon shown Lady Meed, arrayed in scarlet and gold, and adorned with rich jewels, representing 'reward in general, and bribery in particular,' who in the pope's palace is as familiar a friend as Holy Church herself. In the third and fourth sections Lady Meed confesses to a friar, is absolved, and promises in return, at his suggestion, to glaze the window of his friary. The king proposes a marriage between Lady Meed and Conscience, but Conscience objects, exposes the evil which Corruption or Bribery had wrought in Church and State, and finally refuses, saying, 'Unless Reason advise me, rather will I die.' Whereupon Reason is sent for, who persuades the king to give up the match, and to rule his kingdom by the advice of Reason alone.

The first vision ended, the dreamer had a second falling asleep as he babbled over his beads. Again he saw the field of folk and 'Reason preaching to the assembled people, reminding them that the late tempest and pestilence were judgments of God.' In a passage of remarkable power personifications of the Seven Deadly Sins are described as brought to confession. The description is thus summarized by the Rev. Walter Skeat in his valuable introduction to his edition of the poem: 'The first is Pride, who makes a vow of humility. The second is Luxury, who vows henceforth only to drink water. The third is Envy, who confesses his evil thoughts and his attempts to harm his neighbours. The fourth is Wrath, a friar, whose aunt was a nun, and who was both cook and gardener to a convent, and incited many to a quarrel. The fifth, Avarice, who confesses how he lied, cheated, and lent money upon usury, and who, not understanding the French word *restitution*, thought it was another term for stealing. The sixth, Gluttony, who (on his way to church) is tempted into a London ale-house, of the interior of which the author gives a most life-like picture, as distinct as a drawing by Hogarth. Gluttony also repents and vows amendment, but not till after he has first become completely drunk, and afterwards felt ashamed of himself. The seventh is Sloth, a priest who knows rhymes about Robin Hood better than his prayers, and can find a hare in a field more readily than he can read the lives of saints.'[1] In the course of an exhortation to a despairing sinner occur these words:

'Have Mercy in thy mind, and with thy mouth beseech it,
For God's mercy is more than all His other works;
And all the wickedness in this world that man might work or think
Is no more to the mercy of God than in the sea a glede' [i.e. a spark of fire].

The effect of Reason's discourse was that—

'A thousand of men then thronged together,
Cried upward to Christ, and to His clean [pure] mother,
To have grace to go with them *Truth* to seek.'

At first they had no one to guide them. A palmer

---

[1] Page xxix.

whom they met had visited many holy shrines in many lands, but when questioned as to whether he knew St. Truth replied,—

> 'Nay—
> I saw never palmer, with pike nor with scrip,
> Ask after him ere, till now in this place.'

Then Piers the Plowman, the personification of honest and unambitious labour, appears upon the scene. He tells them the way to Truth lies through the Ten Commandments.

In the next passus Piers bids a knight—

> 'Misbede [injure] not thy bondsman,
> Though he be thy underling here; well may hap in heaven
> That he be worthier set, and with more bliss
> Than thou,
> For in charnel [the burial-place, charnel house] at church churles be evil to know,
> Or a knight from a knave."

A gospel of brotherhood and work.

Piers' Gospel of Brotherhood is supplemented by that of Work. He sets all who come to him to labour. Some idle over their tasks, but are soon reduced to submission by the discipline of Hunger, whose influence is portrayed in vivid descriptions of the poor. The climax of this part of the poem is in the seventh passus. Truth—*i.e.* God the Father—commands Piers to stay at home, to continue his work of ploughing and sowing, at the same time sending a bull of pardon, in the benefits of which all honest men, whatever their calling or rank in life—kings, knights, bishops, labouring poor—are entitled to share. A priest demands to see the pardon. It is shown him:

> 'All in two lines it lay, and naught a leaf more,
> And was written right thus—
> "They that have done good shall go into life eternal,
> They that have done evil into everlasting fire." '

A contention ensued between Piers and the priest, in the midst of which the dreamer awoke, and mused on the valuelessness in the Day of Doom of the pope's pardons, indulgences, and penances, compared with a holy Christian life.

The name of the remaining portion of the poem is the 'Vision of Do-well, Do-bet, and Do-best.' The author's own explanation of the names is that he who does a kind action *does well*, he who teaches others to act kindly *does better*, but he who combines both practice and theory *does best*. In the poem of Do-well occurs a passage which excited great interest in the days of Henry VIII. It is one of the curious foresights, or prophecies, contained in the poem that the author foretold the coming of a king who would 'beat the religious orders for breaking their rules, and then should the Abbot of Abingdon receive a knock from the king, and incurable should be the wound.' In the poem of Do-bet the character of the true and honest Piers the Plowman is identified as the truest of all teachers of men, the greatest of all social reformers—Christ Himself; and we are finally told,—

The 'Vision of Do-well, Do-bet, and Do-best.'

'For our joy and our health, Jesus Christ of Heaven
In a poor man's apparel pursueth us ever,
And looketh upon us in this likeness and that with lovely cheer
To know us by our kind heart, and casting of our eyes,
Whether we love the lords here before our Lord of bliss,
For all we are Christ's creatures and of His coffers rich,
And brethren as of one blood, as well beggars as earls.'

'There are not many passages in English poetry,' well observes Mr. Skeat, 'which are so sublime in their conception as the eighteenth passus. In Do-best is described the war with Antichrist, in which the Church is attacked by worldly men and princes. The Castle of Unity, the stronghold of the Church, is assailed by an army of priests and monks. Conscience, the governor of the castle, is driven out, and is wandering in search of Piers the Plowman, when the dreamer awakes in tears.

This remarkable poem of the fourteenth century, as realistic in style as the writings of Browning, and as keen in its satire as those of Thackeray, must certainly be reckoned among the forces that silently prepared the way for the Reformation of the sixteenth century, and doubtless expressed the popular sentiment on the subjects it discusses. It exists in three different forms, full of interest, both as showing the gradual development of the author's design and as illustrating the interest it excited. Dean Milman says, 'The poet who could address such opinions, though wrapt up in prudent allegory, to the popular ear, to the ear of the peasantry of England, the people who could listen with delight to such strains, were far advanced towards a revolt from Latin Christianity.'

When we turn from the pages of Langland and his imitators to those of Chaucer, it is into an altogether different atmosphere. The Black Death, the struggle of labour with capital, and the revolutionary agitations that resulted from or were quickened by the pestilence, are all forgotten in the company of the Canterbury pilgrims at the Tabard Inn in Southwark. All Chaucer's works are redolent of delight in Nature, in green leaves and sweet air, of sunshine and bird-singing; but the cry of the poor, never louder than in his time, is never heard in tale or allegory. No ploughman's story is found in his famous series of realistic poems. He who drew the 'perfect gentle knight,' the young squire, the monk, the friar, the princess, and those of lower degree—the reeve, the miller, and the wife of Bath—has given us no 'Hodge' of his day, no Jack Upland, for the ploughman passingly referred to in the prologue is not the typical peasant of Wat Tyler's time and county. Foxe, who saw in Chaucer a 'right Wicklevian, or else there was never any,' and others who have found reason for reckoning the 'Father of English poetry' among the disciples of the great Reformer, have not taken sufficient account of his indifferentism about the social interests and perplexities of his times. Chaucer must have known Wycliffe, the friend and supporter of his patron John of Gaunt, and the description of the 'poor parson of a town' is often quoted as probably suggested by the known excellences of the Rector of Lutterworth, but it altogether fails to convey the idea of his force of character and polemical power. Chaucer was a courtier rather than a reformer. There is no evidence of sympathetic appreciation on his part of the strivings of Wycliffe. *[margin: Geoffrey Chaucer (1340-1400). His indifference to the social problems of his times.]*

The very absence of reforming intent increases the value of Chaucer's vivid pictures of English social and religious life in the fourteenth century. Few are the monastic abuses which called forth the censure of the Reformers that are not made the subject of the poet's humorous satire. From *[margin: Chaucer's satires.]*

the time of his free translation of the celebrated
'Romance of the Rose,' when he was a youth of twenty,
till that of his ripe old age, when he wrote the prologue
to his *Canterbury Tales*, he never hesitated to banter the
ecclesiastics and religious orders on their corruptions.

The jovial monk. Without prejudice or passion he sets before
us the jovial monk of his day—such a monk
as Scott's Abbot of Jorvaulx in *Ivanhoe*: fat,
bald-headed, hunt-loving, whose golden bridle-bells
jingled in the air as he rode abroad, whose grey-
hounds were swift as birds of flight, and who, though
jewellery was forbidden by his monastic rules, fastened
his hood under his chin with a golden pin, and wore a love
knot in the larger end. The companion pic-
The merry friar. ture is that of the friar, 'wanton and merry,'
with twinkling eyes and pleasant voice, beloved
and familiar with all who kept open house in his allotted
district. Presents of knives and pins he carried with
him to give 'fair wives,' and was ready to entertain any
company with harping or singing. Well he knew the
taverns in every town and every tappestere. Confession
and absolution were easy matters with him. Instead of
'weeping and prayers,' it was sufficient 'to give silver to
the poor freres.' The picture of the fashionable
The fashionable prioress. prioress is that of one 'simple and coy,' with
fair, broad forehead, 'eyes grey as glass,' and
soft, red little mouth. She was, no doubt, a very finished
specimen of refinement, elaborately polite and precise in
her manners and meals, and proud of the French she
could speak—

> 'After the school of Stratford-at-Bow,
> For French of Paris was to her unknowe.'

A good woman, no doubt, she was, in her way, with her
motto, 'Love conquers all.'

> 'She was so charitable and so piteous
> She would weep if that she saw a mouse
> Caught in a trap, if it were dead or bled.
> Of small hounds had she, that she fed
> With roasted flesh, or milk and finest bread.
> But sore wept she if one of them were dead,
> Or if men smote it with a rod smart;
> And all was conscience and tender heart.'

Two other characters are introduced connected with the ecclesiastical life of the times—the summoner and the pardoner. It was the office of the summoner to cite before the ecclesiastical courts all persons who were accused of irreligious or immoral character, and to enforce the penalties awarded on the guilty by those tribunals. Chaucer's typical character of the persons employed in such duties is drawn in the darkest colours; it is that of a drink-loving man, with red-blotched face and narrow eyes: a man of whose appearance children were afraid. For a quart of wine he would hold his silence, and if he found liberal treatment, would tell the offender to have no care for the archdeacon's curse, and in all friendliness inform him that money would clear all. 'Purse is the archdeacon's hell,' said the summoner, a sentiment, though, to which the poet cautiously declines assent: 'Well I wot he lied.' With the summoner there rode a fashionably arrayed pardoner, just returned from the papal court, carrying before him 'a wallet brimful of pardons, come from Rome all hot.' Together, the summoner, with bourdon trumpet voice, and the pardoner, with high clear notes, sang merrily and loud, 'Come hither, love, to me.' Rich was the pardoner in potent relics. In his bag he carried a pillow covered with part of the Virgin Mary's veil, a fragment of the sail of the ship that Peter was in when he stepped forth upon the waters to meet Christ, a glass containing pigs' bones, with which he made more money in one day than the parson in two months. In the story ascribed to him the pardoner is amusingly candid concerning his methods of procedure when preaching and displaying his relics. His text was always the same—'The love of money is the root of all evil,'—his policy, at the same time, to work upon every possible fear and superstition by which he could get his hearers' money transferred to his own pocket. Elsewhere we have shown that in these times of ecclesiastical laxity and scandal some of the clergy were earnest and devout. Chaucer, not unmindful of this, introduces into his pilgrim band the description of a faithful pastor, of whom it is said,—

The summoner.

The pardoner.

A faithful pastor.

> 'Wide was his parish, and houses far asunder,
> But he ne left naught for rain nor thunder,
> In sickness nor in meschief [misfortune] to visit
> The farthest in his parish, moch and lite [rich and poor],
> Upon his feet, and in his hand a staff.
> This noble example to his sheep he gave,
> That first he wrought, and after that he taught.'

Unfortunately the sermon ascribed to this 'good parson,' 'rich in holy life and work,' is a most disappointing performance. It is directly contrary to the supposition indulged by so many writers that John Wycliffe was in the poet's mind. No one knowing the great ecclesiastical Reformer—as Chaucer must have done—would have assigned to him a discourse advocating the necessity of auricular confession, and throughout in thorough accord with papal doctrine. Chaucer, as a man of society, laughed at the abuses of religion and the worldliness of ecclesiastical persons. He was, as Thomson calls him, 'the laughing sage,' a humorous-hearted, generous man, a man of culture, who, as Erasmus after him, had outgrown the superstitions of his day, laughed at them as shams, and helped forward in a way he never intended the coming changes.

The pastor's sermon.

In less prominent degree, yet in a manner that claims at least passing reference, Chaucer's cotemporaries are fellow witnesses to the disorders of the times and the need of reform. Of these, one is John Gower, called by his friend Chaucer, with a touch of his characteristic satire, 'the moral Gower.' His interesting monument in St. Saviour's Church, Southwark, keeps, at all events, his three principal works in remembrance—the *Speculum Meditantis*, the *Vox Clamantis*, the *Confessio Amantis*. Of him a well-known writer says, 'Partly the religious and social reformer, and partly the story-teller, he represents a transition, and fills up the intellectual space between Langland and Chaucer.' 'In his satire of evils and in his grave reproof of the follies of Richard II. he rises into his best strain.' The *Confessio Amantis* is a dialogue between a lover and his confessor, in which, with better intentions than success, the author attacks the Seven Deadly Sins.

John Gower.

With the name of Gower may be linked that of Thomas

Occleve, a writer of kindred aim. Those who are always pointing us to the 'dim ages of faith' might well ponder such a picture of the hireling ecclesiastics and of the miserable condition of the churches as thus presented by Occleve:

Thomas Occleve.

> 'Adayes, now, my son, as men may see,
> One church to one man may not suffice,
> But always he must have plurality,
> Else he cannot live in no wise.
> Attentively he keepeth his service
> In court, there his labours shall not moule
> But to his cure looketh he full foul,
> Though that his chancel roof be all too torne,
> And on the high altar rain or snow,
> He careth not; the cost may be forborne,
> Christ's house to repair or make new.'

When from the elaborate productions of those whose names have taken a place in the literature of our country we turn to such expressions of popular sentiment as are preserved in the Political Poems collected by Mr. Wright for the Rolls Series, we find bitter abuse of the clergy and fierce denunciations of the exactions of the ecclesiastical courts. In the market-places and on the village greens songs and ballads were being sung that show forces were working mightily in the direction of ecclesiastical revolution. Langland, Chaucer, and his friends were the representatives of a generation that had begun to look at life with larger, other eyes than their fathers.

CHAPTER IX.

JOHN WYCLIFFE.

IN the England of Langland's and of Chaucer's days, amidst wasted lands and homes desolated by pestilence, and amid the conflicts of social life that culminated in the Peasant Revolt of 1381, lived John Wycliffe. He has long been spoken of as the Morning Star of the Reformation, as one of the greatest of Reformers before the Reformation, but it is only in the present century, and in the second half of it, that the actual value of his work and the heroic greatness of it are becoming generally understood. It is an Oxford professor who describes him as 'not only the greatest figure in Oxford history, but, along with Chaucer, Shakespeare, and Milton, as one of the four men who have produced the greatest effect on the English language and literature, and still further as wholly unapproached in the entire history of England for his effect on our English theology and our religious life.'[1] A century and a half before the great Reformation, Wycliffe maintained the sufficiency and supremacy of the Holy Scriptures, and was the first to plan, superintend, and send forth a complete translation of the Bible for English-speaking people. Without reserve, he also taught that the doctrine of transubstantiation is unscriptural, groundless, and erroneous. Beyond England the influence of Wycliffe's teaching spread. His writings were carefully copied and circulated in all the universities of Europe, and in their most important and essential doctrine reproduced by Huss and Jerome of Prague, the renowned leaders of the Bohemian Reformation, to whom Luther himself was a debtor. Thus the teaching of Wycliffe in the fourteenth century had its influence in the religious changes of Europe in the sixteenth century.

His position as a Reformer.

The far-reaching influence of Wycliffe's teaching.

It is worthy of note that the public work of Wycliffe,

---

[1] Montagu Burrows: *Wiclif's Place in History*, p. 4.

JOHN WYCLIFFE.

the true father of the English Reformation, did not extend over twenty years; but the training was long and thorough. For ten years (1335–1345) it was that of a student at Oxford, then in the full meridian of its mediæval renown. There the fame of Roger Bacon and of Duns Scotus lingered. Thousands of students, lads and grown-up men, then thronged Oxford, lodging in crowded hotels and living on the barest fare. Amongst them was the future great Reformer, then a youth fresh from Yorkshire. His course of study in the sciences and philosophy of the day was pursued with such success that after being a Fellow of Merton in or about 1360, when about forty years of age, he was appointed Master of Balliol. Thirty years' quiet, persistent work in studying, lecturing, and preaching, prepared him for his later labours as a reformer—first of glaring abuses, and then of erroneous doctrine. The highest academic dignities as doctor of divinity and as a great philosopher were his. No friendly hand has left us any memorials of Wycliffe's work, but his intellectual pre-eminence was such that his adversaries owned him to be 'the greatest theologian of the day, second to none as a philosopher, and incomparable as a schoolman.' In his personal appearance Wycliffe is supposed to have been tall and spare, and is represented with flowing beard. At one time he held the living of Fillingham, in Lincolnshire. This he resigned in 1368 for that of Ludgershall, a village in Buckinghamshire.

His preparation.

As a patriot Wycliffe first appears in history. In 1366 the spirit of the nation had been roused by a demand from Pope Urban V. for the payment of thirty-three years of arrears of tribute, as promised by King John, in acknowledgment of the suzerainty of the See of Rome, in default of which the king, Edward III., was cited to appear before the pontiff, and answer for his conduct as to his feudal lord. King, Parliament, and people united in refusing the demand. Wycliffe, though a priest, shared in the indignant repudiation. He issued anonymously a tract containing the real or conjectured arguments put forth in debate by seven barons in Parliament. Afterwards (*circ.* 1368) he issued his famous and elaborate treatise on the Divine Dominion (*De Dominio Divino*), followed about five years later by another on

As a patriot.

Doctrine of lordship.

the Civil Dominion. All power, he boldly maintained, was of God, who dealt it out to men in their several stations or offices, on condition of obedience to His commands. A favourite expression of Wycliffe's, therefore, was that all dominion is founded in grace. The pope's authority as Christ's vicar upon earth he recognised in things spiritual, but maintained that the king was the minister, the vicar of God, in things temporal, and was, therefore, as much bound by his office to see that temporal goods were not wasted or misapplied by the clergy as the clergy were to direct the spiritual affairs of the king. Still further he carried his arguments, that while the pope and the king are supreme, each in their department, yet every Christian holds 'dominion' of God, and the final, irreversible appeal is, therefore, to the court, not of Rome, but of Heaven.

It is this principle of the dependence of the individual upon God and upon none else that distinguishes Wycliffe's teaching from any other Reformer of the Middle Ages. He alone had the courage to strike at the root of priestly privilege and power by indicating for each separate man an equal place in the eyes of God. By his formula all laymen became priests, and all priests laymen. They all 'held' of God, and on the same terms of service. 'All dominion of man, natural or civil, is conferred upon him by God, as the prime Author, in consideration of his returning continually to God the service due unto Him; but by the fact that man, by omission or commission, becomes guilty of mortal sin he defrauds his Lord-in-chief of the said service, and by consequence incurs forfeiture, wherefore . . . he is rightfully to be deprived of all dominion whatsoever.' Such is the fundamental principle of Wycliffe's famous theory of Dominion. What the doctrine of 'Justification by Faith' was in the hands of the Reformers of the sixteenth century that of Dominion was with Wycliffe. By both there was emancipation to the individual conscience; by both the necessity of a mediating priesthood, the very basis of the Church of Rome, was swept away. The full significance of Wycliffe's doctrine of Dominion was not seen in his day. The education of the individual conscience to independence could not be effected all at once.

In favour with the court and Parliament for the

courage and power with which he had opposed the papal
claim, in 1374 Wycliffe, with John of Gaunt, the king's son, and others, were appointed to meet representatives of Gregory XI. at Bruges, to gain relief from papal extortions through the abuses which had arisen from the papal claim to dispose of English benefices. Wycliffe's commission on this embassy made one of the most picturesque chapters of his life. Like Luther's famous journey to Rome, it brought him into more intimate acquaintance with the corruptions of the papacy, and the mischief of monastic institutions. He returned from the busy centre of trade, and manufacture, and politics, and from his contact with friend and foe, with strengthened patriotism to carry on the work of reform in England. Immediately upon his return from Bruges, he was presented by the Crown to the rectory of Lutterworth, in Leicestershire, with which his name is now so familiarly associated. It is a quiet, pleasant little town, with the church still standing in which he ministered, and where may still be seen the old carved oak pulpit from which the Reformer preached sermons, many of which may still be read, simple and clear in style, full of love to the Redeemer, and earnest in concern for the salvation of souls.

Wycliffe as a royal commissioner at Bruges.

Made Rector of Lutterworth.

The first public attack upon Wycliffe was made in 1377. Wycliffe's defence of the ecclesiastical policy of the Duke of Lancaster, in resisting the arrogance and temporal power of the prelates, was more probably the occasion of the beginning of enmity than his doctrinal teaching. To withstand Wycliffe was to withstand the duke. Convocation, therefore, arraigned Wycliffe, and William of Wykeham, who had incurred John of Gaunt's special indignation, was appointed one of the judges. The tumultuous scene which ensued is well known. It is characteristic alike of the age and of the parties concerned. Early in the morning of the 19th of February prelates, priests, and citizens assembled in the lady chapel of old St. Paul's, the finest cathedral that England ever saw, with its towering spire 500 feet high. Courtenay, Bishop of London, of whom we shall hear again in his opposition to Wycliffe, presided. The cathedral was thronged with 'a main press of people

First attack on Wycliffe.

gathered to hear what should be said or done.' To the surprise and rage of Courtenay, when Wycliffe appeared he was seen to be accompanied by the duke himself. A war of words took place between the bishop and the royal prelate-hater. Amidst the clamour, the court broke up in disorder, and Wycliffe, the accused, retired without having spoken a single word.

Foiled in their first attack, the bishops had recourse to the pope, Gregory XI., the last in Avignon before the Great Schism. Ready with his aid, no fewer than five bulls were issued on one day against Wycliffe, charging him with heresy, and ordering his arrest and imprisonment. The Archbishop of Canterbury, the Bishop of London, the Chancellor of the University of Oxford, and the king, were all called upon to take action against the Reformer. The bulls were signed by Gregory 22nd May, 1377, but before they reached England the aspect of affairs was changed. On 21st June Edward III. died, his grandson, Richard II., was only eleven years old, and the court influence was friendly to Wycliffe. Through various causes of delay, not least being the hesitation of the representatives of Oxford to proceed against their most illustrious member, and their unwillingness to admit the pope's authority to order the imprisonment of any man in England, it was not till the February or March of the following year that Wycliffe was summoned to appear before a court held in the then newly erected chapel of Lambeth Palace. His written defence was laid before the council; but its session was rudely interrupted, not only by the citizens of London, who rallied round Wycliffe as an honoured patriot, but also by a messenger from the mother of the young king, whose influence was great in the council of regency, desiring the bishops not to proceed further, nor pronounce any sentence on the accused. Thus a second time Wycliffe escaped.

Second attack on Wycliffe.

Not long after the trial at Lambeth, Gregory XI. died, and a few months later was seen the strange sight of two rival popes, caused by the election of Clement VII. in opposition to Urban VI. The influence of this event was great upon the history of the Church: it deepened men's convictions of the evils of the papacy, it stimulated Wycliffe to more strenuous

Rival popes, 1378.

endeavours in the cause of reform. To him now the pope was antichrist. 'Stand we firm,' he said, 'in the faith that Christ's law teacheth, for never was there greater need, and trust we to the help of Christ. For He hath begun to help us graciously, in that He hath cloven the head of Antichrist, and made the one part to fight against the other. No doubt the sin of the popes, which has been so long continued, has brought on this division.' Wycliffe's opinion of the schism.

Suggested probably by the influence of the Preaching Friars, in his zeal to promote reform Wycliffe founded what was really a new order—an order of Itinerant Preachers. These preachers were men of culture and learning, chosen from amongst Oxford students, and those ready to enlist themselves as Wycliffe's disciples. Having no benefices, they became known as 'Poor Priests.' Their mission was to the poor, especially to the 'upland folk,' as the peasants were called. Their dress was of the simplest kind—of coarse brown wool—and, after the manner of the Friars, they travelled barefoot. They were constantly moving from place to place, preaching in town and country, wherever they could find an audience, 'God's word,' 'God's laws.' The influence of their teaching was soon felt throughout the country; they stirred up the minds of the people to religious inquiry, and so secured their co-operation in the work of reform. The 'Poor Priests.'

Wycliffe was soon seen to be more than a reformer of ecclesiastical abuses. As the champion of crown and people against Rome, he had been backed by royal and popular sympathy, but his fidelity to the teachings of Scripture and the voice of conscience brought him where he stood alone. With a courage drawn from a sense of duty and from the might of truth, in the summer of 1381 he proceeded to attack and denounce the extreme form of doctrine of transubstantiation, proving it to be contrary to Scripture, and opposed to the testimony of tradition. 'I maintain,' he says in his *Trialogus*, 'that among all the heresies which have ever appeared in the Church there was never one which was more cunningly smuggled in by hypocrites than this, or which in more ways deceives the people; for it plunders them, Wycliffe attacks the doctrine of transubstantiation.

leads them astray into idolatry, denies the teaching of Scripture, and by this unbelief provokes the Truth Himself oftentimes to anger.'[1] In opposition to the Church, he maintained that whilst Christ is bodily present in the Sacrament of the Lord's Supper, the bread never ceases to remain bread.

Doctrine so profoundly at variance with the theological principles of the day could not pass uncondemned. Many of his adherents withdrew their support, even his old friend and patron John of Gaunt, more the soldier than the theologian, desired him not to speak further on the subject. The great Reformer was silenced in his beloved Oxford. His reply to the official condemnation of his doctrine ends with the significant words, 'Nevertheless, I think the truth will prevail.' According to Dr. Lechler, it was Wycliffe's controversy on the subject of transubstantiation that brought him about this time into violent collision with the Friars. In early years he had been on friendly terms with them, now he denounced them as the chief evil of papal rule in England. 'Dead dogs,' they were, of whom the realm should be freed. In his tracts he calls their cloisters 'Cain's Castles,' and exposed their corruption in his *Fifty Heresies and Errors of the Friars*. Once when Wycliffe was thought to be dying a company of exasperated Friars surrounded his bed and exhorted him to repent, but he found strength to raise himself, and with prophetic instinct exclaimed that he should yet live to denounce their errors again.

Wycliffe's denunciation of the Friars.

The onward movement of the Wycliffian Reformation met with a sudden reverse through the great Peasant Revolt in 1381, the cause and effects of which we have already referred to. Caution is necessary in associating this revolt with the widespread influence of Wycliffe's itinerant preachers. Long before the 'Poor Priests' were sent forth, the peasantry were smarting under the sense of their grievances, and the spirit of revolt kindled. Reform with the sword is contrary to all we know of the spirit and teaching of the great Reformer; while his close

Wycliffism and the Peasant Revolt.

---

[1] Quoted in Lechler's *John Wycliffe and his English Precursors*, chap. viii. p. 343.

alliance with the unpopular John of Gaunt in the political action of the times forbids the shadow of a suspicion of any designed connection between the sending forth of the 'Poor Priests' and the revolt of the peasantry. Wycliffe had confined himself to ecclesiastical and doctrinal reform; but the spiritual and the social were too closely bound to be separated. His doctrines led to the recognition of the equal rights of man against the social system of the Middle Ages. This indirect connection between the new religious teaching and the revolt of an oppressed people was made the most of by the Reformer's adversaries.

Almost immediately following the Peasant Revolt an Act was passed for the suppression of the Poor Priests, described as 'divers evil persons who went from county to county and town to town without licence, preaching daily' sermons containing heresies. Of these preachers complaint was made that they would not obey the summons of the ordinaries, 'nor care for their monitions, nor censures of the Holy Church.' It was in consequence enacted that sheriffs and other officers of the king, upon a certificate of the bishop, should arrest all such preachers, 'and hold them in strong prison, till they will justify them according to the law and reason of the Holy Church.' *Act for the suppression of the Poor Priests, 1381.*

Proceedings were also taken against Wycliffe. Resolutely Archbishop Courtenay, successor of Sudbury, executed by the insurgent peasants, set himself to crush Wycliffe and his doctrines. A council was summoned to condemn his heresies, especially those which he had recently advanced as to the Lord's Supper. *Further proceedings against Wycliffe.* The assembly met in the Dominican monastery, Blackfriars, on the 17th May, 1382. In the course of the proceedings an earthquake was felt. Some persons present interpreted it as a sign of Divine displeasure. Courtenay, with ready wit, told them, on the contrary, it was a favourable omen: the shaking of the earth was caused by the expulsion of noxious vapours, and thus the removal of heretics from the Church would contribute to its health. The judgment of a council consisting only of men of acknowledged Roman orthodoxy was a foregone conclusion. Twenty-four points selected from Wycliffe's writings were condemned as heretical or erroneous. A mandate was sent to Oxford ordering that steps should be taken to prevent the dissemination of the doctrines censured. The unwillingness of the university to admit external authority and the popularity of Wycliffe excited a strong feeling of resistance, but the energy of Archbishop Courtenay prevailed. Some of the most prominent adherents of Wycliffe, amongst them Nicholas Hereford, Philip Repyngdon, were condemned for heresy and excommunicated. Wycliffe himself was prohibited from preaching before the university or exercising any academic function.

Probably it was in this same year of Archbishop Courtenay's triumph at Oxford that Wycliffe finished the great work with which his name is for ever associated—his translation of the Scriptures from the Latin Vulgate. From Anglo-Saxon times to his own portions of the Bible in the form of metrical paraphrases had existed, but these were never widely circulated. It is a sign of the general spiritual awakening in the fourteenth century that a priest in the county of Kent, William of Shoreham, about 1325, translated the Book of Psalms; so also did Richard Rolle, the hermit-preacher and poet of Hampole, who died in 1349. It was in the fourteenth century the writer of the *Cursor Mundi* lived, who, according to his light, was a Reformer. He desired his countrymen should have in their own language the histories contained in Scripture, and put forth in the Northumbrian dialect a large proportion of the mediæval religious traditions. His work was the storehouse of the writers of the miracle plays of later years, and has been called 'the Monk's Bible.' Much it contains is in agreement with the Scripture narrative, but the variations and apocryphal traditions show how great was the need of a version of the Scriptures which gave, not their substance merely, but a complete translation. Such was the endeavour in the work put forth under the direct supervision of Wycliffe in the year 1382. What part of the translation was actually wrought with Wycliffe's own pen, and what by his collaborateurs, it is impossible to ascertain with perfect certainty. The translation of the

The manuscript English Bible, 1382.

The Cursor Mundi.

New Testament is regarded as Wycliffe's own work. While he was engaged on that, his friend Nicholas Hereford probably was engaged on the Old Testament, and advanced as far as the middle of the Book of Baruch. Interrupted by the proceedings of Archbishop Courtenay, and summoned to appear before Convocation in London, and subsequently to Rome, he never resumed the work. Wycliffe took it in hand, and the remainder of the Old Testament from Baruch to Malachi is ascribed to him. The contrast between Wycliffe's and his fellow-worker's portions is great. Hereford's is extremely literal—in fact, so literal that without recourse to the Latin text the meaning is frequently unintelligible. Scrupulous anxiety to avoid the charge of altering the Scriptures was probably the translator's motive for such pedantic exactness. Wycliffe's is freer, more idiomatic, and in the everyday language of the thought and feeling of the age in which it appeared. Copies of the translation were made, and as a whole and in portions, according to purchasers' means, it was circulated among all classes of society. As more thoroughly English than even Chaucer's *Canterbury Tales*, Wycliffe's Bible gave shape and character to our English language, and, above all, it lit a light of Scriptural teaching which can never be extinguished. Revision of the work was commenced by Wycliffe, and continued by his trusted friend and assistant in parochial work, John Purvey, who, four years after his master's death, issued the Revision, now generally distinguished as Purvey's, made, as he says, with the 'aid of divers helpers.' Nearly all existing copies of Wycliffe's Bible are of Purvey's revision. The two versions, printed in parallel columns, under the able editorship of Messrs. Forshall and Madden of the British Museum, have been published by the Oxford University Press.

Nicholas Hereford's share in the work.

The influence of Wycliffe's and Hereford's Bible on the English language.

John Purvey's Revision.

The last public appearance of the great Reformer was in November, 1382. The place, again his beloved Oxford. The occasion, a summons to appear before a council held in the church of St. Frideswide. Then his moral greatness shone out as it never could in the days of his popularity. Spare, frail,

Last public appearance of Wycliffe.

emaciated with the strains of conflict, and alone, so far as political influence or support went, he stood before his enemies. Their silence is the convincing proof of their gaining no advantage. No result that affected him personally was come to. Unharmed, as one having a charmed life, he returned to his rectory at Lutterworth.

Two years of life were all that now remained to the famous 'Doctor Evangelicus.' These were devoted with indomitable zeal to revising his version of the Bible, to appealing to the people of England by pamphlets, which, from their extreme brevity, could, by the aid of 'Poor Priests,' be multiplied and scattered almost without limit, even in an age when printing was almost unknown, and to preaching in his own pulpit at Lutterworth sermons, the characteristics of which we know from existing MSS.—simple, clear, often picturesque in style, full of veritable zeal for the glory of God. The end of this noble, busy life was sudden. On the 29th December, 1384, while conducting service in his church, he was struck with paralysis; on the 31st he breathed his last.

Last two years of his life.

'To Wycliffe,' says Prof. Burrows, 'we owe, more than to any one person who can be mentioned, our English language, our English Bible, and our reformed religion.'[1] To attempt any summary of his theological opinions is impossible within the narrow limits of a book like the present. Reference has already been made to his doctrine of lordship, and its application to Church and State. His recognition of the supreme authority of Scripture is seen in his constant appeals to its teaching and his zeal for its translation. In his doctrinal controversy with the Romish Church on the Lord's Supper he rejected transubstantiation, and taught what must be identified as the doctrine of consubstantiation. He held that the sacrament 'is very God's body in form of bread.' 'This sacrament, in his kind [its nature], is very bread and sacramentally God's body.'[2] This teaching is repeated and plain. His doctrine of baptism is free from much modern superstition. He says: 'Bodily baptizing is a figure, how men's souls should be baptized from sin.

Doctrinal views of Wycliffe.

---

[1] *Wiclif's Place in History*, p. 6.
[2] *Select English Works*, iii. 502.

Bodily washing of a child is not the end of baptizing, but baptizing is a token of washing of the soul from sin.'[1] Prayers for souls in purgatory he held of little value. 'Prayer of good life profiteth most of all other; prayer of lips beguileth many.'[2] 'He swept away one by one almost all the peculiar tenets of mediæval Latin Christianity—pardons, indulgences, excommunications, absolutions, pilgrimages; he condemned images—at least, of the Persons of the Trinity; he rejected transubstantiation.'[3] But Teutonic Christianity had to wait more than two centuries and a half before it offered a new system of doctrine to the religious necessities of man.

Wycliffe was a prolific writer. Canon Shirley, the first to propose a society for the publication of all the Reformer's works, in his catalogue enumerates 161. These he divides into two classes, Latin and English; of the former there are 96, of the latter 65. Prof. Lechler extends the classification to six divisions, with numerous subdivisions. Of the Latin works many still remain unprinted in the public libraries of Vienna, Prague, and elsewhere. The English works, possessing a more general interest in connection with the history of our language and of the religious thought of our country, have been published in three volumes, edited by Mr. Thomas, and issued by the Clarendon Press, under the title of *Select English Works of John Wyclif*. These have been supplemented by another volume, prepared for the Early English Text Society by Mr. F. D. Matthew, and containing *The English Works of Wyclif hitherto Unprinted*. His chief works, next to the English translation of the Bible, may be thus classified:—

Works of Wycliffe.

1. PHILOSOPHICAL AND THEOLOGICAL.

Summa Theologiæ, 15 books, containing the important treatise 'On Dominion,' of which *De Dominio Civili, liber* 1, edited by Mr. Reginald Lane Poole, appeared in 1885.

De Ecclesia, edited by Prof. J. Loserth.

Trialogus, first printed at Basle 1525, again at Frank-

---

[1] *Select English Works*, ii. 328.
[2] *Ibid.* ii., 212, 213.
[3] Milman, *Latin Christianity*, viii. 203.

furt in 1753, and re-edited by Prof. Lechler in 1869. This important work is written in the form of a discussion between Truth, Falsehood, Prudence, and may be regarded as a summary of Wycliffe's theological opinions.

De Incarnatione Verbi, edited by Dr. E. Harris, 1886.
De Officio Pastorali, edited by Prof. Lechler, 1863.

II. POLEMICAL.

Dialogus, sive Speculum Ecclesiæ militantis, edited by Mr. A. W. Pollard, 1886.
Tracts, edited by Dr. R. Buddensieg.
Fifty Heresies and Errors of Friars.
De Blasphemia contra Fratres.

III. DOGMATIC AND DIDACTIC.

In this class we place works designed for popular use in the culture of the spiritual life.

On the Sufficiency of Holy Scripture.
The Seven Works of Mercy.
On the Seven Deadly Sins.
Explanation of the Apostles' Creed.
Of the Five Bodily Wits.
Of the Five Spiritual Wits.
Of Faith, Hope, and Charity.
Of Wedded Men and Wives, and of their Children also.
Of Servants and Masters, how each should keep his degree.
A Short Rule of Life.
Of good Preaching Priests.
Why Poor Priests have no Benefices.
The Poor Caitiff, long supposed to be one of the writings of Wycliffe, in the opinion of Shirley, Arnold, Lechler, and others, must be ascribed to some other writer of kindred sympathies.

III. EXEGETIC.

The English commentaries on the Gospels of Matthew, Luke, and John, and on the Apocalypse, long attributed to Wycliffe, are now withdrawn by Dr. Lechler from the list of the Reformer's writings. The following expository fragments are retained ; the English ones may be found in vol. iii. of *Wycliffe's Select Works*, edited by Mr. Arnold :—

Of the Ten Commandments.
Song of Moses (Exod. xv.).
Hymn of Moses (Deut. xxxii.).
Hannah's Song (1 Sam. ii.).
Israel's Song of Thanksgiving (Isa. xii.).
Hezekiah's Hymn of Praise (Isa. xxxvii. 10-20).
Habakkuk's Prayer (iii. 2-19).

Song of the Three Children, or *Benedicite*.
In omnes Novi Testamenti Libros, præter Apocalypsin, Commentarius.
Opus Evangelicum, sive de Sermone Domini in Monte.
Expositio S. Matthew xxiii., *sive de Væ Octuplici.*
Expositio S. Matthew xxiv., *sive de Antichristo.*
Væ Octuplex, Exposition of Matthew xxiii.
Of Ministries in the Church, Exposition of Matthew xxiv.
Ave Maria, 2 tracts.
Magnificat (Luke i. 46-55).
Benedictus (Luke i. 68-79).
Simeon's Hymn (Luke ii. 29-32).
The Lord's Prayer.

The *Te Deum*.
Athanasian Creed.

IV. SERMONS.
Of these copies of some 400 are still extant. Collections of the Latin sermons, delivered in Oxford, have been made by Prof. Loserth and published in three volumes. The English sermons will be found in the first two volumes of Mr. Arnold. They are homilies on the appointed Gospels and Epistles for the Sundays and Saints' Days of the canonical year. Many of the sermons are very short—one is only three lines—and were probably prepared simply as notes for the preacher's use in the pulpit. They are a striking proof of Wycliffe's zeal for preaching, and in their terse, simple style show the manner in which he addressed the middle class and poor of his Lutterworth parishioners.

CHAPTER X.

THE EARLY FOLLOWERS OF WYCLIFFE, OR LOLLARDS.

AFTER the death of Wycliffe there was no organized party to inherit the name and influence of their teacher, but under the name of Lollards his followers so rapidly increased that a contemporary and hostile chronicler says, 'Springing like saplings from the root of a tree, they were multiplied and filled every place within the compass of the kingdom.' They were not without high support. 'The good Queen Anne,' the first wife of Richard II., and the widow of the Earl of Lancaster, were alike favourable to their cause. Many nobles had chaplains who were Lollard preachers, and many merchants assisted the 'Poor Priests,' who travelled from county to county and town to town contending in their preaching and in their teaching for what are to us the fundamental principles of Protestantism—the right of private judgment, with its corresponding responsibility to the one Lord of all. In 1395 the strength and confidence of the Lollards were such that they petitioned Parliament to reform the Church on Lollardist methods.

Rapid increase of Wycliffe's followers under the name of Lollards.

The petition of these early Lollards is of peculiar interest and importance as an authoritative statement of the opinions which exasperated their enemies to deeds of bitter and cruel persecution. In the petition, or protest, the Roman priesthood and its doctrine of celibacy is declared contrary to apostolic precedent. The doctrine of transubstantiation is denounced as a pretended miracle leading men to idolatry. The exorcisms and benedictions so freely used in the Roman ritual are regarded as belonging to the arts of necromancy rather than to a sound theology. Prayers for the dead, pilgrimages, auricular confession, are all set aside as of no avail. War is declared to be unchristian, and such trades as those of the goldsmith and armourer as contrary to the apostolic rule of life. The

The Lollards' creed.

later Lollards also strongly protested against capital punishment. Here, then, we have a summary of the teaching which led the way to the Great Reformation. The opinions of the Lollards were not all alike, but almost all the heresies charged against the Lollards down to the fifteenth century are included in the appeal to Parliament made in the earliest years of their history.

In the intensity of their zeal against papal doctrine some of these early Lollards defied the public sentiments of their day. Images were treated with open insult and used for firewood, and sacramental wafers eaten as common food. We need not wonder that these men aroused the strongest animosity of their opponents. In London, where the Lollards were numerous, the excitement was such that the king, who was then in Ireland, was hastily sent for to quell the disturbance, and to sustain the authority of the Church.

The triumph of the Church over the Lollards was when the revolution of 1399 deposed Richard II. and put Henry IV. on the throne. Then Church and State combined to crush the Lollards, a statute was passed for their suppression, prefaced by the statement that 'False and perverse people of a certain new sect perversely and maliciously preach and teach divers new doctrines and wicked, heretical, and erroneous opinions, and the ways of the Church, with the censures of the Church, do utterly condemn and despise.' It was enacted that no one should preach without licence, or 'anything preach, hold, teach, or instruct openly, or privily, or make or write any book, contrary to the Catholic faith or determination of Holy Church.' The bishop might try any person suspected, and if he refused to abjure, or relapse, he was to be delivered to the sheriff, or mayor, who was to attend the court if required, and who 'the same persons after such sentence shall receive, and then, before the people, in a high place, *be burnt, that such punishment may strike fear in the minds of others.*' This was the terrible statute *De Heretico Comburendo*, under which so many witnesses of Christian truth sealed their testimony during the space of nearly two centuries of English history.

[Sidenote: Statute for the suppression of Lollardy.]

In the opinion of Hallam,[1] the shame of this odious Act

[1] *Middle Ages*, chap. viii., pt. iii., vol. iii., p. 89 (1855).

rests not on the Commons of England. It is directly referred to 'as made at the request of the prelates and clergy,' and there is no proof that the assent of Parliament was ever given to it. Perhaps the most remarkable point in this notorious statute is that it contains no definition of heresy. The ecclesiastical judges could define it as they pleased. Whether through lack of the assent referred to, or from very fear of using the weapon thus forged, the only two executions for heresy in this reign were carried out under power of the king's writ, and not of the new Act.

The first martyr for the Lollard creed by burning in England was himself a priest, William Sawtre. He was a chaplain of the parish of St. Margaret's, Lynn, in the diocese of Despenser, the 'fighting Bishop of Norwich,' who, says Walsingham, 'swore an oath, and never regretted it, that if any of the perverse sect of Lollards should presume to teach in his diocese, he should be given to the fire, or lose his head.' Before the martial bishop Sawtre was frightened into a recantation, and swore never to preach the Lollard doctrines again. Of his recantation he repented, and two years afterwards was found preaching in the diocese of London. It has never been forgotten that in a moment of weakness he denied that he had ever been on trial before. Those who sneer at the denial forget the courage required to lead the way amid the flames of martyrdom. For maintaining 'that in the sacrament of the altar, after the consecration made by the priest, there remained material bread,' and for refusing to admit that the material cross on which the Saviour suffered was worthy of worship, he was condemned, as a relapsed heretic, to be burned. Sentence of degradation was passed upon him: the symbols of each of the seven orders, from priest to sexton, having been successively placed upon him, were ignominiously removed. Then, with a coloured cap put upon his head, as a layman, he was handed over to the sheriff, the first Englishman to suffer death for the expression of religious opinion. The second was an outspoken tailor of the diocese of Worcester, John Badby, who declared that he would never while he lived believe that any priest could make the body of Christ

The first Lollard martyr, 1401.

John Badby, 1410.

sacramentally. In his matter-of-fact way, Badby said that when Christ sat at supper with the disciples He had not His body in His hand to distribute; and said, moreover, 'that if every host being consecrated at the altar were the Lord's body, then there be twenty thousand Gods in England.' He was brought up to London, tried before a court of bishops, presided over by Archbishop Arundel, in St. Paul's, and was condemned as an open and public heretic. Smithfield, or Smoothfield, then the public recreation ground of London, outside the walls of the city, where tournaments were held, was the place of execution, and the second of the long succession of scenes of blood and fire was witnessed in the spring of the year 1410. The Prince of Wales, afterwards Henry V., was present, and at the sound of the poor man's cries of anguish, offered him, not only life, but a pension, if he would recant. The persuasions were in vain: the involuntary cries of suffering were not those of a subdued will. With unconquered fortitude he endured the burning. We get a glimpse of monkish thought concerning such scenes in the pages of Walsingham. There the record concerning Badby is, 'The abandoned villain declined the prince's advice, and chose rather to be burned than to give reverence to the life-giving sacrament. So it befell that this mischievous fellow was burnt to ashes, and died miserably in his sin.'

Such scenes were not without their desired effect. Through the unrelenting severity of Arundel there was a great thinning of the ranks of the Lollards. The recantations were many. John Purvey, the well-known friend of Wycliffe, and the reviser of his Bible, was imprisoned and frightened into a recantation, publicly read at St. Paul's Cross. He, however, recovered his courage, for, in the year 1421, he was thrown into prison again. Sir Lewis Clifford was lost to them, and Philip Repyngdon, the supporter and defender of Wycliffe at Oxford, became, as Bishop of Lincoln, a persecutor of his followers. Yet more serious to the Lollards was the loss of a trusted leader, the Earl of Salisbury. Slain in the first of the many unsuccessful revolts against the throne, his head was carried aloft to London, where the clergy triumphed over his fall in full procession. But the Lollards had

A great thinning of the ranks of the Lollards.

still Sir John Oldcastle, the trusted friend of Henry IV., and one of the greatest soldiers of the day, to look up to as their 'leader and captain.'

In furtherance of the work of repression, Archbishop Arundel in 1408 visited Oxford, where the Wycliffe party showed signs of reviving power. His fears were confirmed. A council was held to inquire into the charge of heresy.[1] In the decrees of the assembly, afterwards sanctioned in the convocation of the province of Canterbury, the archbishop laments the defection of Oxford, as 'bringing forth bitter grapes. He describes the province as being 'infested with divers and unfruitful doctrines, and defiled with Lollardy,' and speaks of the Church as 'like to run into ruin not to be recovered.' The council decreed that no one was to be allowed to preach without a bishop's license, and no manner of person was to presume to dispute upon the articles determined by the Church. No book of Wycliffe's, nor any other, without examination, was to be read within the precincts of the University. No one, on his authority, was to translate any portion of the Scripture into the English tongue, and every head of a college or hall was to inquire at least once a month if there were any Lollards among his students. Any offender was to be first warned; if persisting, he was to be excommunicated. Not without a struggle were these mandates enforced, but Arundel in the end was successful, with the result to Oxford that for the next hundred years nothing great or good was done by the University.

Archbishop Arundel at Oxford.

The spirit of Lollardy had an illustrious representative in Sir John Oldcastle, who in the House of Commons in the year 1404, and again in 1410, moved the application of a portion of the enormous revenues of the Church to the public service. The Commons declared they would pay no more while the bishops, who were abounding in wealth, refused to contribute to the necessities of the State. The Commons also petitioned for a mitigation of the Statute of Heresy. Arundel opposed these proposals with such vigour that they were rejected by the Lords.

Lord Cobham.

While Henry IV. lived, Oldcastle, or 'the good Lord

---

[1] Wilkins, *Concilia*, iii. 114.

Cobham,' as he was popularly called, was protected, but in the year of the king's death (1413) he was accused in convocation of heresy, and of being 'the principal receiver, favourer, protector and defender' of the Lollard preachers. Henry V. did all in his power to protect him, and implored his friend to renounce his heretical doctrine. Finding persuasion vain, the king permitted the bishops to proceed against him. Cobham withdrew to his castle of Cowling, near Rochester. A citation was served on him. He refused to receive it, and was thereupon excommunicated, arrested, and imprisoned in the Tower. His trial was before his old opponent Arundel and a crowded court of prelates. The spirit of the proceedings is vividly set forth in the account preserved by Foxe. In the course of the examination, Wycliffe's name having been contemptuously mentioned, Cobham replied, 'As for that virtuous man Wycliffe, whose judgments ye so highly disdain, I shall say here, both before God and man, that before I knew that despised doctrine of his I never abstained from sin, but since I learned therein to fear my Lord God it hath otherwise, I trust, been with me.' *Lord Cobham's trial.* *Testimony to Wycliffe.*

When questioned concerning the Church and the Pope, losing his self-command, he denounced the wealth of the Church as venom. Asked by Archbishop Arundel, 'What he meant by that venom?' the reply was, 'Your possessions and lordships.' Concerning the popes, he said, 'One hath put down another; one hath poisoned another; one hath cursed another; and one hath slain another, and done much more mischief besides. Let all men consider well this, that Christ was meek and merciful; the pope is proud and a tyrant; Christ was poor and forgave; the pope is rich and a malicious manslayer. Rome is the very nest of antichrist, and out of that nest come all the disciples of him, of whom prelates, priests, and monks are the body, and these shaven friars the tails behind.'

His reply to the test question concerning the sacrament of the altar—'This I say and believe, that it is Christ's body and bread'—clearly shows that the Lollard doctrine was that of consubstantiation.

When cross-examined on the worship of images, a Dominican friar inquired,—

'Sir, will you worship the cross of Christ that He died upon?' 'Where is it?' said Lord Cobham.

The friar replied, 'I put you the case, sir, that it were here, even now before you.' 'A wise man,' said Cobham, 'to put me an earnest question of a thing, yet he himself knoweth not where the thing itself is! Yet once again I ask you, what worship I should do unto it?'

A clerk said unto him, 'Such worship as Paul speaketh of—"God forbid that I should joy but only in the cross of Christ."' 'Sir,' said the Bishop of London, 'ye wot well that He died on a material cross.' 'Yes,' replied Cobham, 'and I wot also that our salvation came not by that material cross, but alone by Him who died thereupon. And well I wot that Paul rejoiced in none other cross, but in Christ's passion and death only.'

Against so prompt and unyielding an opponent nothing was to be gained by discussion. Sentence was pronounced upon him as 'a most pernicious, detestable heretic,' and as such he was delivered to the secular jurisdiction.

His enemies' triumph was not as near as they anticipated. To their consternation, Cobham escaped from the Tower. Their fear was great lest under the leadership of one of the greatest soldiers of the day there should be a general revolt of the oppressed Lollards. The strength of Lollardy in England is shown by the rumour that 20,000 Lollards were about to march on London, and that within the city 50,000 were prepared to assist them. No evidence exists that such a revolution was ever planned, but the scare of such a rising spread, and under its influence, whether believing it or not, a sudden raid was made upon an assembly of Lollards found in St. Giles' Fields, then literally a village in the fields. Numerous arrests followed, and within five days thirty-nine prominent Lollards were executed as traitors.

The Lollard revolt.

Whether real or feigned, this mysterious rising was turned to account by the anti-Lollard party. Alarmed into anger by rumours of treason, rebellion, and meditated assassination, the Commons gave its assent to an Act which strengthened the notorious statute *De Hæretico Comburendo*. Power was given to magistrates to inquire into heresies and to commit heretics; and a conviction of heresy was to entail forfeiture of life and estate. It is a significant fact that the Parliament which passed this Act in April, 1414, met, not where the circumstances of the mysterious insurrection were best known, but at Leicester.

For four years Lord Cobham baffled the efforts of his enemies. At last he was captured in Wales, brought to London, and re-imprisoned in the Tower. His execution was peculiarly barbarous. He was drawn on a hurdle through the streets from his place of imprisonment to St. Giles' Fields; there he was hanged as a traitor and burned as a heretic, he being hung in chains over a slow fire till he was roasted to death. Thus perished the most eminent Lollard of his day; eminent both in social position and in true nobility of character: one whom the people revered as 'Good Lord Cobham,' and the tradition of whom, as known to Shakespeare, is recorded in the words, 'Oldcastle died a martyr.' *Lord Cobham's martyrdom.*

After the death of Lord Cobham the Lollards had no longer a great leader to look to; they had lost the social influence and position they once possessed, yet still were a power in the country. It was with the express view of resisting the current of heresy that Lincoln College was founded, in 1427, by Fleming, the Bishop of Lincoln, who carried out the long-deferred order of the Council of Constance for the disinterring and burning of Wycliffe's bones. Foxe, the martyrologist, who had access to the Register of the Diocese of Norwich, states that between 1428 and 1431, in that diocese alone, one hundred and twenty persons were accused upon suspicion of heresy.

Archbishop Chichely, the founder of All Souls, Oxford, whose tomb in Canterbury Cathedral is remarkable for its sculpture, in which the living and dead man are contrasted, was Arundel's successor, and as severe a suppressor of Lollardy. It was found that many of the poorer rectors and parish priests were Lollards in belief. There was William Taylor, who, for denying the invocation of saints, was burned in Smithfield. There was William White, who laid aside clerical attire, and allowed his hair to grow over his tonsure, who had fearlessly taken to himself a wife. He was brought up in chains before Alnewick, Bishop of Norwich, and was condemned to death. There was Thomas Bagley, also a priest, who bluntly said that if in the sacrament a priest made bread into God, he made a God that can be eaten *Archbishop Chichely. Lollardy among the Clergy.*

by rats and mice. This crime cost him his life. There was John Skilley, a miller, who for having befriended certain Lollards, for seven years was imprisoned in the monastery at Langley. There was Margery Baxter, who, when asked whether she confessed her sins to a priest, replied she had never offended any priest, and therefore she would never confess to any priest, neither obey him, because priests have no power to absolve from sins, for that they daily offend themselves; and men ought to confess to God, and not to priests. Looking through the records of these and other offenders, we find the charges brought against them the usual ones of Lollard doctrine: disbelief in transubstantiation, condemnation of pilgrimages, prayers to images and saints, of confession to priests, and of taking of oaths; their contention for the priesthood of all believers, the right of priests to marry; that the Pope hath no power to bind and loose on earth; that the observance of fast day and festival is not binding; that prayers made in all places are acceptable to God, and that the Catholic Church is only the congregation of the elect, *i.e.*, the faithful.

Many instances are recorded of those who gave way under the pressure of persecuting laws. Foxe gives a list of over a hundred names of those who recanted, of whom, in kindlier spirit than some have spoken, he says: 'These soldiers of Christ, being much beaten with the cares and troubles of those days, although they were constrained to relent and abjure—that is, to protest otherwise with their tongues than their hearts did think—partly through correction and partly through infirmity, being as yet but newly trained soldiers in God's field, yet for the goodwill they bare unto the truth we have thought good that their names should not be suppressed.'[1] For their 'goodwill to the truth,' as Foxe expresses it, they were condemned to do public penance in the towns where they lived by going through the streets and standing in the parish church bareheaded, bareshouldered, barefooted, and with tapers in their hands. In Surrey, Kent, Essex, Buckinghamshire, the spirit of revolt against Rome was resisted by men-at-arms, by burnings and penances, that suppressed, but did not extinguish, the reforming spirit.

Lollard recantations.

[1] Foxe, iii. 588.

CHAPTER XI.

LOLLARD LITERATURE.

INTERESTING evidence of the influence of the Wycliffian Reformation is found in the literature it called forth: a literature of pamphlets in prose and verse, in which the thoughts that stirred men's minds and the arguments which were employed to rouse the people are abundantly illustrated. These religious writings are also an interesting proof that in a greater degree than is generally supposed a certain amount of education existed in the middle, if not lower, classes of the people. If there had been no readers, there would have been no demand for the numerous copies of Purvey's revision of Wycliffe's translation of the Bible, and of other works issued. According to the editors of the Oxford edition of the Wycliffite versions, after the vast destruction of ancient MSS. during past centuries, and notwithstanding the special search again and again made for Wycliffian literature in the times of persecution, there are still about 150 MSS. of the whole or portions of Purvey's revision, the majority of which were written within forty years of its publication. This survival gives some idea of the number of copies once in circulation. Some were written on vellum, in the most elaborate manner, for persons of wealth. Some are copies of only portions of the translation, of single books, and even of fragmentary passages. In the trials of the Lollards of later years we find one charged with having 'the four Gospels in English'; another, 'a book of the Ten Commandments in English'; another, 'the book of the ten plagues of God sent to Pharaoh.' Such was the eagerness with which the Scriptures were studied that persons with retentive memories learned portions, which were turned to account in the secret assemblies for worship. The charge against a certain Alice Collins was that she was commonly sent for to recite unto her assembled friends and neighbours

Purvey's revision of Wycliffe's Bible.

the Ten Commandments and the Epistles of Peter and James.

Just as at one time all the Psalms were generally attributed to David, so for many years the numerous religious writings of the fourteenth century with anything of Gospel fervour in them were attributed to Wycliffe. His was indeed the pen of a ready writer, producing works great and small, learned and popular. But it must be remembered Wycliffe had able coadjutors in Nicholas Hereford, John Purvey, and many of his 'Poor Priests,' for the diffusion of truth by the written word. To them, in the opinion of Professor Lechler, must be ascribed the single commentary on the first three Gospels and on the Apocalypse, hitherto supposed to be the work of Wycliffe. Wycliffe's *Wyckett*, an English tract denying the bodily sacramental presence, was handed down from generation to generation among the Lollards as the most valued defence of their sacramental doctrine. The tract, probably originally a sermon, takes its title from the text concerning the strait gate and the narrow way which leadeth unto life. In it it is said, 'Truly this must be the worst sin, to say that ye make God; it is the abomination of discomfort, that is said in Daniel the prophet, standing in the holy place.'

The Wicket.

In defence of the 'Poor Priests,' a tract, generally ascribed to Wycliffe, was written — *Why Poor Priests have no Benefices*. The defence being that it was against their conscience to hold a living, or, at least, to seek one. The patron, whether prelate or layman, expected some simoniacal return, if not a payment in money to themselves, yet perhaps indirectly—'kerchief for the lady, or a palfrey or a tun of wine.' Another reason which prevailed on the itinerants to decline a benefice was the restraint it would place upon their ministrations. Without that clog, 'they must surely help themselves and serve their brethren, and they are free to fly from one city to another, when they are persecuted by the clerk of antichrist, as Christ biddeth and the Gospels.' For the guidance and direction of the priests several tracts were issued. On the duty of priests as well as laymen Wycliffe wrote a beautiful *Short Rule of Life, for Priests, and Lords and Labourers specially*; also one on *A*

Why Poor Priests have no Benefices.

Tracts for the priests.

Good Preaching Priest, in which he says what is not without its application in the present day, 'God forbid that any Christian man understand that this censing and intoning that men use now be the best service of a priest, and most profitable to man's soul.' For the instruction of the poor in the simple elements of religion *The Poor Caitiff* was written, caitiff then meaning a prisoner, or one in a piteous condition. The book is described by its author, now supposed to be other than Wycliffe, as 'sufficient to teach simple men and women of goodwill the right way to heaven.' It consists of a number of short pieces on the Apostles' Creed, the Lord's Prayer, and other religious subjects.

The Poor Caitiff.

Among the interesting writings of the Lollards, but of later date, certainly after the passing of the Act *De Hæretico Comburendo* is the *Ploughman's Prayer*, preserved in Foxe's *Monuments*. Written probably by one of the Poor Priests, it is of peculiar interest as illustrating the style and character of their teaching. After a summary of the historic faith of the Christian Church, the writer sets forth what is called 'the clear teaching of the Gospel' in seven commandments.

The Ploughman's Prayer.

'The first is this, Thou shalt love thy God over all other things, and thy brother as thyself, both enemy and friend.

'The second commandment is of meekness, in which Christ chargeth us to forsake lordship upon our brethren, and other worldly worship, and so He did Himself.

'The third commandment is in standing steadfastly in the truth and forsaking all falseness.

'The fourth commandment is to suffer in this world diseases and wrongs without resisting.

'The fifth commandment is mercy, to forgive our brethren their trespass as oftentimes they sinneth, without asking of vengeance.

'The sixth commandment is poorness in spirit, but not to be a beggar.

'The seventh commandment is chastity—that is, a forsaking of fleshly likings displeasing to God.

'These commandments enclose the ten commandments of the old law and somewhat more.'

In such teaching there is the witness to the purer faith,

the clearer light, the holier life of the Lollards above that
of their neighbours.

Much of the pamphlet, as the title implies, is in the
form of a prayer, or lamentation to the Lord, concerning
the corruptions of the clergy and the Church. Its closing
petitions thus simply and touchingly express the Lollard's
prayer:

'We poor men pray Thee that Thou wilt send us shepherds of Thine own, that will feed Thy flock in Thy pasture, and go themselves before them. And, Lord, give our king and his lords hearts to defend Thy true shepherds and Thy sheep from out of the wolves' mouths, and grace to know Thee that Thou art the true Christ, the Son of the Heavenly Father, from the antichrist, that is the son of pride. And, Lord, give us, Thy poor sheep, patience and strength to suffer for Thy law the cruelness of the mischievous wolves. And, Lord, as Thou hast promised, shorten these days. Lord, we ask this now, for more need was there never.' *[The Lollards' prayer.]*

Such was the prayer of the Lollards in the days when
Archbishop Arundel, in his province, and Despenser, the
zealous bishop of Norwich, in his diocese, were following
up with bitter and cruel persecution men whose only fault
was the guilt of holding a simpler creed than the recognised one of their time.

To this period, the early part of the fifteenth century,
must be assigned an anonymous plea for the translation
of the Bible into English, and for its diffusion
among the laity. Foxe inserts it in his *Monuments*, as a 'compendious old treatise, showing
how that we ought to have the Scripture in English.' It
contains an enumeration of all possible precedents for the
use of Scripture in the vernacular. Probably at Tindale's,
the Bible translator's, suggestion it was revised and
printed as a contribution to the Reformation controversies
of the sixteenth century. Reference we find to other
tracts in circulation among the Lollards, the possession
and reading of which were made the occasion of accusation. We read of one John Claydon, who had a book
that was well bound in red leather,— of parchment,—
written in a good English hand,' called *The
Lantern of Light*, that was greatly prized as
containing the articles of Lollard belief. Before the days

of Edmund Spenser, there was a *Shepherd's Calendar*,
setting forth that the sacrament was made in the remembrance of Christ. Hampole's *Pricke of Conscience* was
among the forbidden books. Another, now known only
by name, probably, a life of George Podiebrad, King of
Bohemia. *The King of Beeme* also brought its possessors into trouble. Important light on Lollard
doctrine is found in *The Examination of William
Thorpe*, a contemporary and warm-hearted
friend of Wycliffe, and one of his 'Poor Priests.' He
was one of the victims of Archbishop Arundel, and tried
before him in 1407. His intimate knowledge of the
Scriptures and his scholarly acquaintance with the writings of the early Fathers show him to have been a man
of considerable learning. He committed to writing
accounts of his examinations before the Archbishop, in
which the discussions were long and interesting, concerning the five points on which he was charged; viz.,
that, when preaching at St. Chad's Church, Shrewsbury,
he had said that the sacrament of the altar, after the
consecration, was material bread; that images should in
no wise be worshipped; that men should not go on
pilgrimages; that priests have no title to tithes; and
that it is not lawful to swear in any wise. Thorpe's
defence was long treasured by the Lollards, and read by
them in hand-written copies. In the sixteenth century it
was revised by Tindale, and published in printed form.

Of productions in verse in Lollard literature there are
two of special interest—*Peres the Ploughman's Creed*, and
The Ploughman's Tale. The *Creed*, frequently
confounded with Langland's more famous
Vision of William concerning Piers the Ploughman, already referred to, is a much shorter poem, written
at a later date, about 1394, and by an unknown writer,
of Lollard sympathies. The poem abounds in points of
interest. The writer describes in vivid, picturesque language the experiences of a poor man, who, knowing his
A B C, his *Paternoster* and his *Ave Maria*, desired to learn
the Creed, and who, in the end, got better instruction from
a poor ploughman than from any of the four orders of
friars. The friars he found living in luxury, and each set
denouncing all the rest. Leaving them, he found a poor
ploughman toiling in a field with his wife, under such

circumstances of cold and poverty that as the woman walked barefoot over the frozen ground the tracks of her feet were stained with blood. The poem furnishes us with a vivid picture of the stately magnificence in which the friars lived, and of the jealousies existing between the different religious orders, and is of pathetic interest in the picture it presents of the condition of the labouring poor. The Creed, as expounded to the inquirer by the ploughman, is an orthodox paraphrase of the Apostles' Creed, with an additional clause setting forth the Wycliffian doctrine of the sacrament. According to some copies of the poem, the friars themselves were in dispute as to the Real Presence.

Ascribed to the same author now, though inserted in early editions of Chaucer, is *The Ploughman's Tale*, or *The Complaint of the Ploughman*. The poem is of considerable length, and has been reprinted in Mr. Wright's Political Poems. It paints popes, cardinals, prelates, rectors, monks, and friars, who call themselves followers of Peter, and keepers of the gates of heaven and hell, and pale, poverty-stricken people, cotless and landless, who have to pay them for spiritual assistance. Of them, says the ploughman in his prologue,—

The Ploughman's Tale.

> 'They make us thralls at their lust [desire],
>   And say we may not else be saved;
>   They have the corn, and we the dust;
>   Who speaketh them against, they say he raved.'

The Lollard character of the writer is very apparent in a dialogue introduced between the fierce Griffin of the dominant Church and the gentle Pelican of Lollardy. Of this poem Lechler says, 'It is an almost prophetic glimpse of the apparent defeat of the Lollard movement, followed by the phœnix-like reappearance of its spirit as the animating power of the Reformation.'

CHAPTER XII.

THE LATER LOLLARDS.

IN the midst of the turmoil, bloodshed, and sorrow of the Wars of the Roses, from 1440 to 1485, every man had to look after his own. For the bishops in that time of chaos there was little leisure to trouble themselves about heretic Lollards. Because no instances of death for expression of religious opinion occurred for half a century, the assertion has too often been repeated that the suppression of Lollardy was complete; but, in the beautiful language of Fuller, it is true of the Lollards, 'The very storm was their shelter.' Bishop Pecock's elaborate *Repressor of over much Blaming of the Clergy*, written about the year 1450, is proof in itself of the presence and power of Lollardy in the land.

Abatement of persecution during the Wars of the Roses.

Bishop Pecock's Repressor of over much Blaming of the Clergy.

Bishop Pecock's position as a 'repressor' is unique: it involved him in a charge of heresy. He was a man of great proficiency in learning and of singularly independent judgment. As Bishop of Chichester, he was brought into actual contact with the Lollards. The position which he took up towards them was adverse, yet not heartily papal. By reason rather than force he sought to influence them. With scrupulous anxiety to be just to his opponents, he made himself acquainted with their doctrines, and his endeavour was to meet them with common-sense argument. 'The clergy,' he said, 'shall be condemned at the last day, if by clear wit they draw not men into consent of true faith, otherwise than by fire, and sword, and hangment: although I will not deny these second measures to be lawful, provided the former be first used.' He had the boldness to affirm that the interpretation of Scripture must in all cases be accommodated to reason, and that the faith of the Church might be tested by the Scriptures as to whether it was the very faith which Christ and His apostles taught or no. His testimony to the Wycliffe

Bible is that those who had read therein had found it 'much delectable and sweet: it drew its readers into a devotion and a love to God, and from love and fondness of the world.' By his books, sermons, and tracts Bishop Pecock raised such a storm of displeasure, that he was accused of heresy, tried, and convicted. He was offered the choice whether he would abjure or be delivered to the secular arm. Bewildered, the condemned bishop stood for a few moments motionless. At length he replied, 'I am in a strait betwixt two, and hesitate in despair as to what I shall choose. If I defend my opinions and position, I must be burned to death; if I do not, I shall be a byword and reproach.' He chose the latter alternative, which was made as humiliating as possible. In the presence of a vast concourse of people, assembled at St. Paul's Cross, he knelt before his brother bishops, and made his public recantation. A fire was then kindled, and with his own hands he delivered the offending book and other of his writings to be burned. Deprived of his bishopric, he was sent to Thorney Abbey, in Cambridgeshire. There he was kept in close confinement, and the power to offend again with his pen effectually prevented, by withholding from him the use of all materials for writing.

Bishop Pecock charged with heresy.

His recantation.

When peace was restored to England on the accession of Henry VII., it is evident that the religious principles of the reforming party had a deep and strong hold on the minds of a great number of persons. The bishops again were busy as victim after victim was haled before them.

Renewed persecution of the Lollards.

Within a few months of the king's accession a Lollard was burnt in London. Soon the number of burnings there, and in Canterbury, and in Norwich, rapidly increased. Neither age nor sex was spared. The honours of fourscore years were not allowed to plead exemption for a venerable lady, Joan Boughton, who, as 'a disciple of Wycliffe,' was committed to the flames in Smithfield. Such was the honour in which she was held that during the night of the day following her burning the ashes of the fire were collected as treasured memorials. At Canterbury the king himself argued with a condemned priest, who, it is said, recanted, but was nevertheless burnt.

In Buckinghamshire, in 'among the beech-crowned slopes of the Chiltern Hundreds,' the number and influence of the Lollards were such that they attracted the attention of the bishop of the diocese, William Smith, who instituted proceedings against them. *The Buckinghamshire martyrs.* The first to suffer was William Tylsworth, who was burned at Amersham in 1506. By a refinement of cruelty, his persecutors compelled the condemned man's daughter to fire the faggots which were to burn her own father. About sixty Lollards bore faggots to the place of burning as a part of their penance.

The severity of these proceedings had the desired result of causing many to recant. Of those who made submission and were sentenced to do penance, a large number were branded on the cheeks with a hot iron, and were compelled to wear badges *The 'Great Abjuration.'* of green cloth on their sleeves, as a permanent mark of disgrace. Others were compelled to undertake pilgrimages to the shrines they had derided. In some cases the penance amounted to perpetual servitude in a neighbouring monastery, the precincts of which the penitent was never to pass.

The year of the 'Great Abjuration,' as it was called, was not that of the extinction of Lollardy. Hunted like wild beasts from hiding-place to hiding-place, beset by informers, imprisoned, or subjected to aggravated humiliation, 'the Known Men,' 'the Just Fast Men,' as the Lollards were variously called, struggled on through the early years of the sixteenth century. Evidently Lollardy was not extirpated when Henry VIII. was on the throne: in the year 1519 seven persons, including one woman, were burned on the same day at Coventry for teaching their children the Lord's Prayer and Ten Commandments in English. *Lollardy in Henry VIII.'s reign.* In 1521, Bishop Longland of Lincoln felt 'no little discomfort and heaviness' from the number of heretics, as he deemed them, within his diocese. Other bishops must have felt the same, for within five and twenty years six persons suffered death in Kent, five in the eastern counties, two in Wiltshire. With these later Lollards, as with those of the fourteenth century, the points of accusation were the same. Excepting certain extravagant expressions of thought and superstition upon the part of some of their number, the thoughts and characteristic habits of the later Lollards were the same as those expressed in their petition of 1395. The earlier and later Lollards were one in their bold denunciations of transubstantiation, pilgrimages, and of worship before shrines and images. They were one in the vehemence with which they inveighed against prayers for the dead, auricular confession, priestly celibacy, and the exercise of religious functions by men whose lives were a reproach to their holy calling. And they were one in their belief in the simple sufficiency of the Scriptures as a guide to salvation.

The influence of Lollardy was mainly confined to the midland and south-eastern parts of the country. The north of England seems to have been wholly untouched. Westward of Sussex, along the coast, there is no trace of Lollard persecutions, but in Wiltshire and in the counties northward as far as Leicestershire, its influence in varying degree prevailed.

The area of country over which Lollardy prevailed.

In process of time the power of truth in the Lollard teaching would have brought about a national Reformation, but it was hastened by the influence of the Lutheran Reformation and by political events in England. Unquestionably the suppressed but by no means extinguished Lollardy prepared the way in thousands of homes for the great religious reforms of the sixteenth century. In the darkest night of religious superstition the 'Lollard Bible-men' were witnesses to the truths dear to all Protestants. Brave, heroic men and women they were, for the most part of the middle classes, of the traders in the towns, of the farmers in the country, who 'in their travails, their earnest seekings, their burning zeal, their readings, their watchings, their sweet assemblies, their love and concord, their godly living,' laid the spiritual foundations of the Great Reformation, and prepared the public mind to eagerly welcome Tindale's Testament, and the rapid succession of versions of the Scriptures that followed. Undeniably it was in the eastern counties and other counties where the Lollards most abounded the principles of the Reformation were most welcomed, and in the dark days of Mary most heroically held.

Connection of Lollardy with the Great Reformation.

A MAP OF ENGLAND,
showing the counties over which the influence of Lollardy extended.

Part III.

THE GREAT REFORMATION OF THE SIXTEENTH CENTURY.

CHAPTER XIII.

OXFORD REFORMERS.

WHILE the Lollards were holding their meetings for Bible reading and mutual exhortation in places of concealment, in peasants' huts and secluded fields, a fresh and independent movement for reform had arisen in Oxford. Scholars were there who had studied in Italy, and were in full sympathy with the newly awakened interest in learning. Within a space of time not exceeding the ordinary term of a man's life, a succession of events had taken place that was changing the intellectual condition of all Europe. The conquest of Constantinople by Mahomet the Second, and the consequent coming into Europe as refugees of scholars of the East, rich in classic learning, who found a ready welcome in Italy, especially at Florence; the discovery of America by Columbus, and of the new route to India round the Cape by Vasco de Gama; and last, but not least, the invention of the printing press in Germany, broadened men's sympathies, quickened aspiration for knowlege, and though not at once, yet surely, prepared men to look with bewilderment and disgust upon the childish fables and the impostures of the Church which they had so long tolerated. Not without reason is such a period described as that of the Renaissance—the new birth.

<small>New movement for reform at Oxford.</small>

Amongst those brought under the influence of this movement was John Colet, Dean of St. Paul's Cathedral, and the founder of St. Paul's Grammar School. In his early years, after the completion of his course at Magdalen College, Oxford, he had travelled in Italy, and returned to his university with enthusiasm, not only for the revival of literature, but also for the reformation of religion. We know him as a man of deep and fervent piety, of self-sacrificing ways, of great ability, and of varied learning. It is a probable conjecture that when in Italy

<small>John Colet at Oxford, 1496.</small>

he had heard Savonarola, the prophet monk and preacher of Florence, and that moved by his impassioned eloquence, Colet determined to take up a like work of reform in his own country and in his own university. All who favoured the new learning were enthusiasts in the study of Greek, then regarded as a novelty, and the language of 'pagans and heretics,' by those to whom the Latin of the Vulgate was a sacred language. Probably there were not half a dozen persons in England at this time acquainted with the original language of the New Testament. Colet's position was therefore a pronounced one when, upon his return to Oxford in 1496, he began a course of expository lectures on the Epistle to the Romans. Setting aside the allegorical and mystical interpretations of the scholastic commentators, the young expositor-lecturer, not then in deacon's orders, sought to explain the book as a whole, and not in textual fragments. Such a method gave a sense of reality to the apostle's writings that arrested attention and drew to his lectures monks, and priests, and students, with note-books in hand, all eager to hear—some to learn, some to accuse. His enthusiasm for the Scriptures, especially for the writings of St. Paul, and their literal interpretation, was intense. 'Keep firmly to the Bible and the Apostles' Creed, and let divines, if they like, dispute about the rest,' was his advice to the young men of Oxford who came to him in their theological perplexities.

Colet's expository lectures.

Though less known than many of the Reformers, as Mr. Seebohm in his scholarly volume on *The Oxford Reformers* shows, Colet's influence was important in preparing the way for the great changes so shortly to follow. Among those influenced by the work of Colet in Oxford was the afterwards famous Erasmus, and in a less degree, Thomas More, afterwards Sir Thomas More. Erasmus, frail in constitution, and diminutive in stature, but keen and quick-witted, and Colet, the staid, devout theologian, were about the same age, but Colet's intellectual development was so rapid that as soon as they were brought together Erasmus became a pupil of Colet. In the course of subsequent events the pupil accomplished more than the master, but to Colet belongs the honour of befriending Erasmus as a poor foreign scholar at Oxford, and by his

His influence upon others.

private intercourse producing an impression on the mind of his friend that affected the whole course of his mental and spiritual history. More was but a lad of seventeen, preparing for his future profession, a lad of fascinating character, full of wit and genius. Upon him the earnestness of Colet produced impressions which led, in after years, to enduring friendship and fellow work. The awakening influence of Colet's teaching may also have been shared by another young student, twenty years younger, then at Oxford, William Tindale, whose life work was to be that of biblical interpretation as a translator of the New Testament Scriptures. Contemporary with Colet, and also at Magdalen College, was Thomas Wolsey, the afterward celebrated cardinal, with whom through life there was a degree of intimacy amounting almost, if not positively, to friendship.

More prominent, and possibly more difficult work, awaited Colet in London. Four years before the close of Henry VII.'s reign he was made dean of the cathedral of the city of which his father had been lord mayor. In London, as at Oxford, he pursued his course as a religious teacher and reformer; in his cathedral sermons he went through the 'Gospel History,' the 'Apostles' Creed,' and the 'Lord's Prayer.' The scripturalness of his teaching, his simple style of dress, his earnest reproofs of ecclesiastical wickedness in high places, his discountenancing the worship of saints and relics, won the sympathetic admiration of the persecuted Lollards, who counselled one another in their secret assemblies to go and hear the dean. The dean, though, knew not the Lollards. Unconscious class prejudice may have prevented him inquiring sufficiently into their position and aims, for though never their persecutor, he spoke of them as 'men mad with strange folly.'

Colet as Dean of St. Paul's, 1499.

High in honour as the name of Colet deserves to be for his influence as a theologian, his claim is yet greater as a leader in the great work of educational reform, the influence of which in bringing about the Reformation is seldom sufficiently emphasized. Dean Colet it was who first set aside the exclusive claim of the priesthood to the training of the young, by directing that the governing body of his school should

An educational reformer.

be 'married citizens of established reputation.' He was
the first to direct the teaching in English the Articles of
the Faith, and the Lord's Prayer, and the Ten Commandments. The far-reaching influence of such reforms
may not have been discerned by Dean Colet, but honour
to him to whom it is due, for the impulse thus given to
educational reform in our land. It was in a spirit of
noble self-sacrifice he devoted immense wealth
to the endowment of a school for 153 scholars;
his intent being an advance upon existing
educational methods, especially in the teaching of the
classics, also, as he himself has left on record, 'to increased knowledge and worshipping of God and our Lord
Jesus Christ, and good Christian life and manners in the
children.' And as if to keep this end always prominently
in view, an image of the child Jesus was carved over the
master's chair, with the words, 'Hear ye Him.'

<small>Founder of St. Paul's School, 1510.</small>

William Lily, the eminent grammarian, was appointed
head-master, and the help of the illustrious Erasmus and
Linacre secured in the preparation of school books.
Finding his learned friend Linacre's Latin grammar too
long and too learned for his little beginners, Colet himself wrote one, as he thought, easier, in the 'proem' to
which he says to those for whom it was written, 'I pray
you, little children, lift up your little white hands for me
who prayeth for you to God.' The result of this movement thus initiated is seen in the many grammar schools
founded within the following thirty years—more than had
been in the three hundred previously. 'The piety and
charity of Protestants,' says his biographer, Knight, 'ran
so fast in this channel that in the next year there wanted
rather a regulation of grammar schools than an increase
of them.'

At the time Colet was busily occupied in carrying out
his plans for his school, his friend Erasmus' famous
satire, *The Praise of Folly*, appeared. Its clever, vivacious
author claims for it that it was not written with
serious intent; that it was a mere *jeu d'esprit*,
cast off during a seven days' visit at More's
house; that a copy of it, snatched from his hand, was
passed on to a Parisian printer, who published it in
1512. Its circulation was enormous: within a few
months seven editions were called for, twenty-seven

<small>Erasmus and his *Praise of Folly*, 1510.</small>

ERASMUS.

in all during the author's life. With the keenest satire, men of all classes are attacked, and abuses of all kinds exposed. Theologians, monks, popes, and with them nobles, princes, and kings, all pass under the lash.

Erasmus endeavoured to screen himself from the consequences of his bold utterances under the pretext that they were ascribed to 'Folly,' and were to be taken as such. Yet there were those who shrewdly suspected that 'Folly' and Erasmus were of the same mind. It is not easy to estimate the effect the satire of Erasmus had upon the public mind of his day. Written in Latin, it was in circulation in every university and country in Europe; it became the common talk of men everywhere, and led to the saying, afterwards current, that 'Erasmus injured the pope more by joking than Luther by scolding.' Effect of the satire.

In manners more courageous, though in language less picturesque than that of his illustrious friend, Colet urged the necessity of radical reform in the Church. Warham, the learned primate, of whom Erasmus says that he was a man of learning and of mild goodness, and (both in morals and piety) a worthy prelate, destined to see and to take conspicuous part in the casting off the yoke of England's allegiance to the pope, appointed Colet to preach before a convocation called to meet in St. Paul's for the 'extirpation of heresy.' In Colet's treatment of the subject there was no encouragement to the persecuting party. He fearlessly addressed the assembled bishops, abbots, and clergy of high degree, priests and prelates sitting robed and mitred before him, many of whom were notoriously worldly, self-seeking politicians, on the necessity of ecclesiastical reform. The sermon is of peculiar interest as an authentic setting forth of the state of the clergy in the beginning of Henry VIII.'s reign; for, spoken to the clergy themselves, the charges or statements made must have been indisputable, else they would have been refuted. If the satires of Erasmus be regarded as overdrawn, the convocation sermon of a royal chaplain may be read as a corrective. Speaking first of 'conformation to this world amongst the clergy,' the preacher complains of their breathless race from benefice to benefice; of their giving themselves up to feasting and banqueting, gaming and jesting, hunting and hawking, and describes them as 'drowned in the delight of this world.' Worse in their influence than the heresy of the Lollards were the vicious and depraved lives of the clergy! Then passing on to speak of the reformation required, he declared it must begin with the bishops. Addressing them, he said: 'If you keep the laws, and first reform your own lives to the law and rules of the canons, [you] will thereby provide us with a light, in which we shall see what we ought to do—the light, *i.e.*, of your example.' He complains that men unfitted for office had been admitted to holy orders, and that promotion in the Church had not been made with just regard to merit, as might be seen when 'boys instead of old men, fools instead of wise men, wicked instead of good men, reigned and ruled.' The simony in their midst he compares to a 'dire pestilence creeping like a cancer through the minds of the priests. When the clerical and priestly part of the Church are reformed,' he said, 'we shall then with better grace proceed to the reformation of the lay part.'

To speak with such out-spokenness as Colet did against incapable priests, to discountenance the worship of saints and relics, to translate articles of faith into English, was to identify oneself, in his day, with the 'detestable heresy' of Lollardy. Colet's school was denounced by one bishop as a 'temple of idolatry'; and the Bishop of London, Fitzjames, the Lollard burner, with two other bishops, united in laying a charge of heresy against the offender—charges that against a poor Lollard might have resulted in burning; but, fortunately for the Dean of St. Paul's, he had for his friend Warham, the gentle and learned primate, who dismissed the charge.

Colet charged with heresy, 1512.

While Colet was in conflict with men of the old school of thought, now called the Old Learning, in distinction from the doctrines of the Renaissance, which were denominated the New Learning, his friend Erasmus had been engaged as Professor of Greek at the University of Cambridge. As Gibbon epigrammatically puts it, 'Erasmus learned Greek at Oxford to teach it at Cambridge.'

Erasmus' Greek Testament, 1516.

At Cambridge Erasmus was busily engaged in the preparation of a revised text of the Greek Testament, a work that more than any other of his time contributed to the cause of the Reformation among the learned. Diligently Erasmus collated such MSS. as he could obtain, and personally superintended the printing of his work at Basle. Of the labour involved he says, 'If I told you how much sweat it cost me, you would not believe me.' The result appeared in 1516 in a volume dedicated to Pope Leo X., containing in parallel columns the Greek text with a Latin translation. To these he afterwards added expository notes. It is easy, in these days of thorough recensions of the New Testament, to say of this, one of the earliest, it has no critical value; but to it belongs the value and honour of all true pioneer work. For centuries the Vulgate translation of the Scriptures had been the only one in use, and its authority regarded as sacred. The text of Erasmus carried home to the minds of the reading public of his day, lay and clerical, that at best the Vulgate was 'but a second-hand document,' and in places even an erroneous document. Previous to that published by Erasmus, the only printed text was that in the fifth volume of the famous *Complutensian Polyglot*, published in 1514. The publication of this great work, of which only six hundred copies were printed, was in progress for fifteen years, the last volume appearing in 1517. The first edition of Erasmus' New Testament was followed by a second in 1519. The two together consisted of three thousand three hundred copies.

Printed and published at Basle.

Rapid sale of the Greek Testament.

The Greek Testament of Erasmus made him hosts of enemies. Priests used their influence at the confessional to warn young students against it. In one of the colleges at Cambridge it was forbidden by solemn decree to bring the book 'by horse or by boat, on wheels or on foot.' The monks made themselves conspicuous by the zeal of their opposition; and none, characteristically says Erasmus, 'barked more furiously than those who never saw even the outside of the book' they condemned.

Opposition to Erasmus' Testament.

Among those who read the much-talked-of book was Thomas Bilney, a name not then known beyond the circle of college student friends at Cambridge. Of the impression it produced upon his mind we have the record in a letter to Bishop Tunstall, who, with Colet, and More, and Warham, was a friend of Erasmus. Bilney, writing of his college days, says: 'I heard speak when the New Testament was first set forth by Erasmus, which when I understood to be eloquently done by him, being allured rather by the Latin than by the word of God—for at that time I knew not what it meant—and at the first reading, as I well remember, I chanced upon the sentence of St. Paul, "It is a true saying, and worthy of all men to be embraced, that Christ Jesus came into the world to save sinners." '[1] The far-reaching results of the impression produced upon Bilney's mind will be seen in subsequent chapters. The noble work of Erasmus also laid the foundation for that of his great admirer, Tindale, whose English version of the New Testament was based on the third edition of Erasmus's Greek Testament; and the time was not far distant when, by royal authority, a copy of his *Paraphrases on the Gospels and Epistles* was ordered to be placed in every parish church.

Thomas Bilney.

No doubt the results of the labours of Erasmus went beyond his intentions; but none need question the earnest religious intent expressed in the 'Exhortation' prefixed to his edition of the New Testament: 'I utterly dissent from those who are unwilling that the sacred Scriptures should be read by the unlearned translated into their vulgar tongue, as though Christ had taught such subtleties that they can scarcely be understood even by a few theologians, or as though the strength of the Christian religion consisted in men's ignorance of it. . . . I long that the husbandman should sing portions of them to himself as he follows the plough, that the weaver should hum them to the tune of his shuttle, that the traveller should beguile with their stories the tedium of his journey.'[2]

Purpose of Erasmus in publishing Greek Testament.

An important sign of the times in their social and religious aspect is seen also in Sir Thomas More's famous

---

[1] Foxe, *Acts and Mon.*, iv. 635.
[2] Quoted in Seebohm, *Oxford Reformers*, p. 256.

SIR THOMAS MORE
(*After the portrait by Holbein*)

CARDINAL WOLSEY.
(From the portrait by Holbein.)

in the church of which Wycliffe made his last public
appearance. Soon after another bull allowed him to suppress monasteries with fewer than seven inmates; and twenty were found whose funds were appropriated to the founding of the new college at Oxford, to be known as Cardinal's College. This was soon followed by another bull, authorizing the suppression of monasteries which had fewer than twelve inmates, the funds thus obtained to be employed in founding twenty-one new bishoprics.

<small>Suppression of monasteries begun by Wolsey, 1524.</small>

Thus it was within the Church and under papal sanction the revolutionary act of the dissolution of monasteries began. It was an outward sign of the prevailing demand for Church reformation, whose onward course was clearly foreseen. In the picturesque language of Fuller, Wolsey's measure 'made all the forests of religious foundations in England to shake, justly fearing that the king would fell the oaks when the cardinal had begun to cut the underwood.'

If Wolsey's intention had been fulfilled, Cardinal College at Oxford would have exceeded in its magnificence and in the range of subjects taught every other in Europe. As a feeder to the college, Wolsey founded another on a smaller scale at Ipswich, where he proposed to prepare boys for Oxford, after the model of William of Wykeham's foundation at Winchester. Had Wolsey remained in power, no doubt monastic revenues would have been increasingly diverted to his great scheme of educational and diocesan reform. Another thought of the fertile brain of this great statesman, which would have had a vast influence upon the cause of Church history had it ever been carried into effect, was that of a united Church, or Patriarchate, of England and France.

How all these schemes came to naught is a matter of familiar history. On the fall of the great chancellor, who was at one and the same time cardinal, Archbishop of York, Bishop of Winchester and of Durham, and Abbot of St. Albans, all his work fell with him. The name of his college at Oxford was changed to that of Christchurch, its property, with that of the college in progress at Ipswich, shared the common fortune of forfeited estates. He retired to the house at Sheen, near Richmond, which Colet, his friend, who died nine years pre

<small>Fall of Wolsey.</small>

viously, had built for his own 'nest.' He died a broken-hearted man at Leicester Abbey, in the November of 1530, a victim to the wanton caprice of one whom he had served only too faithfully; and with him the most notable of the Oxford reformers disappeared.

The Oxford reformers, Colet, Erasmus, Wolsey, More, like many other great men, from the time of Grosseteste downwards, wrought mainly for reform within the Church, for a reformation of discipline. But the hour was now near at hand when the reformation was about to be carried into the dogmas of the Church, in the rejection of the fundamental principles of the old Church in its sacramental and sacerdotal claims, and in the assertion of the individual conscience and of the written word.

Work of the Oxford reformers.

CHAPTER XIV.

CONTEMPORARIES AT CAMBRIDGE.

From the University of Oxford the spirit of reform passed to that of Cambridge. The celebrated band of Oxford reformers—Colet, Erasmus, Wolsey, More—conscious of the evils within the Church, wished for and advocated a reformation of manners of bishops, clergy, and people. They never attempted definition of doctrine, nor tried to enforce dogma. They probably would have tolerated the largest liberty of thought that could have been allowed within the pale of the Romish Church. In this their position differed from that of the Cambridge reformers, who, under the influence of the Lutheran movement, were reformers of doctrine, boldly attacking dogmas which lay at the root of the worst corruptions of the Church.

Cambridge reformers, reformers of doctrine.

Whatever deduction may be made from Erasmus' panegyric in 1513, that Cambridge was not inferior to any university in Europe, it cannot be doubted that great progress had been made there in theological learning. Within seven years of that time there was a band of men at Cambridge whose names became conspicuous as holders and teachers of new doctrine. Of these was Thomas Bilney, of Trinity Hall, familiarly known as 'little Bilney,' from his diminutive stature, and as 'Saint Bilney,' from his devoutness of life, who expressly attributed his conversion to the influence of Erasmus' New Testament. William Tindale, some years Bilney's senior, drawn, it may be, by the fame of Erasmus, removed from Oxford and settled at Cambridge, where he became famous for his knowledge of Greek. George Stafford, divinity lecturer, whose expositions of Scripture were similar in their effect with what was done by Colet at Oxford. Robert Barnes, a prior of the Augustinian Friars, and a convert of Bilney, who took a foremost, if not always honourable, place among the reformers of his day as a writer and preacher. Miles Coverdale, his friend, and a member of the same order, who stood by his side in 1526, when Barnes was in trouble before Wolsey for a sermon he had preached, and afterwards became eminent as a translator of the Scriptures. John Rogers, the intimate friend of Tindale, who edited the Bible known as Matthew's Bible, and was the first who suffered for his religion in the reign of Queen Mary.

Cotemporary with these, though not at the time one in sympathies with them, was Thomas Cranmer, a fellow of Jesus College, living a quiet, studious life, busy with lectures and examinations, and with no thought of the distractions and perils of high office that awaited him. There was also Stephen Gardiner at Trinity Hall, where his honour was great as a student of the classics, with whom Cranmer was destined to do battle unto life's end. And another—then in residence at Cambridge, who by his preaching became the most popular of English reformers, and by his martyrdom endeared his name to all lovers of religious liberty—was Hugh Latimer, the University cross-bearer, 'as obstinate a papist as any in England,' whose oration on taking his degree of bachelor of divinity was devoted to an attack on the opinions of Melanchthon.

Bilney's influence as a leader in reform has been little recognised; his gentle spirit prevented him taking a foremost place in public teaching, but his persuasive influence was such that he won many disciples. Around him there gathered a little band of Cambridge students, whose custom it was to meet at an inn known by the sign of the White Horse, afterward dubbed 'Germany,' from the Lutheran sympathies of those accustomed to meet there. Most distinguished among Bilney's converts was Latimer. Bilney sought him out, asked him for 'God's sake to receive his confession,' it being customary with the clergy to choose their own confessor. The interview had the desired result. Latimer heard his confession, and by it, he says, 'I learned more than before in many years.' The opponent of Lutheran beliefs in the spring of 1524 was won over to the side of the reformers. Previous to this Bilney had made disciples of Thomas Arthur of St. John's, John Lambert of Queen's, and Robert Barnes, Prior of the Augustine Friars at Cambridge. To these must be added the name of John

Bilney's influence at Cambridge.

Fryth, who became a companion of Tindale, and under circumstances of shameful treachery was the first of the new reforming party to suffer martyrdom for denying the doctrine of transubstantiation.

Nicholas Ridley, afterwards Bishop of London, was one of Latimer's hearers, and acknowledges his obligations to him. It was at Pembroke Hall he committed to memory in their original language all the Epistles of St. Paul and the other Epistles of the New Testament. Becon, afterwards chaplain to Cranmer, and John Bradford, afterwards Ridley's chaplain, both traced their conversion to Latimer's sermons.

Drawn by the inducements to students in connection with Wolsey's magnificent college at Oxford, some eight or ten promising young students of Cambridge, all of them more or less Lutheran in sentiment, left for Cardinal College. Among them was John Fryth, to whom reference has already been made, and Richard Taverner, whose name has some celebrity as a reviser of Coverdale's and Matthew's Bible. Richard Cox was another, who had afterwards a varied and eventful life, being at one time tutor to Prince Edward, then an exile who took a prominent part in the 'Frankfort Troubles,' and subsequently Bishop of Ely. The result was that in both Universities 'heresy,' or Lutheranism, rapidly increased; not in defiant contradiction of the ordinary teaching of the Church's creed, nor in departure from the customary ceremonies of religious worship, but in careful study of the Scriptures, and the comparison of their teaching with that of the religion that existed around, and in the eagerness with which the writings of German and Swiss reformers were sought after. As early as the March of 1521 Archbishop Warham, writing to Wolsey, complained that both the Universities were 'infected' with the 'pestilent doctrine of Luther.' *Cambridge men drawn to Oxford.*

Whether from latent sympathies with the great reforming sentiment influencing younger minds, or from wisdom far-seeing enough to discern that the new doctrine could not be put down and stamped out by persecution, the great cardinal's action was mercy compared with that of the bishops towards the Lollards, and of his own successors against *Wolsey's policy towards heretics.*

the Lutheran reformers. Wolsey satisfied himself by prohibiting the circulation of the offending books, and commanding all who 'had any books written or printed of Luther's heresies and errors' to give them up to the bishop of their diocese.

About the time of this searching for Lutheran books, and in prospect, possibly, of the gathering storm, Tindale, as an ordained priest, and as one suspected of heresy, left Cambridge, returned to his native county of Gloucester, and for awhile lived with Sir John Walsh in the manor-house of Little Sodbury, near Bristol. There he found a circle of society in which his admiration for Erasmus and sympathy with reforming sentiments met with contemptuous opposition. Ignorant priests, in whose opinion it 'was better to be without God's laws than the Pope's,' worried him, and he was cited for heretical doctrine before the bishop's chancellor at Bristol, but through the influence of his friends the plot against him failed. At Sodbury his great purpose of translating the Greek Testament of Erasmus was matured. To further its accomplishment, he came up to London, hoping to find in Tunstall, the newly appointed bishop of that diocese, one who, as a friend of Erasmus and patron of the new learning, would befriend him in his undertaking. He soon found, though, as he himself says, 'there was no room in my lord of London's palace to translate the New Testament—nay, no place to do it in all England.' To all intents and purposes the Bible at this time was an interdicted book. No one was allowed to publish a translation of the Scriptures 'until the said translation had been approved by the ordinary of the place.'

Tindale's withdrawal from Cambridge and publication of his English New Testament, 1521-1525.

While seeking in vain episcopal sanction for his scheme in London, Tindale dwelt with Humphrey Monmouth, a wealthy cloth merchant in the east end of the city. In the spring of 1524 Tindale left London for Hamburg, and thence 'got him straight to Luther' at Wittenberg, for encouragement and direction in his great undertaking. The work of translation must have been far advanced before Tindale left England, for within two years of Tindale's arrival in Germany the whole was in print, and being brought over with all possible secrecy and speed by German merchants to this country, where it

WILLIAM TINDALE.
(From the portrait in Hertford College, Oxford.)

soon took the place of the fragmentary unprinted transcripts of Wycliffe's and Purvey's versions.

While the noble-minded, indefatigable Tindale was pursuing his work with a heroism which should make his name dear to Englishmen, exciting scenes were taking place among his friends at Cambridge. Latimer had unexpectedly one day West, Bishop of Ely, as a hearer. On seeing him enter the church, the preacher adroitly changed his subject for that of the priesthood of Christ as an example to all priests and bishops. The bishop was sagacious enough to thank the preacher 'for the good admonition he had received,' but at the same time asked him to preach a sermon against Lutheranism. Latimer declining to do this, was told he 'smelt somewhat of the pan,' and shortly afterwards was prohibited by the bishop from preaching in his diocese. The silencing of the most popular preacher in the University became the occasion of much local excitement. Prior Barnes, whose Augustinian friary, like many other religious houses, was exempt from episcopal jurisdiction, invited Latimer, on the Sunday following the prohibition to preach for him, Barnes himself preaching elsewhere a sermon in which with characteristic impetuosity he launched out into a furious denunciation of the whole body of clergy and bishops, and especially of Cardinal Wolsey. For the offending sermon he was taken under arrest, tried before Wolsey, and the alternative put before him of 'reading a recantation or being burned.' Firmly refusing for a time, Barnes at last yielded, consenting to submit to any penance which might be inflicted upon him.

Exciting scenes at Cambridge.

Prior Barnes and Latimer, 1525.

The scene of penance, held in St. Paul's Cathedral, was made as public and solemn as possible. 'With six and thirty abbots, mitred priors and bishops,' Cardinal Wolsey presided; he attired in purple, they in damask and satin. Before them was Barnes, bearing a faggot on his shoulder, signifying the sentence he had escaped by his recantation; with him were four German merchants, likewise bearing faggots, and under arrest for having brought into this country Lutheran books. Near at hand were 'great baskets full of books'—prohibited books that had been seized and brought

Prior Barnes' penance, 1526.

up to London from Cambridge and elsewhere. After a sermon preached by Fisher, Bishop of Rochester, Barnes and his companions were led thrice round a great fire made before the northern door of the cathedral, as a warning of what they might expect if they relapsed; but for this time books were burned instead of men. Unhappy Barnes, after his humiliating recantation, was thrown back into prison, from which escaping, he took refuge in Germany, where he became intimate with the leading reformers. Some years after he returned to England, was welcomed by Latimer, but his rash impetuosity brought him into conflict with Gardiner, as it had done with Wolsey, and became the occasion of his martyrdom.

A few months after the solemn scene of penance and book-burning Bilney and Latimer were summoned to London to answer for themselves before Cardinal Wolsey and Bishop Tunstall. The shrewdness, wit, and wisdom of Latimer so won upon Wolsey that, reversing the Bishop of Ely's prohibition, he gave him special licence to preach throughout England. Bilney was less fortunate. No punishment was inflicted, no public recantation was exacted, but he was induced to promise on oath 'not to preach any of Luther's opinions, but to impugn them everywhere.' The condition was ignominious, and proved more than he could bear.

Bilney and Latimer before Wolsey.

Not long after Bilney was again in trouble. Before Cardinal Wolsey and a large assembly of bishops, lawyers, and divines, he was charged as a preacher of heresy; with him on this occasion was his friend and convert, Thomas Arthur. Both recanted in their hour of fear; and on the 8th December, 1527, went through the same humiliation as Barnes, standing bareheaded on the same spot, and each bearing a faggot, as a sign of the sentence they narrowly escaped. Arthur was kept in confinement at Walsingham, where five years afterwards he died. Bilney for a year was kept in prison, and upon his release returned a heartbroken man to Cambridge, there to rejoin his friend Latimer.

Bilney and his troubles.

Touching is the story of Bilney's repentance. A deep sense of melancholy settled upon him. For 'a whole

HUGH LATIMER.

year,' says Latimer, 'he was in such an anguish and agony that nothing did him good—neither eating nor drinking, nor even communication of God's Word: for he thought the whole Scriptures were against him, and sounded to his condemnation. Whatsoever any man could allege to his comfort seemed to make against him.' Then, gathering courage, publicly he showed his contrition and allegiance to the Reformed doctrine by openly preaching the doctrines he had abjured in his native county of Norfolk. He was apprehended, tried, condemned to death as a relapsed heretic. On an August day of 1531, in a low valley near the city of Norwich, commonly called the Lollards' Pit, from previous executions that had taken place there, Bilney was burned alive in the presence of the assembled crowds, sitting down on the surrounding sloping ground. Calmly, nobly, he atoned for his times of weakness by the courage with which he met his end.

While Bilney was passing through his troubles his distinguished disciple Latimer was availing himself of Cardinal Wolsey's permission to continue his preaching at Cambridge. Confining himself principally to the inculcation of practical righteousness and the censure of crying abuses, there was little that could be controverted in his discourses. Two sermons of his preached in the Christmas of 1529, known as the 'Sermons on the Card,' in which after his manner he proposed to explain to his hearers how they might play with Christ's cards, so as to be winners, and not losers, excited such a stir beyond university circles that in the spring of the following year he was summoned to preach before the king at Windsor. There the vigour of his style, its homely terseness, its abounding humour, made him as popular as at Cambridge. Henry was so pleased with the sermon that after it 'he did most familiarly talk with Latimer.' Latimer, always kindly-hearted, seized the opportunity of the royal presence and the royal favour to procure the pardon of a poor woman, in whom his friend Bilney was especially interested, as he believed unjustly accused, who was imprisoned on the charge of murdering her child. Her pardon Latimer had the joy of taking back upon his return to Cambridge. The king's favour towards him was such that in the

Latimer's rising fame.

year 1530 he was made one of the royal chaplains. The influence this position gave him he at once sought to use in the interest of reform. In a remarkable letter to the king Latimer protested against those who were 'making it treason to have the Scriptures in English, and urged the king to sanction their free circulation.' Mr. Froude describes this letter as 'an address of almost unexampled grandeur.' 'With no authority,' says Mr. Froude, 'but his own conscience, and the strong certainty that he was on God's side, Latimer threw himself between the spoilers and their prey, and wrote to the king protesting against the injustice which was crushing the truest men in his dominion.' The letter had no effect upon the king's action at the time, but the years were not many before he granted to all his subjects to read the English Bible in simply a revised edition of Tindale's version, which it had so often been declared penal to possess.

Latimer's letter to the king, 1530.

Once we find Latimer's courage failing him. It quailed under a charge of heresy brought against him in convocation in 1532, the year after Bilney's death at the stake. The enemies of Latimer procured his excommunication and imprisonment. To save his life from peril, he signed certain Romish articles, against which other Reformers testified even unto death. Justly does Mr. Demaus, in his admirable biography of Latimer, observe, 'It cannot be denied that his conduct' on this occasion 'was unworthy of his character and of his position.' Latimer had yet to attain unto the courage of his friend and spiritual father Bilney.

Latimer's hour of weakness, 1530.

While the storm was gathering which broke upon Wolsey in 1529, and while More, Gardiner, and Tunstall were eager to suppress what they deemed heresy, Tindale was earnestly working at a translation from the Hebrew of the Old Testament. In this he had the help of his young friend Fryth, to whom reference has been made as a student of Cardinal's College. Being suspected of heresy, he left England in 1528, and joined Tindale at Marburg. A translation of the books of the Pentateuch was printed at Marburg in 1530, and of the Book of Jonah in 1531. This was the last of Tindale's published labours in connection with the Old Testament, though he is believed to have left behind him in MS. other portions of the Old Testament, subsequently edited by his friend Rogers.

In the same year as Latimer was received into royal favour his cotemporary at Cambridge, Cranmer, unexpectedly was brought into prominence. His decided opinion in favour of Henry's divorce from Catherine, and a suggestion of his that the question should be referred to the universities and canonists of Europe for their decision, brought him under the king's notice. The suggestion was eagerly taken up by the king, and won for Cranmer the royal favour he never lost. He was appointed one of the royal chaplains, and was directed to take the matter of inquiry in hand. In 1531 the result of the inquiry was laid before Parliament. In the summer of the following year Archbishop Warham died, and the king almost immediately afterwards intimated to Cranmer, who was away in Germany, his nomination to the vacant see. No one could have been more surprised at such intelligence than Cranmer himself. He had just married the daughter of a prominent Lutheran Reformer, Osiander, and a married archbishop might well seem to him an impossibility. He sent his wife to England, but delayed his own return in the vain hope that another appointment might be made. But the king's command was inexorable. No one was ever more sincerely reluctant to be made Archbishop of Canterbury than Cranmer. As the creature of circumstances he yielded to the imperious will of Henry. The pope granted the usual bulls, and on the 30th March, 1533, Cranmer was consecrated Archbishop of Canterbury. Instead of taking the usual oath, first of allegiance to the pope, and then to the king, Cranmer swore allegiance to the pope only in so far as that was consistent with his supreme duty to the king.

Rapid promotion of Cranmer.

Suggestion concerning the divorce, 1529.

Made Archbishop of Canterbury, 1533.

Henry's motive in the promotion of Cranmer is manifest. Under the new archbishop in April, convocation, though not with absolute unanimity, declared in favour of divorce. On May 23rd, Cranmer declared the king's marriage with his brother's widow null and void. Less than a week after Anne, whom Henry had already married privately, was crowned queen.

In all this Cranmer's subserviency is pitiful, but there is no reason to cast discredit upon what it is wellnigh certain was his conscientious and deliberate conviction concerning Henry's marriage with Catherine. It ought not to be forgotten that the onus of this miserable divorce business lies with the papal court that sanctioned a marriage forbidden by the Divine law. In the expressed conviction of many of the best and wisest men of the day, the dispensation granted by Julius II. for Henry's marriage was, as dispensing with a law of God, utterly void, and of no effect. Cranmer's predecessor, Warham, the foremost canonist of the age, when the marriage was in prospect, pronounced it as one abhorrent to religion, and as an outrage against even the letter of Scripture. Before Anne Boleyn appeared on the scene, doubts as to the validity of the marriage had been raised from time to time. Two of the greatest princes of Europe had taken exception to alliance with the daughter of the king—the Princess Mary—on the ground that her legitimacy was doubtful. Gardiner, Bonner, and, above all, Cardinal Wolsey, tried every possible means to secure the result that Cranmer is unsparingly blamed for effecting. On the other hand, there were those who with sounder and true-hearted sentiment felt that worse than the illegality of the marriage at first was the proposal to disturb it after eighteen years of wedlock. The courageous and throughout honourable conduct of Catherine won her many friends, and no slight impression was produced by Bishop Fisher's heroic declaration of his willingness to stake his life that the marriage was perfectly valid. While to many others the presence of Anne Boleyn, more than political and canonical expediency, was the real occasion of the great question being raised.

Cranmer's character. In Cranmer's action we see his character clearly displayed; he was a man of learning and zeal, always honest in intention, but pedantic, technical, making more of precedents than of principles. Such a man was sure to take the position Cranmer did with regard to the divorce question. He may justly be accredited with sincerity, though wisdom be lacking.

As a Reformer, Cranmer was borne along by the current of events, rather than a leader. His was a mind not eager for spiritual discoveries, but surely receptive of increased measures of truth, as they were presented to him. That he was sincerely religious there can be no doubt. Amid the harsh tempers and personal enmities of the times in which his lot was cast, moderation and forbearance graced his character in an eminent degree. It gives vividness to our thoughts concerning one whose position is so prominent in the history of the great Reformation to remember that he was a man of short stature, fair complexion, and fond of field sports, able when archbishop to ride the roughest horse as well as any of his household.

Not least among the difficulties great and manifold in which Cranmer as archbishop found himself involved was that of the trial of young Fryth, eminent among the early Reformers for his extraordinary abilities and great learning. A short treatise of his, on the sacrament of the body and blood of Christ, setting forth the view of the sacrament that had been taught by Zwingli, called forth a reply from Sir Thomas More, ever resolute in suppressing heresy, in which he asserted that Fryth had taught 'all the poison that Wycliffe, Huskyn [*i.e.*, Œcolampadius], Tindale, and Zwinglius had taught concerning the blessed sacrament of the altar, not only affirming it to be very bread still, as Luther doth, but also, as these other beasts do, saith it is nothing else.' Fryth, just as he was on the point of returning to the Continent, was arrested near Southend-on-Sea, and imprisoned in the Tower. From the Tower he was taken to the archbishop's palace at Croydon, there to be examined before Cranmer, Stokesley, Bishop of London, and Gardiner, Bishop of Winchester. The last of these had been Fryth's tutor at Cambridge, and persecution was alien to the spirit of Cranmer. A plan of escape, with the promised connivance of the two persons in whose charge he was placed, was suggested to him. But he bravely refused to act on the advice offered. He had been desirous to escape, he said, but now that he had been taken and delivered into the hands of the bishops only for religion and doctrine's sake, he was bound to maintain and defend his cause. 'If I should now start aside and run away, I should run from my God and the testimony of His Holy Word.' By personal

[margin: John Fryth.]
[margin: Controversy with Sir Thos. More.]
[margin: Arrested.]

argument and persuasion Cranmer strove hard to save Fryth, but he absolutely refusing to recant or modify his utterances, the penalty was inevitable. He was condemned by the Bishop of London. On the afternoon of July 4th, 1533, he was taken into Smithfield; there, with a young man, too illiterate to argue with his accusers, but who persisted that he believed 'even as John Fryth doth,' he suffered. A London rector exhorted the spectators not to pray for the sufferers any more than they would pray for a dog, 'at which words Fryth, smiling, desired the Lord to forgive him.' It is one of the paradoxes of history that the time came when Cranmer suffered death for the very doctrine he had condemned in Fryth, and when his writings were used by him in controversy with Gardiner on the subject of the sacrament of the Lord's supper.

Martyred, 1533.

Two years after the death of Fryth there appeared, 'unheralded and unanticipated,' the whole Bible in English. It was the work of Miles Coverdale, the friend of Prior Barnes, who pleaded for him before Wolsey. Beyond the fact that he was ordained priest at Norwich in 1514, nothing is known of the life of Coverdale from the time of his leaving Cambridge until the publication of his translation of the Scriptures in 1535. The conjecture is probable that, finding it unsafe to remain in England, he went abroad, and there, forestalling Tindale's purpose, produced a complete secondary translation of the Scriptures. Of the merits of his translation, made from the 'Douche and Latyn,' some account is given in another chapter. It was published with a dedication to Henry VIII.

Coverdale's Bible, 1535.

Whether Tindale ever saw Coverdale's translation is unknown, for the year of its publication was that of his arrest and imprisonment in the great State prison at Vilvorde. For sixteen months, in the dreary confinement of his prison, Tindale, with such few books as the governor of the castle allowed him to have, toiled on at his life's great work, leaving his MSS. to his friend John Rogers. On 6th October, 1536, he was led forth to die. His last words, 'uttered with fervent zeal, and in a loud voice, were, "Lord, open the King of England's eyes,"' perhaps not knowing that already Coverdale's Bible had appeared under the patronage of Cromwell and dedicated to the king. Or perhaps desiring that fuller recognition of royal approval, granted within less than a year of Tindale's death, when there appeared at the foot of the title-page of Matthew's Bible published in 1537, three-fourths of which was Tindale's own work, the words, 'Set forth with the king's most gracious license,' and when by royal decree a copy of the whole Bible was ordered to be placed in every parish church.

CHAPTER XV.

THE REFORMATION PARLIAMENT AND CONVOCATION, 1529-36.

Early character of Henry VIII.

For the first twenty years, or more than half his reign, Henry was popular in the highest degree, a jovial young king, handsome, frank, accomplished in all manly exercises of the time, and in the new learning. He had been carefully educated by good scholars, and he believed himself to be a special master of theology. In the international affairs of his time he took a keen interest. He had Wolsey, that 'great child of honour,' as Shakespeare calls him, great also as a statesman in wisdom and energy, and under his rule England rose to a leading position in Europe. 'Bluff King Hal,' according to the painters of his portraits, possessed a beauty that commended itself to the taste of those times, and made him a favourite with his people. His popularity it was that helped him in his quarrel with the pope, and in those troubled years of his declining manhood when transformed into the bulky, self-willed despot.

With the movement toward religious reform advancing among the people Henry had not even the degree of sympathy that Wolsey showed. His zeal for orthodoxy is known by his famous controversy with Luther, and by the title 'Defender of the Faith' bestowed upon him in solemn conclave by Pope Leo X., in the year 1521. In the first eighteen years of his reign, until his quarrel with the pontiff, he maintained the supremacy of the pope, and until the end of his days he was rigidly orthodox in the Roman doctrine of transubstantiation, celibacy of clergy, and auricular confession. To speak of Henry as ever other than a papist is to overlook the fact that there were almost as many martyrs to the Protestant faith in his as in Mary's reign.

The terrible storm of Henry's wrath against the papal court in 1529 broke upon Cardinal Wolsey. He was discarded, accused of having exercised, contrary to law, legatine authority in England, was deprived of his office of lord chancellor, and finally accused of high treason. His position as a minister of State was due entirely to the king's favour; when that was withdrawn he was an utterly ruined man.

Tired and suspicious of ecclesiastics in the high offices of State, Henry made a layman, Sir Thomas More, Cardinal Wolsey's successor as high chancellor, and the Dukes of Norfolk and Suffolk his chief ministers. After the fall of Wolsey, it is the figure of Thomas Cromwell that rises into prominence. To him is accredited the daring policy for the abolition of the papal supremacy in England, whereby not only the question of the divorce might be easily settled, but the allegiance of the clergy, divided between their sovereign and the pope, might be wholly claimed by the former. Cromwell, who as a steady working dependant of Wolsey obtained his introduction to the affairs of State, after his great master's death threw in his lot with the Reformers, zealously supporting their cause as the patron of Coverdale in his work of Bible translation, and as the suppressor of monasteries. Policy, though, rather than spiritual sympathy, was his motive for advancing the cause of the Reformers. Rapidly he rose to a position of power that for ten years rivalled that of Wolsey. 'In wisdom, diligence, faithfulness, and experience,' as Cranmer said of him, 'no prince ever had such a servant,' and it might be added, nor one with a harder heart. His portraits present him to us as having small eyes and firmly compressed lips, eyes keen to follow the course on which he had entered, lips that show the firmness of resolve with which his ruthless policy was pursued.

Thomas Cromwell.

In the November of 1529 assembled perhaps the most memorable Parliament that ever sat. In the course of a few years it abolished appeals to Rome, declared the king supreme head of the Church, instead of the Bishop of Rome, and prepared the way for the dissolution of the monasteries. Of this Parliament Mr. Froude writes, 'The election had taken place in the midst of great and general excitement, and the members chosen, if we may judge from their acts and their petitions, were men of that

The Reformation Parliament.

broad, resolved temper who only in times of popular effervescence are called forward into prominence. It would probably have been useless for the Crown to attempt dictation or repression at such a time. Under the actual circumstances, its interest was to encourage the fullest expression of public feeling.'[1] Both king and Parliament were in a mind to promote needed ecclesiastical reform, and the work went on apace. The Parliament, which sat at intervals from 1529 to 1536, passed a series of statutes which soon effectually set England free from the dominion of the pope.

In 1529, after 'sore debatings,' the power of the ecclesiastical courts was curtailed with regard to probate duties and mortuaries; the latter, a peculiarly obnoxious form of clerical impost, the priests claiming the value of the last dress worn in life by persons brought to them for burial. The clergy were also prohibited from following secular employments, residence was enforced, and pluralities forbidden. These were measures of practical reform Colet had urged in his famous convocation sermon eighteen years before. The clergy, though, had sinned away their opportunity, and now, notwithstanding the protest of convocation, and the bitter indignation of the bishops against the interference of laymen, the reforms were resolutely made by a power they could not resist.

Power of ecclesiastical courts curtailed.

In its next session, 1531, the Reforming Parliament passed an Act against proctors and pardoners who sold indulgences; and in the same session made itself memorable by an act of oppression, not to be overlooked because its victims were ecclesiastics. On the pretence that the clergy were involved in the premunire for having acknowledged Wolsey's legatine function, they were required to pay an enormous fine, amounting to a million of our money, and, moreover, to acknowledge the king's supremacy in ecclesiastical affairs. Unjust as was the first command, the clergy at once submitted; against the second they struggled hard; but the Cromwellian policy for the complete separation of the Church of England from that of Rome prevailed. The convoca-

Act against the sale of indulgences.

Clergy heavily fined.

[1] *History*, i. 207.

tion of both provinces of Canterbury and York formally acknowledged the king supreme head of the Church, with the qualification 'as far as the law of Christ allows.' This Act of convocation has since been known as the 'Submission of the Clergy.' By it the Church was left free, as far as Rome was concerned, for the admission of those alterations in doctrine, government, and worship which ultimately followed. Sir Thomas More, seeing the course events were taking, in the rigidity of his devotion to the Roman Catholic religion resigned the office of chancellor.

<small>'Submission of the Clergy.'</small>

Evidence of the strong reforming spirit abroad in the land is seen in the petition against the clergy presented to the king by the House of Commons in the spring of 1532. The grounds of complaint were twelve, the principal charges being—(1) That the convocation made Church laws without the consent of the king and the laity. (2) That the fees of the ecclesiastical courts were excessive, and that sums of money were demanded for administering the sacraments. (3) That the bishops made simoniacal contracts in presenting to benefices, and filled too many with their relatives. (4) That the number of festivals and holidays was excessive, and became the occasion of 'many great, abominable, and execrable vices.' These were so numerous that it has been estimated that a fourth of the time of the people was consumed in a manner detrimental alike to their national and social life. (5) That persons were imprisoned by the ecclesiastical authorities without knowing the charge against them, and had no power of recovering damages for unjust accusations and imprisonments. (6) That persons charged with heresy were unfairly dealt with by 'subtle interrogatories and prejudicial witnesses.' In consequence of these charges the king required that all existing Church laws should be submitted to his approval, a demand which the bishops effectually resisted; the important compromise arrived at being, that in future no canon should be made by convocation without the royal assent, and that a commission of sixteen clergy and sixteen laymen should be appointed to consider those already in force. The commissioners were appointed, but

<small>Complaints against the clergy.</small>

<small>No canon to be made by convocation without royal assent.</small>

the result of their labours was never legally sanctioned; consequently to this day the ancient canon law of the Church is binding where it is not contrary to the statute law, and does not interfere with the right of the Crown. The complaint of the severity and lack of charity with which charges for heresy were conducted was met by an Act which, instead of leaving the initiative to ecclesiastics, provided that lay persons should be empanelled to present heretics to the ordinary on oath. Upon such presentments, which were to be founded upon the oaths of two witnesses, the ordinary might proceed to conviction; but the proceedings were to be open, like those of secular law courts. But the final issue was still the same. If a person convicted did not abjure and do penance, he was to be burned as formerly. The Act did not define heresy positively, but declared negatively that 'No manner of speaking or holding against the Bishop of Rome, or against any laws called spiritual laws made by authority of the See of Rome, shall be taken to be heresy.' The effect of this statute was to open a wider gate than was intended: it opened the way for the denial of any doctrine of the Roman Catholic faith. To counteract such a measure of toleration, a few years later the famous Act of the Six Articles was passed.

Law concerning heresy.

The course of ecclesiastical reform was now rapidly advancing. In the same year an Act was made whereby the payment of *annates*—i.e., a year's income exacted from every clerical person on his preferment to a benefice—was forbidden to be paid any longer to the pope. Though, to the clergy's honour, this declaration of independence originated in a resolution of convocation, they derived no personal benefit from it, as the payment of the impost still had to be made, though to the king, instead of to the pope.

Act concerning annates.

In the same session was passed what was perhaps, from the constitutional point of view, the most important statute of the Reformation—that which prohibited appeals to Rome. Though the statute was in part suggested by the appeal of the unhappy Catherine in the divorce case, it is equally certain that it was a necessary consequence of the king's supreme headship, which had been made in the preceding year. Unquestionably, also, it was the restoration of

Appeals to Rome prohibited.

one of the ancient rights of the English Church. It was under Stephen, when the right to the Crown itself was in controversy, that the practice of appeals to Rome came in. Henry II., before and after his contest with Becket, withstood it. From John's time appeals to Rome became common, until the original independence of the nation was restored by the Act which declared that no English subject was to appeal from an English court to a court beyond the realm. All disputed cases such as had hitherto been made subjects of appeal to Rome were to be settled by the ecclesiastical courts of this country. Appeals were possible, as formerly, from archdeacon to bishop, and from bishop to archbishop, but there the right of appeal stopped. Subsequently provision was made for a final appeal from the court of the archbishop to 'the king in chancery'—that is, to judges nominated or delegated from time to time by commissions issued in the king's name out of the court of chancery. Thus the judicial authority of the pope over England was altogether extinguished.

In the following year, 1533, another long source of contention was put an end to by the abolition of papal authority in the appointment of bishops. Nominally the appointing of English bishops had always been by English sovereigns, but bulls from the pope confirming the election were considered necessary. These bulls, being exceedingly costly, were sometimes used as a means for delaying or preventing a consecration. The Act of 1533 abolished any interference on the part of the pope, and it was enacted that when a see became vacant the king had a right to send down to dean or chapter leave to elect (*congé d'élire*) the candidate named in the letter of licence to the vacant office. It is under this power of nomination bishops are still appointed. *Abolition of papal authority in appointment of bishops, 1533.*

Step by step, the way was thus cleared for the great statute by which the royal supremacy, already formally acknowledged by convocation, was set forth in the Act of Parliament passed in 1534, which ordered that the king shall be the only supreme head on earth of the Church of England. In the same remarkable session Parliament passed 'an Act concerning the king's succession,' which *Act declaring royal supremacy, 1534.*

declared the Princess Mary, the daughter of Catherine of Aragon, to be illegitimate, and settled the succession on the Princess Elizabeth, the infant daughter of Anne Boleyn. Another Act, generally known as the Treason Act, declared it to be high treason to question the king's supremacy over the Church. Any man could be called upon at any time to take an oath that he assented to the king's supremacy. Earnest, devout Catholics there were who refused to violate their conscience by acknowledging Henry's supremacy over that of the pope. A noble band of nine or ten Carthusian monks, including the Prior of the Charterhouse and the Prior of Beauvale, were ruthlessly put to death by the cruel and disgusting method then usual in cases of treason; and Fisher also, the aged Bishop of Rochester, than whom, though somewhat narrow-minded, there was not a man of more saintly life in England. He had been a staunch friend to Queen Catherine as her confessor, and as one who fearlessly opposed the divorce. His sympathetic interest in the prophesying Nun of Kent, who foretold the king's death and the triumph of the pope, was made the occasion of an accusation of treason, from which he narrowly escaped. For refusing to take the oath of supremacy he was imprisoned in the Tower, where he was scandalously ill-treated. Tottering with age, he was carried in a chair to Tower Hill, and there, on the 22nd June, in the year 1535, he was beheaded. A yet more illustrious victim was Sir Thomas More, whose speech at the opening of the Reformation Parliament had been hailed with enthusiasm. From his celebrated home at Chelsea, where he had welcomed and entertained his Oxford friends, and where the garden was in which the king had sauntered about with him with his arm round his neck, More was taken to the Tower, and there imprisoned for a whole year, in the very cell, it is said, where he had racked victims for heresy. A hale man, 'a dauntless soul erect, who smiled at death,' he went forth to the fatal spot on Tower Hill, on 16th July, 1535. He was characteristically cheerful to the last. The awkwardly erected scaffold shook as he ascended the ladder. 'I pray you, Master Lieutenant,'

Act concerning the succession.
The Treason Act.
Resistance to the Supremacy Act.
Execution of Bishop Fisher, 1535.
Execution of Sir Thos. More, 1535.

said More, 'see me safe up; for my coming down you may let me shift for myself.' After repeating the fifty-first Psalm on his knees, and just before the fatal blow, he carefully moved his long beard out of the axe's course, saying, 'It has never offended,' and so laid his noble head on the block. 'How many souls hath that axe wounded which cut off More's head?' wrote Erasmus, when he heard of the death of one whose loss he and others mourned as that of 'their own father or brother.'

The final important measure of the first Reformation Parliament was the Act in 1536 for the dissolution of the smaller monasteries. The fall of the monasteries followed the abolition of the pope's supremacy almost as a natural result. Long before the sixteenth century it had been found that public policy required some restraint to be put upon the action of the monastic system, for it was gradually absorbing the lands of the country to an enormous extent. It is estimated that two-thirds of the entire area of London was occupied by convents and hospitals, and one-third of the whole area of England. In addition to the excessive wealth of the monasteries, there was excessive liberty: they were, for the most part, exempt from all episcopal control, and subject only to that of the pope, who could only exercise his jurisdiction by deputy. Excessive wealth and liberty had led to evils that were notorious all over Europe. Popular writers had satirized the follies and vices of the monks, and grave statesmen and ecclesiastics had urged a reformation of the various orders. The storm that broke upon the monasteries in 1536 had long been gathering.

Suppression of the lesser monasteries, 1536.

The case for the dissolution of the monasteries on national and ecclesiastical grounds was strong, but it was disgraced by the oppressive manner in which it was carried out. Acting on the precedent set by Wolsey, the smaller monasteries were first abolished, the dissolution being preceded by a general visitation.

Under the authority of Cromwell, commissioners were appointed to visit the monastic houses throughout the country, to examine into their state, moral and religious, and to report upon the administration of their revenues. Articles of inquiry, eighty-six in number, were placed in the hands of the visitors.[1] Fuller probably sums up the character of these visitors correctly, that 'they were men who well understood the message they went on, and would not come back without a satisfactory answer to him that sent them.' They went sometimes singly, sometimes in pairs, and at other times in greater numbers. A great many religious houses were visited by them in the four months which elapsed between their appointment and the meeting of Parliament. Making, though, the greatest allowance for their activity, they could not have visited all, nor one-half, of the monasteries; yet they presented such a report to Parliament of the state of the monasteries in general that when its contents were heard the thrill of horror found expression in the cry, 'Down with them! Down with them!' That the reports in the notorious 'Black Book,' fabled to have been destroyed from politic motives in the days of Queen Mary, but still existing, according to Mr. Gairdner,[2] in certain documents called 'comperta,' were many of them conjectural and grossly exaggerated may be taken for granted; but it may be safely alleged, from evidence more unimpeachable than that which is furnished by the visitors, that England was weary of the covetousness and licentiousness of the monastic institutions. The reports of Cromwell's commissioners would have been powerless but for the popular knowledge of the superabundant corruptions.

The result of the commission was the passing of an Act in 1536 for the suppression of all religious houses in the country with incomes under the annual value of £200. Of the thousand monastic houses then existing in England, 376 fell under this enactment. Their annual revenues, amounting to £32,000, and their jewels and plate, valued at £100,000, passed to the Crown. Without entering into calculation of the comparative value of money in those days and these, it may be safely said that these sums represent twelve times as much as they do now. Thus the value of the property confiscated amounted to more than a million and a quarter of modern money. Before the end of the year all the smaller houses had been dismantled, and their inmates, not turned pennilessly adrift, as is

Suppression of 376 monasteries.

[1] *Church History*, ii. 214, (1837).
Letters and Papers of Reign of Henry VIII., vol. x. p. 42.

generally supposed, but pensioned according to their position.

Such was almost the final act of the memorable Reformation Parliament, which began its sittings in the November of 1529, and was dissolved in the April of 1536. It was the Parliament which gave ecclesiastical independence to England without doctrinal change, and established for a while a system epigrammatically described as 'popery without the pope.'

It must not be supposed that the work of the Reformation Parliament proceeded without opposition. 'There was much murmuring.' Many thought 'that the Bishop of Rome would curse all Englishmen, and that the emperor and he would destroy all the people.' *Resistance to Reform.* The submission of the clergy generally to the reforming measures was easy; but, as we have seen, there was a small and noble band of men ready to die as martyrs rather than acknowledge the king's supremacy in matters of Church government. Reginald Pole, himself of royal blood, did his best to bring about a Catholic crusade against England, and thereby enforce obedience to the papal power. In his *Reginald Pole on The Unity of the Church.* book on *The Unity of the Church*, Charles V., Henry's avowed enemy, was called upon to invade England, and fight against the enemy of Christendom. Henry's subjects were urged to rebel against a tyrant more wicked than Saul, who killed the priests; more sacrilegious than Dathan. The vigorous style of the book caused Cranmer to mourn over it, as written 'with that eloquence, that if it were set forth and known to the common people, it were not possible to convince them to the contrary.' Pole's service to the papal cause was appreciated in the proper quarter. He was summoned to Rome, and was made a cardinal. Henry, unable to wreak his displeasure upon the absent offender, discharged the violence of his wrath upon those nearest and dearest to Pole at home. His aged mother, the Countess of Salisbury, and his eldest brother, Lord Montague, were beheaded as traitors for corresponding with him.

In many parts of the country the summary measures used by the commissioners for the suppression of the monasteries roused the people into a state of indignation

that found expression in open rebellion. It was Cromwell who had to bear the brunt of the storm.
Hated by the old nobility as 'a low-born
knave,' and popularly held responsible for all the troubles of the times, it was against him the tide of indignation turned. The first rising was in Lincolnshire, in the autumn of 1536. At Lincoln the bishop's palace was attacked and pillaged, and the town occupied by a gathering of from fifty thousand to sixty thousand persons. But their very strength proved their weakness. 'There had been no forethought: there was no efficient leader; they had no commissariat: each man had brought a few days' provisions with him, and when these were gone the multitude dissolved with the same rapidity with which it had assembled.'[1]

Catholic uprisings.

The few that remained the Duke of Suffolk had no difficulty in suppressing. The most serious rising was that in the North, known as the Pilgrimage of Grace. Priests took a prominent part, bearing crosses and banners, in which were worked a chalice, a host, five wounds, a crown of thorns, and the sacred monogram *I.H.S.*, and below all the letters *I.G.* (*Itinerarium Gratiæ*). 'The chalice and the host were in remembrance of the spoiling of the Church; the five wounds to the couraging of the people to fight in Christ's cause.'[2] The insurgents were under the leadership of Robert Aske, the son of a Yorkshire gentleman of ancient lineage. York was seized; then Pontefract Castle, where the archbishop had taken refuge; and then Hull. At Doncaster an open conference was held on the bridge over the Don, the king's forces and the insurgents being in array on either side of the river. The demands of the malcontents were set forth in twenty-four articles, which clearly show the anti-Reformation spirit of the rising. The first was for the suppression of the heresies of Wycliffe, Huss, Luther, Melanchthon, and other Reformers, and to have the works of Tindale, Barnes, and others destroyed. The second, to have the Act of Supremacy repealed. The third, to have the suppressed abbeys restored. Another, that the Lord Cromwell and the lord chancellor should have 'condign punishment as subverters of the good laws

Pilgrimage of Grace.

---

[1] Froude, *History*, vol. ii. p. 526.
[2] *Ibid*, ii. p. 518.

of this realm, and maintainers of the false sects of these heretics, and first inventors and bringers-in of them.' Other than religious grievances found expression in the demands, one being for the restoration of all the common lands inclosed since the fourth year of Henry VII. Partly by negotiations, in which demands were conceded and promises of pardon made, partly by sheer weariness through the prolonged proceedings, the insurgents were dispersed. Then came the punishment of the offenders: whole districts were given up to military violence; the leaders tried, condemned, and executed, and severities committed which found their revenge, and intensified the Catholic reaction sixteen years later, in the days of Queen Mary.

CHAPTER XVI.

REFORM OF DOCTRINE.

Latimer's sermon. A FAMOUS Reformation sermon was preached by Latimer, the most popular preacher of his day, before the Convocation of Canterbury in 1536. It was a critical time, that of the meeting of the first Reformed convocation after the overthrow of the papal supremacy, and at a time when the effects of the abolition of the lesser monasteries were beginning to be felt in the agitation that soon culminated in open insurrection in the Northern dioceses. Archbishop Cranmer chose a brave man for the occasion; one who hesitated not to make good use of it, before rulers of the Church who had sought his life. His subject was the same as that of Tindale's widely circulated book, *The Wicked Mammon*—the parable of the unjust steward. His treatment of it is an earnest, vigorous inquiry of the representative clergy whether they had been faithful in the discharge of their duties. Like Colet, in his famous sermon of four and twenty years before, Latimer dwells on the abuses that had long called for reform. 'Abuses in the court of arches and in the consistorial courts of the bishops; in the ceremonies so often defiled by superstition; in the holidays so generally abused by drunkenness and gambling; in the images, and pictures, and relics, and pilgrimages extolled and encouraged by the clergy, to the deception of the ignorant; in the religious rites of baptism and matrimony celebrated in an unknown tongue, and not in the native language of the people; in the most solemn services of religion, masses, openly sold in violation of the most express ecclesiastical law.'[1] Boldly the preacher denounced abuses connected with purgatory as 'a pleasant fiction, and from the beginning so profitable to the feigners of it that there hath been no emperor that hath gotten more by taxes and tollages of them that were alive than these,

---

[1] Quoted by Demaus, p. 222.

the very right and right-begotten sons of the world, got
by dead men's tributes and gifts.' Bold words these from
a bishop in days when face to face with Gardiner, Bonner,
and Tunstall.

At the royal theologian's dictation, so it is generally
believed, and under Cranmer's leadership, a series of Ten
Articles was passed by this convocation. The
object of these articles, as set forth in their *Ten Articles, 1536.*
title, was to 'establish Christian quietness and
unity, and to avoid contentious opinions.' They are of
remarkable interest, as setting forth what was thought to
comprise the truth, and what was regarded as error, and
as the predecessors of the present Thirty-nine Articles
of the Church of England. Five of the articles relate to
doctrine, treating of faith, baptism, penance, the Lord's
supper, and justification; and five concerning images, the
honouring of saints, the praying to saints, rites and
ceremonies, and purgatory. As the source of doctrine and
foundation of faith, the Bible and the three creeds—
the Apostles', Nicene, and Athanasian—are declared to be
'infallible words of God.' Those denying this are declared
to be 'infidels or heretics, and members of the devil, with
whom they shall perpetually be damned.' The article on
baptism is in accord with that now held by the Church of
England. In the article on penance, confession to a priest
is declared necessary, 'if it may be had;' and bishops and
preachers are directed to instruct and teach the people
that the words of absolution are as 'the very words and
voice of God Himself speaking unto us out of heaven.' In
that on the altar, the doctrine of transubstantiation is
strongly affirmed. A gleam of Protestantism is seen in the
setting forth of the doctrine of justification as 'signifying
remission of our sins, and our acceptation or reconciliation
into the grace and favour of God; that is to say, our perfect renovation in Christ,' not only in outward good works,
but in inward holiness. In the articles referring to matters
of custom and ritual, it is admitted that, while circumstances might justify the destruction of images, according
to Old Testament precedent, that yet it was desirable to re-
tain them, 'especially the images of Christ and Our Lady.'
Prayer 'to saints in heaven everlastingly living' is regarded as laudable, provided they are not thought to be more
merciful than Christ, or that any saint doth serve for one

thing more than another. On the debated subject of purgatory, prayers and masses for the souls of the dead, though we know not where they are, are commended; but it is especially intimated that the Bishop of Rome's pardons 'are not necessary for obtaining everlasting life, or for delivering the souls of men out of purgatory and the pains of it.' The supposed value of masses said at *Scala Cœli* is also deprecated.

Though these articles are in the main in accord with the opinions and practices of the Roman Catholic Church, yet in their emphatic intimation that 'no ceremonies have power to remit sin,' and in their silence on four out of the seven so-called sacraments, there is the sign of manifest advance in religious thought since the time when the king wrote his *Assertion of the Seven Sacraments*, and Latimer's life had been endangered by a charge of heresy. In the words of Strype, 'The sun of truth was now but rising, and breaking through the mists of that idolatry, superstition, and ignorance that had so long prevailed in this nation and the rest of the world, and was not yet advanced to its meridian brightness.'

For the further instruction of the clergy and of the public mind, an exposition of doctrine was published in the following year, under the title of *The Institution of a Christian Man*. This book was drawn up under the direction of a committee of bishops and other divines, Gardiner and Bonner, as well as Cranmer and Latimer, taking part in the work. No small amount of success attended the result of their deliberations. It contains a beautiful paraphrastic exposition of the Apostles' Creed, the Lord's Prayer, and the Ten Commandments, the commandments being set forth, not according to the Roman method, but in that familiarly known among Protestants. In the exposition of the second commandment, though the use of images is not forbidden as an incentive to devout thought, image-worship is thus rebuked: 'We be utterly forbidden to make or to have any similitude or image to the intent to bow down to it or worship it.' In the recognition of seven sacraments there is a concession to the Romanists more than in the Articles, they, as before observed, referring only to three. The *Ave Maria* is carefully explained not as a prayer to the Virgin. All the Ten Articles of

The bishops' book, The Institution of a Christian Man, 1537.

1536 are incorporated with the various portions of the work to which they relate. Apart from its wavering as to the number of the sacraments, and its manifest reluctance to abolish superstitious ceremonies, the *Institution* is, as a contemporary styled it, 'a right godly book of devotion.' Cranmer's was probably the moulding mind. 'To him,' says Latimer, 'if anything be praiseworthy, a large share of the praise is justly due.' Though submitted to the king, for some reason not fully explained the book appeared without his formal sanction, and lacking this it was popularly known as the 'Bishops' Book,'—possibly, also, because of the diligent use of it required by many of the bishops. The Bishop of Exeter directed his clergy every Sunday to read portions of it 'in the English tongue, or in the Cornish tongue where the English tongue is not used.' Bishop Bonner required all his clergy to procure the book, 'and to exercise themselves in the same.'

A revised and extended edition of the *Institution* was published in 1543 under the new title, *A Necessary Doctrine and Erudition for any Christian Man*. This contains some additional articles on the subjects of faith, free-will, and good works. Faith is defined as a persuasion wrought in man's heart that there is a God, and that the words and sayings of Scripture are infallible truth. It is the belief of what was taught by the apostles and confirmed by the universal consent of the Church, 'wherein man leaneth not to his own natural knowledge, which is by reason, but leaneth to the knowledge attained by faith;' as Isaiah saith, 'Unless ye believe ye shall not understand.' This passage from Isaiah is according to the Vulgate. The article on free-will is Augustinian, but temperate. It ends with the admonition that preachers are neither 'so to preach the grace of God that they take away thereby free-will, nor, on the other side, so extol free-will that injury be done to the grace of God.' To distinguish this publication from that of 1537, it was called the 'King's Book.' Between these two dates the decidedly Catholic statute of 1539, known as the Six Articles, had been passed. It is probable Gardiner had greater influence in the preparation of this work than in either of the former, for its bent is decidedly towards the Catholic position.

The king's book, A Necessary Doctrine and Erudition for any Christian Man.

There was also at this time a reaction in the king's own mind, brought about by the very means used by Cromwell and Cranmer to strengthen the Protestant party. The noble ambition of Cranmer was to unite all the Reformed Churches, as he said, 'in one sound, pure, evangelical doctrine conformable to the discipline of the primitive Church.' To effect this much labour was expended by Cranmer, aided by Cromwell, in conference, both at home and abroad, with Continental Reformers, which resulted in thirteen articles of religion being drawn up as a basis of union. But nothing came of these negotiations. The king took part in the discussion; but the old anti-Lutheran bias was too strong to be overcome. On three points—viz., the denying of the cup to the laity, private masses, and the celibacy of the clergy—he would not give way. About this time, Lambert, a convert of Bilney, the Norwich martyr, and a friend of Fryth and Tindale, was charged with denying the doctrine of transubstantiation. Henry presided at his trial. Refusing to recant, Lambert threw himself on the king's mercy, with the only result that the king blurted out that he would be 'no patron of heretics.'

The reactionary influence on the mind of Henry led to the ferocious statute of 1539, known as the Six Articles, or the 'Whip with the Six Strings.' This Act, remarkable as 'the first attempt to make religious doctrine part of the statute law,' reimposed on England all the leading doctrines of the Roman Catholic faith, declaring:—

The Act of the Six Articles.

1. That in the Lord's supper 'the natural body and blood of Christ are present.'
2. That communion in both kinds is unnecessary.
3. That priests might not marry.
4. That vows of celibacy ought to be observed.
5. That the use of private masses ought to be continued.
6. That auricular confession is expedient and necessary.

It enacted that all who denied the first article should be burned as heretics, and that those who persistently refused assent to the others should be hanged as felons.

The immediate consequence of this infamous Act was that many young and zealous Reformers left the country, where they could no longer remain without endangering their lives or compromising their consciences. Abroad in Germany and Switzerland their intercourse with ardent Continental Reformers, especially those of the Zwinglian school, had an influence upon the subsequent course of the English Reformation. At home it led to Latimer resigning the bishopric of Worcester, and Shaxton that of Salisbury. It compelled Cranmer to send back his wife to her German relatives, and but for the constancy of the king's friendship towards him, he must have suffered as many others. Though the cruel provisions of this Coercion Act were not enforced with the relentless severity that some historians have supposed, yet in a short time more than five hundred persons were imprisoned. It was under this Act that the gentle, accomplished Anne Askew suffered so heroically.

In 1539 a new set of commissioners was appointed, under whose irresistible pressure the surrender of many of the larger monasteries was obtained. Especial pains were taken to excite popular prejudice by the exposure of the monkish frauds in supposed relics and miraculous images, which had long been a fertile source of revenue to their possessors. At Hales Abbey, in Gloucestershire, a constant succession of pilgrims had been shown a phial, reputed to contain the blood of Jesus, but invisible to all in mortal sin. In the presence of Latimer it was examined, and found to be a phial, having a dark and clear side, which, at the will of the exhibitor, had revealed or concealed a fluid, consisting of honey coloured with saffron. Such was the object of devotion famous all over the West of England as the Blood of Hales. Another rare treasure was a taper at Cardigan, which had burned for nine years without wasting or going out, till at last, on some one swearing falsely by it, the taper at once went out, and never could be re-kindled again. Upon examination, the taper was found to be a piece of painted wood, and when a light was applied by a Reformer's hand it burned readily enough. In the South of England no image was in higher repute than the Rood of Grace, at Boxley Abbey, in Kent. The figure rolled its eyes, bowed its body, knitted its forehead into a frown, and dropped its lower lip, as if to speak. According to the verse of a contemporary,—

Suppression of the great monasteries.

Destruction of images and relics.

> 'He was made to juggle,
> His eyes would goggle,
> He would bend his brows and frown;
> With his head he would nod,
> Like a proper young god,
> His shafts would go up and down.'[1]

In Maidstone market-place this wonder-working image was publicly exhibited by the commissioners, where it roused wondrous detestation and hatred in the people when they saw how they had been duped. Other wonder-working objects of devotion were taken to London and placed by the most celebrated pulpit in England, St. Paul's Cross, where they were lectured upon, their mechanical contrivances exposed, and finally thrown among the people to be torn in pieces. Such exposures were death-blows to the system that had made them possible.

With rough but certain stroke the destruction of shrines followed, by an order to the magistrates and sheriffs of each county. Within a year of the issue of the order, in 1538, all were levelled to the ground—not one escaped the hammer. The only shrines now remaining—those of Edward the Confessor, in Westminster Abbey, and of St. Albans, in the cathedral bearing his name—being ingenious reconstructions of restored fragments. At Canterbury the gorgeous shrine of St. Thomas, that for nearly four centuries had drawn pilgrims of every class, from royalty downward, was dismantled. Like the reputed blood of Christ at Hales, that shown as the blood of the murdered archbishop was found not to be blood at all, and the so-called martyr must have been as miraculous as the monks had pretended, if they had told the truth, for it was found that, besides the head they had shown to the pilgrims as his undoubted and genuine head, another was in the shrine. So great was the accumulated treasure of gold, silver, and precious stones, that they filled two coffers, borne on the shoulders of seven or eight men; and for the removal of the rest of the spoil six and twenty carts are said to have waited at the cathedral door. The vacant space of pavement, splintered by the

Destruction of shrines, 1538.

---

[1] *Phantasie of Idolatries.*

violence of the destroyer, and worn by the knees of millions of worshippers, is now all that remains to tell of the glory of the shrine renowned as the richest in England, and perhaps in all Christendom. Nor was this all: the saint, the hero of a triumph of papacy over the Crown, was proclaimed a traitor, his name obliterated in the service-books, his festival ordered to be disregarded, even every window in which his figure appeared blazoned in glass was ruthlessly ordered to be destroyed.

Rome's retaliation was the issuing, in 1538, of the long-prepared bull of excommunication and deposition, which, for three years, for politic reasons, had been suspended. Its only effect upon Henry was to cause him to proceed with greater earnestness and severity with Cromwell's policy of coercion. The next year, 1539, he obtained an Act, not, indeed, to suppress the larger monasteries, but to grant and confirm to him all such monasteries as had been, or should be, surrendered. Many monks and abbots were induced by fair means or foul to leave their monasteries, and others were driven out by force. The abbots of Glastonbury, Reading, and Colchester paid the cost of their refusal with their lives, and were hanged for not accepting the king's supremacy. Within four years from the time that the first commission was issued, in April, 1536, not a monastery was left in England, great or small. Tewkesbury and St. Albans were bought back by the people. Six hundred and sixty in all fell to the rapacious king. Yet in the first Act of Parliament the greater houses had been described as 'great and honourable,' wherein 'religion was right well kept.' Now they were all dismantled, the buildings unroofed, the accumulated treasures of centuries in jewels and plate inventoried and sent away in long arrays of wagons; the bells and lead sold, and the ruins left to be pilfered by neighbouring inhabitants as long as any door, window, iron, or glass remained. The inmates of the different monasteries were provided with annuities, the amounts of which were fixed in proportion to the possession of the houses and the rank of the persons.

The king excommunicated, 1538.

It would be unjust to the memory of the leading Reformers to pass unnoticed the fact that they withstood the wholesale confiscation of the vast spoils to the king's treasurer. Cranmer proposed that all such houses as were not of royal foundation should be turned into schools and colleges for education, or hospitals for the sick and the poor.[1] Latimer pleaded with Cromwell to spare the abbey of Great Malvern, 'not for monkery—God forbid!—but to maintain teaching, preaching, study with praying;' adding, 'Alas! my good lord, shall we not see two or three in every shire changed to such remedy?' But the Reformers were at a disadvantage. It was the Parliament that passed the Six Articles that gave authority for the dissolution of the greater monasteries. The Romish party, led by Gardiner, was for the time in the ascendant, and being overborne by them, the Reformers were as powerless to modify the policy pursued in the appropriation of the funds of the abbeys as they were to oppose the law of the Six Articles passed in the same year.

[1] Strype, *Cranmer*, i. 160 (1694).

CHAPTER XVII.

EARLY REFORMATION LITERATURE.

IN the autumn of the year 1525, in the Lutheran city of Worms, appeared the first printed English New Testament. It was published anonymously and in two forms—in quarto and octavo. That it was the work of Tindale was an open secret among Reformers. Great was the impulse to the cause of Reform, from the putting into circulation of six thousand copies of this work. Brought into England chiefly through the eastern ports—Yarmouth, Harwich, and Norwich—in the spring of the following year, by a system of private colportage, it was soon on sale in all parts of the country. In London, in the universities, in the country towns, the volumes passing from hand to hand were 'read with great application and joy.' In the humble homes of the Lollards Tindale's Testament took the place of the fragmentary transcripts of Purvey's revision of Wycliffe and Hereford's version. In the rooms of university students, in merchants' mansions and baronial halls, in monasteries and convents, the first printed English New Testament was read with curious and often eager interest, all the more so for the strenuous efforts that were being made for its suppression. The chief authorities in the Church preached against it, prohibited it, publicly burnt it, but the demand for the suppressed book increased enormously. Independent of Tindale's control, several unauthorized editions were issued by Antwerp printers in 1526 and the two following years. Much to Tindale's annoyance, in 1534, just as he was on the point of publishing a revised edition of his work, usually known as the second, a Protestant refugee, George Joye, issued a revised reprint of Tindale's New Testament. Tindale's own revision, of which the first title runs, 'The Newe Testament, dylygently corrected and compared with the Greke by Wyllyam Tindale,' contains side-notes, prologues to the different books, and translations of the por-

Tindale's English New Testament, 1525.

tions of the Old Testament contained in the Sarum service-book. A third edition, known among bibliographers as the G. H. edition, and having two titles—the first dated 1535 and the second 1534—appeared in 1535. The first title-page has these words, 'The Newe Testament yet once agayne corrected by Willyam Tindale;' and the little volume in all probability represents the last revision of the great translator. From this edition also the New Testament text of Matthew's Bible is taken.

Stringent measures were taken for the suppression of these successive editions of English New Testaments. Though the Catholic clergy deprecated the translation of the Scriptures, no doubt their grave objection was to the 'prologues' and 'glosses' which accompanied the translation. Of these Archbishop Warham complained, as being 'nefarious and distorted comments.' Bishop Tunstall, the friend of Erasmus and the patron of learning, whose patronage Tindale had vainly sought for his undertaking, denounced the book as the work of 'many children of iniquity, maintainers of Luther's sect, blinded through extreme wickedness, wandering from the way of truth and the Catholic faith,' and required all persons within the bounds of his diocese to deliver up all copies in their possession under pain of excommunication. In 1529 awkward attempts were made by the bishops, who clubbed together towards the expense to buy up as many copies as they could of the New Testament before they left Antwerp. These were publicly burned at Paul's Cross in the May of 1530, in the presence of and under the superintendence of Tunstall.

Such was the treatment to which Tindale's great work was subjected, of which in eloquent words Mr. Froude says: 'Though it has been many times revised and altered, it is substantially the Bible with which we are all familiar. The peculiar genius—if such a word may be permitted—which breathes through it, the mingled tenderness and majesty, the Saxon simplicity, the preternatural grandeur, unequalled, unapproached in the attempted improvements of modern scholars, all are here, and bear the impress of the mind of one man, William Tindale.'[1]

Ten years intervened between the publication of the

---

[1] Froude, *History*, vol. ii. p. 498.

MILES COVERDALE.

first edition of Tindale's Testament and the first complete printed English Bible, which appeared in 1535 as a small folio volume. It is printed in an uncommon black-letter, and is adorned with woodcuts and maps. It was the work of Miles Coverdale, one of the band of Cambridge Reformers, who subsequently became Bishop of Exeter. This translation was made principally from the Latin Bible of Pagninus of 1528, and the Zurich Bible (Swiss-German) of 1524–1529. In the New Testament and the Pentateuch free use was made of Tindale's version. The place where it was printed is still unknown, though the late Mr. Henry Stevens believed it to have been the work of Jacob Van Meteren, of Antwerp,[1] and it appeared, possibly at the instigation of Cromwell, with a dedication to Henry VIII. as 'Defendour of the Fayth, and under God the chefe and supreme head of the Church of Englonde.' In this version, for the convenience of reference, each book is divided into sections, and the sections into paragraphs. Coverdale's translation of the Psalms, remarkable for its rhythm and often for its vigour, is still in familiar use, being that largely retained in the Book of Common Prayer. Familiarly, Coverdale's version is known as the 'treacle' Bible, as the first of successive versions rendering the passage, 'Is there no balm in Gilead?' as, 'There is no more triacle at Galaad,' the word 'triacle' being used in its old sense of a medicine to counteract poison, hence, a remedy. Though issued with the approval of Cromwell, and dedicated to the king, it was not until the third edition in 1537 that the wished-for words appeared on the title-page, 'Set forth with the king's most gracious license.'

Wolsey ner's 539.

Coverdale's Bible, 1535.

Proof of the widespread desire for the Scriptures in English is seen in the issue of another version within two years of the first edition of Coverdale's. It appeared as a fine full-sized folio volume, containing the whole Bible 'truly and purely translated into English by Thomas Matthew.' The real editor was John Rogers, a friend of Coverdale, cotemporary with Coverdale, Barnes, and others at Cambridge, who became identified with the Reformation movement. For some months before Tindale's imprison-

'Matthew's Bible' (John Rogers), 1537.

---

[1] See *Bibles in the Caxton Exhibition*, pp. 36–40.

Rogers was associated with him at Antwerp, and ably, in his hour of danger, appointed by him his literary executor. At all events, the Bible edited by Rogers is of peculiar interest, as containing the translation before unpublished of the Old Testament Scriptures from Joshua to the end of Chronicles, ascribed by general tradition, corroborated, says Bishop Westcott, by internal evidence, to Tindale.[1] As the work contains Tindale's translations of the Pentateuch and of the New Testament, more than half the book is his; the remaining portion, from Ezra to Malachi, except the Book of Jonah, is mainly a reprint from Coverdale's Bible. Roger's contribution to the work is principally in notes of an advanced Protestant character, and in the addition of marginal references and a concordance. The books are divided into chapters and sections, distinguished by letters of the alphabet, and the whole was adorned with many woodcuts.

It is one of the curious paradoxes of history that this Bible, containing the whole of Tindale's translations denounced by More, Tunstall, and Warham as heretical, and with notes of a zealous Protestant character, should have had all obstacles which could hinder its sale or reading removed by royal license. Cranmer recommended Matthew's Bible to Cromwell as more to his liking than any translation heretofore made. Cromwell showed the book to the king, who ordered that it 'shall be allowed by his authority to be bought and read within this realm.' And the public acceptance of it was such that within a short time one thousand five hundred copies of the fine folio volume, containing the whole of the before proscribed translations of Tindale, were sold. 'From Matthew's Bible itself, a combination of the labours of Tindale and Coverdale,' says Bishop Westcott, 'all later revisions have been successfully formed. In that the general character and mould of our whole version were definitely fixed. The labours of the next seventy-five years were devoted to improving it in detail.'

Licensed by Royal Authority 1537.

The first of these revisions, prepared by a lawyer, Richard Taverner, met with considerable favour. Taverner was also one of the Cambridge students of Lutheran

---

[1] *History of the English Bible*, pp. 184, 185 (Second Edition).

sympathies, and one of those invited by Cardinal Wolsey to his new college at Oxford. His work as a revisionist of Matthew's Bible has the reputation of being able and vigorous in the New Testament portion, but of less merit in reference to the Old. Taverner, in his dedication, says he undertook the work of revision at the request of the printers, who may have realized the too polemical character of Matthew's annotations, and desired their suppression, as well as changes in translation. *Taverner's Bible, 1539.*

One of the mysterious features of Cromwell's character is that while manifestly so unmindful of the righteous and merciful precepts of the Bible, he was so impressed with its worth that he is said to have committed to memory the whole of the New Testament. Certainly to his zeal in no small measure is owing the publication of the 'Great Bible,' so called from its size—a noble volume, printed under the superintendence of Miles Coverdale as editor, and of Richard Grafton as a skilled printer. Letters of Cromwell show how deeply interested he was in the work. The printing was begun in Paris, and portions of the printed sheets were sent home by Bonner, who was then at the court of Francis I., as ambassador's luggage; but the work was interrupted by the inquisitor-general, and the sheets already printed ordered to be seized and burned. Through the connivance of the authorities, who probably wished to avoid any unpleasantness with the English king, the finished sheets were sold to a haberdasher to 'lap his caps in,' and from him 'four great dry vats full' were purchased, and brought over to England with the presses. The work, completed in London, was issued in the April of 1539. The title-page, designed by the celebrated Hans Holbein, presents a pictorial study of historic interest, as illustrating the spirit of the times. *The 'Great Bible,' or 'Cromwell's,' 1539.*

The 'Great Bible' is printed in black letter; every chapter is prefaced by a summary of its contents. The text is Coverdale's revision of his own translation and Tindale's, with the help of S. Münster's Latin translation, and of the famous *Complutensian Polyglot*. The fact is interesting, both in reference to Tindale's merits as a translator and to Coverdale's own grace of spirit, that the 'Great Bible' follows more Tindale's version than Coverdale's own. Another characteristic is the frequent introduction of readings from the Vulgate. A third, the absence of all polemical annotations.

With the energy that characterized Cromwell in all his undertakings, while this revision was being printed an injunction was issued, requiring the clergy to provide by a certain date, in each parish, 'one book of the whole Bible of the largest volume in English,' the cost, equal to about £6 of modern money, to be divided between the parson and the parishioners. It was further required that the Bible should be set up in a convenient place within the church for general reading, and that the clergy should 'expressly provoke, stir, exhort every person to read the same.' Fifteen months after its publication Cromwell went the way of Wolsey. His policy, not only in the matter of the king's marriage with Anne of Cleves, but in home and foreign politics, disappointed Henry's expectations. His fall was sudden and overwhelming. Unheard he was condemned as a traitor. He who had shown no mercy learned what it was to receive none. From the Tower he wrote to his old master, 'With the heavy heart and trembling hand of your highness's most miserable prisoner and poor slave, I cry for mercy! mercy! mercy!' But none was shown. As a traitor he died upon the scaffold, his head hacked off, rather than chopped, by a clumsy executioner. Cromwell's avarice, unscrupulous ambition, his heartless cruelty can scarcely be painted in colours too dark. Yet to him, in no small degree, England owes release from the ecclesiastical empire of Rome. His title, *Malleus Monachorum*, expresses the popular estimate as to who suppressed the monasteries. His figure on the title-page of the first edition of the Great Bible is the memorial of the prominent part he took in giving to England the blessing of an open Bible. From his intimate connection with it, not without reason the first edition of the Great Bible is generally known as Cromwell's Bible.

Fall of Cromwell, 1540.

For the second edition of the 'Great Bible,' issued in 1540, a prologue was written by Cranmer, reprinted in all subsequent editions. In it an earnest appeal is made to all classes to avail themselves of the opportunity of becoming acquainted with the Holy Scriptures as the great remedy for the evils of

Cranmer's Bible, 1540.

human life. Copies containing the archbishop's prologue are distinguished from those of the first edition as Cranmer's Bible.

Four great versions of the Bible, and these in tens of thousands of copies, were now in circulation among the people. Without the fear of prison, the scourge, or the stake, the Bible for a brief while was an open book to all who could read. For those who could not, there were the public readings by laymen and others in the churches. In St. Paul's six copies of the Great Bible were set up by Bishop Bonner. These any one was at liberty to read in the hearing of others, provided it was not to the disturbance of Divine service. 'Many well-disposed people,' we are told, 'used much to resort to the hearing thereof, especially when they could get any that had an audible voice to read them.' Mr. Green in his *History*[1] points out what an immense effect these popular readings had upon the knowledge of the people. One who wrote within old men's recollections of the time says: 'It was wonderful to see with what joy the book of God was received, not only among the learneder sort, and those that were noted for lovers of the Reformation, but generally all England over, among all the vulgar and common people; and with what greediness God's Word was read, and what resort to places where reading of it was. Everybody that could bought the book, and busily read it, or got others to read it to them, if they could not themselves, and divers more elderly people learned to read on purpose. And even little boys flocked among the rest to hear portions of the Holy Scripture read.'[2] This time of exultant liberty, as we shall shortly see, did not last long.

Before passing to the time of the Protectorate, it will be well to observe the abundant evidence of a spiritual awakening found in the popular literature of the time, and especially the writings of the early Reformers. It is a true sign of the popular character of the Reformation when we find that while the keen, relentless satires of Erasmus were giving expression in Latin, the literary language of the upper classes, to the pre-Reformation

---

[1] *History of the English People*, vol. iii. pp. 9-12 (1886).
[2] Strype, *Life of Cranmer*, p. 64 (1694).

feeling respecting monks and friars, other writers in the home-born language of the people were expressing the same sentiments. Prominent among these was John Skelton, the first poet-laureate, and one of the greatest scholars of his time. Erasmus calls him the 'glory and light of English letters.' The scholar poet spoke home truths to his countrymen, not always characterized by strict regard to propriety of expression, in his *Colin Clout*, a merciless satire on the ignorance of the clergy and the corruptions of the Church. Of this poem it has been remarked that it 'represents the whole popular feeling of the time just before the movement of the Reformation took a new turn by the opposition of the pope to Henry's divorce.' In what the author calls 'ragged rhymes' there is set forth the appeal of the country Colin and of the Clout, or mechanic, of the town against the ecclesiastical evils of the times. Priests, prelates, monks, all pass under the poet's lash on account of their luxury, profligacy, tyranny, and neglect of duty. The poem closes with the prayer that 'our Saviour Jesu' will send His grace

[margin: John Skelton's Colin Clout.]

> 'To rectify and amend
> Things that are amiss
> When that His pleasure is.'

A famous pamphlet of early Reformation times was *The Supplication of the Beggars*, by Simon Fish, a lawyer. The 'supplication' is addressed to the king, setting forth in bold and spirited manner the danger to the nation and the throne from the grasping avarice of the religious orders, of whom the writer says they 'had begged so importunately that they had got into their hands more than the third part of all the realm.' A calculation is set forth to show that the alms given to the begging Friars amounted annually to £43,233 6s. 8d. The use made of all this wealth by 'this greedy sort of sturdy, holy, idle thieves,' is said only to be to 'exempt themselves from obedience to the king,' and 'to translate all rule, power, and dignity from him to themselves.' Merciless charges of immorality are brought against the accused, and the doctrine of purgatory satirized as 'an invention of the priests for their

[margin: Fish's Supplication of Beggars.]

ends.' 'If the pope with his pardons may for money deliver one soul thence, he may deliver him as well without money; if he may deliver one, he may deliver a thousand; if he may deliver a thousand, he may deliver them all, and so destroy purgatory; and then he is a cruel tyrant, without all charity, if he keep them there in prison and in pain till men will give them money.' Copies of this pamphlet were scattered in the London streets, and widely circulated. One came into the king's hands, who is said to have protected its author against proceedings by the ecclesiastical authorities.

The influence of Simon Fish's *Supplication of the Beggars* was such that it called forth a reply from the foremost Englishman of the day, Sir Thomas More, entitled *The Supplication of Souls*, an imaginary appeal of souls in purgatory, lamenting there was so little faith on earth that the relief of destitute bodies should be placed before that of suffering souls. He argued, too, for the necessity of the existence of purgatory, from the fact that men's sufferings in this life are not sufficient to make satisfaction for their sin. *[Sir Thomas More's Supplication of Souls.]*

The youthful and learned John Fryth then took up the controversy in his *Disputation of Purgatory*. Against the doctrine of purgatory he set that of the sufficiency of Christ's atonement, setting forth that faith alone was necessary to receive it. The true purgatory, he said, is the Word of God. Christ makes His Church clean by His Word. Faith is the purgatory of the heart. Reference has been made, in the account of his tragic death, to his remarkable treatise in which he maintained and defended the doctrine of the sacrament, subsequently adopted in the Book of Common Prayer. *[Fryth's Disputation of Purgatory, 1531.]*

The effect produced in England by the writings of the German Reformers was great. The writings of Luther, together with those of Huss, of Zwingli, of Melanchthon, and of many anonymous authors, the writings were smuggled into England and industriously scattered abroad. Luther's *Babylonian Captivity of the Church of God* was published in 1520, the same year in which he publicly cast the papal bull of excommunication into the flames. The main thought of the book *[Influence of German Reformers.]*

is expressed in the title. Picturesquely the Church is described as led into bondage by the pope and curia, as the Jewish people were taken into Babylon. Under the same bondage were the sacraments, which likewise ought to be delivered. A copy of this treatise Luther sent to Leo X., with expressions of personal respect, and invoking him to set about a work of reformation in his corrupt court, which is styled a 'licentious den of robbery.' This was the work that called forth in the following year the famous tract of Henry on the *Seven Sacraments*. Rapidly this reply passed through several editions, was translated into German, and, so said one admirer, 'filled the whole Christian world with joy and admiration.' With characteristic vehemence and bluntness, Luther replied to his royal assailant, in his reply exclaiming: 'I cry, Gospel! Gospel! Christ! Christ! and they cease not to answer, Usages! Usages! Ordinances! Ordinances! Fathers! Fathers! The Apostle St. Paul annihilates with a thunderstorm from heaven all these fooleries of Henry.' Sir Thomas More and Bishop Fisher then joined in the conflict, More, in a manner so rabid that Atterbury says, 'He threw out the greatest heap of nasty language that was perhaps ever put together.' A prohibited book which called forth such exalted antagonists, every one, of course, was eager to see, and large numbers found their way into England. Luther's famous *Commentary on the Epistle to the Galatians* belongs to the later years of his life. No one who reads its pages can wonder at its becoming a work of historic interest in connection with the Reformation. In its passionate vehemence it stirred the hearts of thousands to a true and living idea of faith as the all-controlling principle of the Christian life. Of its doctrinal teaching some account will be found in the chapter on the Doctrines of the Reformation.

A long catalogue of prohibited books under date of 1529 shows the sympathetic interest with which in England the Reformation movement on the Continent was watched and studied. In addition to numerous controversial and other works by Luther appear the titles of various works of Melanchthon, whose zeal, learning, and

[margin: Luther's Babylonian Captivity of the Church.*]*

[margin: Henry's Assertio Septem Sacramentorum, *1521.]*

[margin: Luther's Commentary on Epistle to the Galatians.]

gentleness have placed him next to the heroic Luther as an agent in the work of the Reformation. The commentaries of Bugenhagen, another of Luther's most intimate friends, appear in the list; also those of Brenlius, and of Martin Bucer, the friend of Cranmer, of whom Cardinal Contarini said, 'That he was able to contend alone with all the doctors of the Romish Church.' There is also the mention of exegetical works, by Conrad Pellicanus, one of the most distinguished Hebraists of his time, and of the controversial works on the nature of the Lord's supper by the great Swiss Reformer, Zwingli, and his friend John Hausschein, called Œcolampadius. Bitterly Sir Thomas More complains of the large circulation of such publications: 'Of these books of heresies there be so many within these few years, what by Luther himself, and by his fellows, and afterwards by the new sects sprung out of his, which, like the children of Vippara, would now gnaw out their mother's belly, that the bare names of these books were almost enough to make a book.' Of the production and circulation of these books he says, 'Albeit they neither can be there printed without great cost, nor here sold without great adventure and peril, yet cease they not with money sent from hence to print them there, and send them hither by the whole vatsful at once, and in some places, looking for no lucre, cast them abroad by night.'

Next to Tindale's translation of the New Testament, no book rendered greater service to the Reformers' cause than his *Obedience of a Christian Man.* This was published in the same year (1528) as another memorable book of his, *The Parable of the Wicked Mammon,* an exposition of the parable of the unjust steward, in which the doctrine of justification by faith is set forth with great acuteness. Both books were written with an earnestness and force that caused them to be eagerly read in England by all who were friendly to the Reformation, and as eagerly condemned by the Church authorities as 'frantic,' 'pestilent,' 'contagious,' and 'damnable.' But Tindale's masterpiece is his *Obedience.* It was an inestimable advantage to the Reformers to have such an able defence against the common imputation they had to endure of disloyalty, of treasonable and of socialistic teaching, for

Tindale's Obedience of a Christian Man, 1528.

it brought into prominence 'the two great truths which
constitute the very essence of the English Reformation —
the supreme authority of Scripture in the Church, and
the supreme authority of the king in the State.'[1] The
book abounds also in noble precepts, expressed with manly
and practical directness rather than with grace of style.
In it martyrs found comfort and support that strengthened
them to brave the flames. Into the fainting heart of poor
Bilney it inspired fresh life, and when Bainham, another
martyr of some ten years later, publicly withdrew a recantation made at his trial, it was with a New Testament
in his hand and Tindale's *Obedience of a Christian Man*
in his bosom. The moulding influence of Tindale's writings on the thought of those engaged in the Reformation
struggle is seen in the way this teaching was popularized
and illustrated in the pulpit utterances of Latimer and
other Reformation preachers.

Sir Thomas More, at Bishop Tunstall's suggestion, put
forth his strength to refute the anti-papal writings of
Tindale in an elaborate defence of the doctrines
and practices of the Church of Rome. It
appeared in 1529, bearing the title, 'A Dialogue of Sir Thomas More, . . . wherein
he treated divers matters, as of the veneration and worship
of images and relics, praying to saints and going on pilgrimage, with many other things touching the pestilent
sect of Luther and Tindale, by the one begun in Saxony,
and by the other laboured to be brought into England.'
Tindale was ready with his answer in 1531. Naturally,
the language in which this was couched was unpalatable
to More. More, seen at his weakest in his controversial
work, indignant at Tindale's charges, speedily issued the
first part of an elaborate *Confutation*, which grew into a
book 'ten times the size of the one it was intended to
demolish,' and even excelling his opponent's in the use
of bitter words. On which side the victory lay is seen
in the fact that within four years the royal supremacy
was formally acknowledged in England, and only a few
years later the Scriptures took their place as the ultimate
authority in all matters of faith and practice.

Tindale's pen was, beyond question, one of the great

[1] Demaus, *Tyndale*, p. 266 (1886).

potencies of the time. His translations, his treatises, his tracts exercised an influence recognised by his adversaries as necessitating strenuous opposition, and rejoiced in by his friends as a leader of their cause. Sometimes he showed a fiery intolerance of the opinions of others as sincere in their convictions as himself, but his merits far outweigh his discourtesies in controversy. He showed how disinterested was his boldness in the position he took on the great question of the king's divorce. We hear much of Cranmer, who stepped at once into the path of promotion by counsel, given, there is every reason to believe, in all sincerity of conviction; but the testimony of Tindale is often overlooked. More to him than the king's favour, more to him than the joy of returning to his native country, more than the interests of the religious party to which the service of his life had been given, was the testimony of a clear conscience. His *Practice of Prelates*, published in 1530, and having for its sub-title, *Whether the King's Grace may be separated from his Queen because she was his Brother's Wife*, was emphatic in its conclusion that there was no warrant for the contemplated divorce in Scripture, and that to defy the Word of God was to insure speedy and terrible judgment on the land. The publication of this book was the occasion of the issue of an order for his apprehension by the enraged king, and it was through no lack of will on Henry's part that Tindale's death did not occur then, instead of six years later. In his *Practice of Prelates* Tindale thus picturesquely portrays the growth of the papal power, comparing it to the ivy, 'which springeth out of the earth, and then awhile creepeth along by the ground till it findeth a great tree; then it joineth itself beneath alow unto the body of the tree, and creepeth up a little and a little, fair and softly. . . . And then it sendeth his branches along by the branches of the tree, and overgroweth all, and waxeth great, heavy, and thick, and sucketh moisture so sore out of the tree and its branches that it choketh and stifleth them, . . . and becometh a seat and a nest for all unclean birds, and for blind owls, which hawk in the dark, and dare not come to the light.'

Tindale's great influence as a Reformer.

On the Romanist side, in the early history of the Reformation, excepting the writings of Sir Thomas More, the champion of Roman orthodoxy, very little theological literature was published. More's desire, expressed in his epitaph, to be remembered as 'troublesome to thieves, murderers, and heretics,' is fulfilled by his voluminous and violent attacks upon Tindale, not one of whose works escaped his censure.

Romanist writers.

Bishop Fisher's principal contribution to the literature of his day was a pamphlet, widely disseminated on the Continent, and secretly circulated in England, on the subject of the king's divorce. In defence of the doctrines of his Church he wrote a considerable number of controversial tracts against Luther and Œcolampadius. Gardiner, Bishop of Winchester, whose name is so prominent in connection with the history of the Reformation in England in the two great controversies concerning the king's divorce and the king's supremacy, though a firm Romanist, was on the opposite side to Bishop Fisher. He sat with Archbishop Cranmer in court when the marriage of Catherine was pronounced null and void. In vindication of the divorce, the marriage with Anne Boleyn, and the repudiation of the Roman dominion, he wrote his celebrated treatise, *De Vera Obedientia* (Of True Obedience), for which Bonner prepared the preface. At a later period, when in prison, he wrote various tracts in defence of the doctrine of transubstantiation against Cranmer, some of which were published abroad under the name of Marcus Antonius Constantinus.

Bishop Fisher.

Bishop Gardiner's position.

The most eloquent and accomplished of the defenders of the papal power in England was Reginald Pole. His tract, that grew into a book, on the Unity of the Church, has been referred to in connection with the events that called it forth. His not less remarkable scheme for the 'Reformation of the Church,' set forth in 1556, and his work on 'Justification,' advocating doctrinal views closely allied with those of the Reformers, advanced by him and other eminent Romanist representatives at the Council of Trent, belong to a later period than that at which we are glancing.

Reginald Pole.

In the religious discussions of early Reformation times the help of the drama was called in for the defence of both the old and the new doctrines. The mystery plays, representing scenes from scriptural history, were followed by the moralities, short plays in which the characters were those of allegorical personages, and interludes in which historical characters and those from real life were introduced—a distinction, though, not rigidly observed. A famous morality on the Romanist side was *Every Man*, the work of an anonymous writer in the reign of Henry VIII., possibly earlier. In it the author says of priests:

The drama and the Reformation.

> 'God hath to them more power given
> Than to any angel that is in heaven;
> With five words he may consecrate
> God's body in flesh and blood to take,
> And handleth his Maker between his hands.
> The priest bindeth and unbindeth all bands,
> Both in earth and in heaven.'

Again:

> 'God gave priests that dignity,
> And letteth them in His stead among us be.
> Thus be they above angels in degree.'

On the Protestant side John Bale, afterwards Bishop of Ossory, in 1538 wrote *A Brief Comedy, or Interlude, of John Baptist's Preaching in the Wilderness, opening the Assaults of the Hypocrites, with the Glorious Baptism of the Lord Jesus Christ*. The aim of the writer is manifest in the opening lines:

John Bale.

> 'The kingdom of Christ will now begin to spring,
> Which is the preaching of His New Testament;
> Now shall Messias, which is our Heavenly King,
> Appear to the world in manhood evident.'

With vigour the Baptist's denunciations of hypocrites, Pharisees, and other classes are paraphrased, and applied to the priests, Friars, and others of the Catholic Church. The whole closes with these lines:

> 'Give ear unto Christ, let men's vain phantasies go,
> As the Father bade, by His most high commandment.
> Hear neither Francis, Benedict, nor Bruno,
> Albert nor Dominic, for they new rules invent.
> Believe neither pope nor priest of his consent.
> Follow Christ, and therein fructify,
> To the praise of God, and His Son Jesus' glory.'

Fifteen other dramatic productions followed from the prolific pen of Bale. No writings were more obnoxious to the Catholics than those of 'Bilious Bale,' as he has been nicknamed. From the time he was twenty-five till that of his death in 1563 he was an active and bitter controversialist. More than sixty pamphlets in Latin and English are ascribed to him. He played a rough part in the religions controversies of his time, but rendered a permanent contribution to the literature of our country in his *Most Illustrious Writers of Great Britain* — the earliest work of its kind.

EDWARD THE SIXTH.

CHAPTER XVIII.

THE PROTECTORATE, 1547-1553.

ON the death of Henry, his son Edward VI., a child nine years old, nominally reigned in his stead. The young prince was of fair complexion, short in stature, gentle in disposition, and of precocious abilities. When eight years old, he wrote in Latin to his godfather, Cranmer, and at nine he knew four books of Cato by heart. By the reformers he was hailed as the young Josiah of his times. The will of Henry, for his protection, had named merely a council of regency, chosen from men of both parties. Of this council Cranmer and Tunstall, and Wriothesley and the Earl of Hertford, the young king's uncles, were leading members. Almost immediately the Council appointed Hertford 'Protector of the Realm,' and ordered that he should be made Duke of Somerset. The sympathies of the Protector were decidedly Protestant, and under him, with Cranmer to take the lead in ecclesiastical matters, the work of religious reform was rapid. At once persons imprisoned under the Six Articles were set at liberty. Amongst them was Latimer, who for nearly a year had been in the Tower, and for seven years a silenced preacher—'a bell without a clapper,' as he styled himself. To leave no question as to the acknowledgment of the royal supremacy, notices were served upon all the bishops, requiring them to take out new commissions from their new sovereign.

The boy-king.

The Protector.

Progress of religious reform.

Next followed the important step of a general visitation of the churches by commissioners appointed by the Crown. The visitors were both clergy and laymen, and with them went selected preachers. The country was divided into six circuits, and the authority of the bishops, being subject to the king's pleasure, was suspended while the visitation was being conducted. The injunctions issued,[1] which

General visitation of the churches.

---

[1] Given in Cardwell, *Documentary Annals*, vol. i. pp. 4-31.

had the force of an Act of Parliament, are a valuable record of the state of religion, both as an indication of a former state of things, and of approaching changes. A glimpse of ancient use is found in the requirement that all the clergy were to have 'one sermon every quarter of the year at least, wherein they shall purely and sincerely declare the word of God,' and show that 'pilgrimages, offerings of money, candles, or tapers to relics or images, or kissing and licking of the same, praying upon beads, and such like superstitions, have no promise of reward in Scripture.' 'Two lights upon the high altar before the sacrament' were to be allowed, but all 'images abused with pilgrimages, or incensed unto, were to be taken down.' On holy days, when there was no sermon, the priest was 'to plainly recite in the pulpit' the Lord's Prayer, the Creed, and the Ten Commandments in English, 'to the intent the people may learn the same by heart,' and all parents and householders were to be exhorted to teach them to their families and servants. The sacraments were to be 'reverently and duly administered,' and where it had not already been done, 'one book of the whole Bible of the largest volume in English' was to be procured within three months, and within twelve months 'the Paraphrase of Erasmus, also in English, upon the Gospels.' These were 'to be set up in some convenient place in the church,' and no one 'authorized and licensed thereunto' was to be discouraged from reading.

The injunctions.

Light is thrown upon the habits of the parochial clergy by injunctions prohibiting their frequenting taverns and ale-houses, and spending their time at dice, cards, tables-playing, or any other unlawful games, and requiring them to buy, every one for his own use, within three months, a Latin and English New Testament. It was further required of them to keep a register of 'all weddings, christenings, and burials.' Chantry priests, instead of occupying themselves in singing masses for the dead, were 'to exercise themselves in teaching youth to read and write.' All non-resident clergy were to contribute a certain proportion of their income to the poor of the place whence it was derived, and whoever had a hundred a year in Church prefer-

Concerning the clergy.

ment—equal perhaps to more than a thousand now—was to give an exhibition to a poor scholar at Oxford or Cambridge.

For Divine service injunctions were made that prepared the way for the coming Book of Common Prayer. In the meanwhile, King Henry's Primer was to be the devotional manual of the people, while the ordinary service was proceeding in Latin. *Concerning Divine service.* Processions in or about the church were forbidden, and all ringing of bells during the service, except that of one just before the sermon. A characteristic sign of the Reformation movement is seen in the requirement that in every church 'a comely and honest pulpit was to be set' for the preaching of God's word, and one of the forthcoming homilies was to be read every Sunday. In exhortations to their parishioners, the clergy were to correct the abuses associated with 'pilgrimages, relics, and the adoration of images.' Some customs, half superstitious, half imaginative, were not forbidden; but the people were to be warned against putting any trust for salvation in such practices as 'casting holy water about one's bed, upon images and dead things, or bearing about holy bread, or St. John's Gospel, or making crosses of wood upon Palm Sunday, in time of reading the passion, or keeping of private holy days, as bakers, brewers, smiths, shoemakers, and such others do,' *i.e.* in honour of their patron saints; 'on ringing of the holy bells, or blessing with the holy candle, to the intent thereby to be discharged of the burden of sin, or drive away devils, or to put away dreams and phantasies.' Those who look upon the pre-Reformation Church with a sense of loss might learn from such a list of vain and foolish superstitions that the former days were not better than those that succeeded.

For the relief of the poor, it was required that 'a strong chest with a hole in the upper part thereof' be provided, into which the parishioners were to put their alms for the poor, and men making their wills were to be exhorted to leave for the general *Provision for the poor.* relief of the poor such sums as formerly they would have given in 'blind devotion' for pardons, pilgrimages, decking of images, offering of candles, etc. If more was received than was required for the poor, the surplus was to be devoted to the repairs of the highways.

The records, and even the fabric of many parish churches bear witness to the effect of these injunctions.

<small>Wholesale destruction of carving and loss of church plate.</small> The removal of all monuments of 'feigned miracles, pilgrimages, idolatry and superstition,' was required, 'so that there remains no memory of the same on walls, glasses, windows, or elsewhere.' The first year of Edward VI. was in many churches one of much whitewashing and painting, covering up the frescoed figures of saints and angels, taking down roods, removing images, and in not a few a crashing of 'blasphemous pictures in church windows.'

A typical example occurs, for instance, in Bishop's Stortford Church, where the churchwardens' accounts, under date of 1547, show that whitewashing and painting were the principal items of expenditure. Entries of profit, in the same year, arising from the sale to various purchasers of a cross of silver, a chalice of silver gilt, censers, a ship of silver or incense boat, and other church plate, possibly were to meet the extra expenditure incurred, or may be regarded as proof of foresight on the churchwardens' part of coming changes. Even the monumental brasses were in some instances sold by churchwardens. To such an extent was this kind of traffic carried on by avaricious or needy clergy and their churchwardens, that early in Edward's reign it was forbidden by the Council, and instructions issued to cause 'due search to be made what hath been taken away, sold, or alienated out of any church or chapel, and to what use the money coming thereupon hath been employed, and by whom used.' In fact, there can be little doubt that to the barbarous zeal or avariciousness of the authorities of Edward's reign, rather than, as so often asserted, to the Puritans of the seventeenth century, must be ascribed the wholesale destruction of much costly and beautiful carving, and much precious plate and glass.

Though Edward ascended the throne in January, 1547, it was not until the November of that year Parliament <small>Repeal of the Six Articles, 1547.</small> met. One of its first acts was the repeal of the Six Articles, with every other penal act relating to doctrine and matters of religion. It might have been hoped the intention was to abolish the punishment of death for religious belief, but subsequent events in the reign proved such was not the case. The principles of religious toleration had yet to be learned.

Another Act of Parliament carried into effect Cranmer's proposal made in the previous year, to restore the administration of the communion in both kinds to the laity. The use of the cup by the officiating priest only was a custom slowly introduced. Till the beginning of the twelfth century it was almost unknown in this country, and long after, to conciliate the laity, unconsecrated wine was given them. Cranmer's proposal therefore was for the restoration of an ancient right; it was agreed to by Convocation, and then enjoined by statute. In the following year, 1548, the office for Holy Communion, as described in the next chapter, was published in English. 'The laity,' it has been picturesquely said, 'were called up into the chancel. The mass became a " communion " of the whole Christian fellowship. The priest was no longer the offerer of a mysterious sacrifice, the mediator between God and the worshipper; he was set on a level with the rest of the Church, and brought down to be the simple mouthpiece of the congregation.'[1] *The communion to be administered in both kinds, 1547.*

An important alteration was also made in the law for the appointment of bishops. We have seen that a statute of 1533 secured to the Crown the power of nomination to all English bishoprics. The royal license for election, with a letter naming the person whom the king desired to be elected, was still to go ' as of old had been accustomed ;' but it was now made obligatory to elect the person thus nominated. This was among the Acts repealed by Queen Mary, and not revived by Queen Elizabeth; so that the mode of election established by Henry resumed its force, and is still the law of the Church of England, though no longer that of the Protestant Church of Ireland. *Act for the appointment of bishops, 1547.*

A statute was also enacted for the appropriation of the endowments of all colleges, free chapels, or what we should now call chapels of ease, chantries, and of all guilds and confraternities. These had been granted to the late king just before his death; but as the grant was to him alone, an- *Appropriation of the endowments of colleges,*

[1] J. R. Green, *History of the English People.*

other law was required to secure this surrender. The chantries, with the fraternities attached to them, had undoubtedly become subject to much abuse. Their priests were an order of clergy whose sole work was celebrating masses for the benefit of souls in purgatory. At altars inclosed by screens, or in small chapels specially built for the purpose, and generally containing the founder's tomb, the mass priest officiated, and candles were burned proportionably to the obits founded. Upon the question of the suppression of these and other superstitious institutions, and the appropriation of their revenues to better objects, Protestant Reformers could give but one answer.

<small>free chapels, chantries, etc., 1547.</small>

As closely associated with the beliefs and practices of the old religion, the property of the numerous social or religious guilds was also confiscated. These societies were composed of men and women of all ranks for mutual assistance in all times of urgent need, especially in old age, in sickness, or of loss occasioned by 'fire, water, and shipwreck,' and in what must have been no uncommon experience in those rough, rude days of strife, 'wrongful imprisonment.' The social guilds were the benefit clubs of the Middle Ages, each bearing the name of some patron saint; and each having its badge, which the members wore at funerals, pageants, and feasts. If the guild were rich enough, it had a hall or 'guild house.' All over the country, in town and village, these societies sprang up. In Norfolk there were nine hundred and nine, in Cambridgeshire there were fifty. In the thought of the usefulness of their social objects, the intimate connexion of these institutions with the beliefs and practices of the old Church has often been overlooked. Wycliffe, in the fourteenth century, had complained of the abuses among the guilds. Chantries were founded or helped by them for the maintenance of priests, to say masses for the welfare of the members of the guild, and for the repose of the souls of the departed. 'The performance of miracle and other plays, setting out of pageants, and providing of minstrels, were undertaken by many of the social as well as by the craft guilds.' As institutions concerned in the support of anti-Reformation beliefs, they suffered in this country as in others.

<small>Social guilds.</small>

The Act for the suppression of these and kindred institutions proposed that the revenues should be devoted 'to godly uses,' in erecting almshouses, grammar schools, in further augmenting the universities, and making better provision for the poor. Cranmer, who had in vain interposed to rescue the lands of the monasteries for religious purposes, foreseeing how the property would go that it was now proposed to acquire, was anxious that the measure should be deferred until the king attained his majority; but his efforts were fruitless. With the exception of the two universities, Winchester, Eton, and St. George's, Windsor, all lands and possessions of colleges were made over to the Council. Out of these funds it was that the King Edward's grammar schools, in all fifty-three, were founded; but a large proportion of the property went merely to the enrichment of avaricious and time-serving courtiers. *King Edward's grammar schools.*

It can be no matter of surprise that the Reformation movement soon restored to the clergy a liberty long withheld, though often claimed—the right to marry. In England, marriages had been so general among the clergy, that in the twelfth century it was observed that 'the greater and better part of the English clergy were clergymen's sons.' In that century, though, in a synod held at Westminster, canons were passed, forbidding the English married clergy to live with their wives, yet, as public documents show, after that many of the clergy were married men. Their position was anomalous, the legality of the marriage being recognised neither by Church nor State, yet by many persons no aspersion was cast upon their moral character. Where a clergyman was living otherwise a blameless life, there were many who did not think the worse of him for having recognised the sanction of a higher law than the Roman rule. Mr. Froude points out that the common surnames of Clark, Parsons, Prior, Bishop, Monk, etc., are all memorials of clerical marriages. *Clergy allowed to marry, 1548.*

As the time of Reformation drew near, often the first sign of a clergyman joining the Reforming party was that he took to himself a wife. Archbishop Cranmer, as we have seen, was a married man long before he became in any sense of the word a Protestant; and from an expression in one of Cranmer's letters, the probability is

that his predecessor Warham was so likewise. In common
fairness, it ought to be remembered that the sweeping
charges of immorality often made against the clergy of
the sixteenth century rested rather upon violation of the
canon law than of the moral law, and that while monks
bound themselves by vow to celibacy, no such obligation
was required of the clergy. In the first year of the Protectorate the question of the celibacy of the clergy was
raised in Convocation, and a resolution passed against its
being made compulsory; and in the following year, 1548,
all prohibitions 'forbidding marriage to any spiritual person' were removed, though somewhat grudgingly, by Act
of Parliament.

In the January of 1549 an Act of momentous importance was passed, the first Act of Uniformity. After having
received the assent of Convocation, the changes
of creed and ritual embodied by Cranmer and
his colleagues with elaborate care in the Book
of Common Prayer were discussed by Lords and Commons. To the book itself we shall refer in the following chapter. Aiming after the impossible, its use was
enjoined by an Act inflicting heavy penalties on those who
should refuse to use, or should 'deprave it.' Though
eight of the bishops strongly protested against the fram-
ing of the Act of Uniformity, it does not appear that any
refused to use the new liturgy. Their policy, and that of
others dissatisfied with the changes that were made, appears to have been, after making their protest, to comply.
It can be no matter of surprise that in many parts of
the country the calling in of the old service-books and
the introduction of the Reformed service met with more
strenuous opposition.

First Act of Uniformity, 1549.

Other causes of discontent were also at work in the
land. The bitterness on account of ecclesiastical changes
was intensified by the social grievance, in part occasioned
by the dissolution of the abbeys. The monks were easy
landlords, but the new owners to whom the abbey lands
fell were eager to reap their full value by rise
of rents, and by inclosing large tracts of common lands for pasturage (the wool trade having become
considerable) deprived cottagers of old and valued rights
of pasturage. Latimer, in a sermon preached before the
king in the year 1549, gives a glimpse of the circumstances

Rise in rents.

of the times. He told his majesty that his own father was a farmer in Leicestershire, where he paid a rent of £3 by the year, and was able to bring up his children in comfort, and could always find a man and a horse for the king's service; but that the man who now held the same land was paying £16, and was a beggar. The distress was deepened by a general rise of prices that fol- *Debasement* lowed on the debasement of the coinage, which *of coinage.* had begun with Henry, and went on yet more unscrupulously under Somerset.

Of this we may be sure—more felt the evil of the times than could explain them. In the eastern counties, where the Reformed doctrines were popular, the *Revolt in the* grievance to the front was the inclosure of *eastern coun-* the common lands, and the evictions from *ties, 1549.* them by the new landlords. Somerset's sympathies were with the oppressed peasantry, but he did not know how to help them. Sixteen thousand men, under the leadership of Robert Ket, rose in defence of their rights, and were not dispersed till nearly a fourth of their number had fallen in a desperate fight near Norwich. It is a characteristic of the spirit of the times that, to quell this agrarian revolt, the help of Italian and German mercenaries was obtained.

In the west of England, where the religious changes that had so rapidly followed one another *Revolt in the* were the great cause of complaint, another *west of Eng-* insurrection, even more formidable, was in *land, 1549.* progress. Many, believing that all the evils were owing to the Reformed religion, protested against the changes, and by open revolt demanded the restoration of the mass and the Six Articles, and a partial re-establishment of the suppressed abbeys. Not without great difficulty was the revolt suppressed. Exeter was laid siege to, and was on the point of being taken, when Lord Grey, aided by Italian musketeers, relieved it, and defeated the insurgents on Clifton Down, and afterwards at Bridgwater. In one month four thousand Devonshire and Cornish men were killed in the battle of resistance against the Reformed religion.

A ghastly memorial of the conflict long remained in the parish of St. Thomas, near Exeter. For many years after there dangled from the church tower the remains of its vicar, condemned by court-martial as a rebel, and hanged in his popish apparel.

The details of Somerset's growing unpopularity that brought about his overthrow and execution in 1552 must be sought in the general histories. His name is perpetuated in Somerset House, which stands on the site of a palace the Protector began to build, but did not live to see completed. For its erection neighbouring monasterial buildings were demolished, and a cloister of old St. Paul's torn to pieces to provide material; and he is said to have threatened St. Margaret's, Westminster, with like destruction, but either by bribes or fears was prevented.

The remaining year and a half of Edward's reign was under the protectorate of the Duke of Northumberland. The change of protectors, however, brought no change of system.

Meanwhile one of the greatest changes that had yet been made was exciting the attention of all worshippers in the parish churches. In recognition of the primitive idea of the Lord's supper—still preserved where it might least be expected, in the pope's own cathedral of St. John Lateran—and in protest against the sacrificial idea of the mass, an order was issued for the removal of all stone altars, 'and instead of them,' so runs the order, 'a table to be set up in some convenient part of the chancel, . . . to serve for the ministration of the blessed communion.' The change had been publicly recommended by Bishop Hooper, in a sermon preached before the court.

Substitution of tables for stone altars, 1550.

In this discourse, after first arguing that no sacrifices were left to be done by Christian people, but such as ought to be done without altars, the sacrifices of thanksgiving, of charity, and the mortifying their own bodies, he continues: 'Seeing Christian men have none other sacrifices than these, which may and ought to be done without altars, there should, among Christians, be no altars; and therefore it was not without the great wisdom and knowledge of God, that Christ, His apostles, and the primitive Church lacked altars, for they knew that the use of altars was taken away. It were well then that it might please the magistrates to turn the altars into tables, according to the first institution of Christ, to take away the false persuasion of the people they have of sacrifices to be done upon the altars; for as long as the altars remain, both the ignorant people and priest will dream always of sacrifice.'

This had already been done in some places, as the following entries show, taken from the records of St. Michael's, Bishop's Stortford, under date 1548:

	s.	d.
Item for taking down of the altars		x.
Pd. to William Balam and his son for making [good] the places where the altars did stand		xiiij.
Pd. for planks for the table		xxij.
Pd. to Cornelius for making the table	iij.	viij.

In the diocese of Rochester, and afterwards in that of London, Bishop Ridley had insisted that all the altars should be removed, and communion tables put in their stead.

The order of 1550 had thus been anticipated; the only prominent opposition which it encountered was on the part of Bishop Daye of Chichester, who declared 'he could not conform his conscience to do' what was required of him. Time for deliberation and conference was given him. These failing to influence, he was committed to the Fleet Prison, in company with Heath, Bishop of Worcester, whose objection was chiefly to the new Ordinal. Upon being deprived of their bishoprics, Heath became the guest of Ridley, with whom he said he dwelt more like a son than a subject, and Daye was sent to reside with the lord chancellor.

With the issue of the revised Prayer-Book in 1552 was passed a second Act of Uniformity, 'obliging the subjects to be present at the reading of it,' under penalties of censure or excommunication. Persons who attended any other rendered themselves liable to imprisonment. *Second Act of Uniformity, 1552.* Of the additions made to the services, and of the retrenchment in the matter of ceremonial, particulars are elsewhere given.

While the famous Council of Trent was formulating the creed of the Romish Church, the English Reformers in 1553 set forth their confession of faith in forty-two articles, that form the basis of the present creed of the Church of England. Cranmer's desire was for *The Forty-two Articles. Undertaken in 1551; published in 1553.*

a representative confession of faith of all the Reformed Churches, and as an authoritative statement of Protestant doctrines in contradistinction to those of Rome. A conference, or Protestant council, was proposed, to which the most distinguished foreign Reformers were invited. For the purpose of such a conference Calvin said he would willingly cross ten seas. Though the plan of the proposed conference fell through, Cranmer preserved the spirit of the intention, as seen in the free use made of the Augsburg Confession drawn up by Melanchthon. The question has been raised whether these articles were ever sanctioned by Convocation.[1] Dr. Cardwell, and so recent and able an authority as Canon Perry, give good reasons in support of the assertion that they received full ecclesiastical sanction. The point is of importance, because by Article XXXV. formal sanction was given to the newly issued Prayer-Book, referred to as 'The book which of very late time was given to the Church of England by the king's authority and the Parliament, containing the manner and form of praying, and administering the sacraments in the Church of England, likewise also the book of ordering ministers of the Church, set forth by the foresaid authority, are godly, and in no point repugnant to the wholesome doctrine of the gospel, but agreeable thereunto, furthering and beautifying the same not a little; and therefore of all faithful members of the Church of England, and chiefly of the ministers of the word, they ought to be received, and allowed with all readiness of mind and thanksgiving, and to be commended to the people of God.'

Historically, the Forty-two Articles are a valuable index to the chief points of controversy which engaged the attention of the English Reformers, as against the Church of Rome on the one side, and the more revolutionary sects of Protestantism on the other side. The doctrine of transubstantiation is denied, as 'repugnant to the plain words of Scripture:'

'Forasmuch as the truth of man's nature requireth that the body of one and the selfsame man cannot be at one time in divers places, but must needs be in some

[1] *Synodalia*, i. p. 3.

one certain place: therefore the body of Christ cannot be present at one time in many and divers places. And because (as Holy Scripture doth teach) Christ was taken up into heaven, and there shall continue unto the end of the world; a faithful man ought not either to believe or openly to confess the real and bodily presence (as they term it) of Christ's flesh and blood in the sacrament of the Lord's supper. The sacrament of the Lord's supper was not commanded by Christ's ordinance to be kept, carried about, lifted up, nor worshipped.'

Four of the articles (XXXIX.-XLII.) on the following points were afterwards omitted in the revision under Elizabeth: That the resurrection of the dead is not yet accomplished. That the souls of the departed neither die with their bodies nor sleep until the day of judgment. That millenarians are heretics. That they also are worthy of condemnation who teach that all men shall be saved at last. Otherwise in spirit and in form the Forty-two Articles are one with the authoritative expression of faith set forth in the Thirty-nine Articles of the Church of England.

In the same session as the Forty-two Articles were passed, a noteworthy Act was passed concerning feasts and fasts. It was enacted that Sunday and the other holidays were to be religiously observed, that the bishops were to censure offenders, and to impose such penance on them as should seem expedient: notwithstanding it was to be lawful for any husbandman, labourer, fisherman, etc., to labour, ride, fish, or work on the foresaid holidays, not only in the time of harvest, but at any other time of the year when need shall require. The eves of the holidays were to be observed as fasts, and abstinence from flesh was enacted both in Lent and on Fridays and Saturdays.

<small>Act concerning holy days and fasts.</small>

A sad picture of the state of the Church and the nation in these times is given in another Act of the same session, enacting 'that if any persons should quarrel, chide, or brawl in any church or churchyard, he should be suspended *ab ingressu ecclesiæ* if he were a layman, and from his ministration if he were a priest; and that if any person should strike another with any weapon in the church or churchyard, he should be punished by the loss of one of his ears.

The last year of Edward's reign of six and a half years was marked as the first had been, by a visitation, not, though, one of inquiry and injunction, but of spoliation. Notwithstanding the confiscated wealth of richly endowed colleges and chantries, and the assertion of royal or national rights over the wealth of bishoprics, the miserable administration of the Protectorate was almost at a standstill for want of money. Amongst other means of replenishing the treasury was the appointment of commissioners professedly to examine and register 'all manner of goods, plate, jewels, bells, and ornaments yet remaining in every church;' in reality to gather in all that was of value, and not absolutely required for the celebration of the reformed services.

A visitation of spoliation, 1553.

In the autumn and winter of 1552-3, throughout the country, the commissioners were busy at this work, inquiring after and securing vestments, copes, plate and jewels, and everything of church property that could be secured. Even the bells of the churches shared the fate of other furniture, and were taken either to be melted down for the sake of the silver, or sold for exportation. Out of three hundred and ninety old churches in Essex, ninety-eight have but one bell remaining, one being sufficient to call the people to service.

The result of the commission was not, after all, so profitable as anticipated. The commissioners only gleaned where others had gone before, who, following royal example, had helped themselves, or purchased for their private use goods and plate belonging to various parish churches. 'Many private men's parlours,' says an early historian, 'were hung with altar cloths; their tables and beds covered with copes, instead of carpets and coverlids; and many made carousing cups of the sacred chalices.' Much treasure was simply secreted by pious clergy, churchwardens, and other persons, who quietly awaited in hope the coming days when it would again be honoured in use.

Few sadder scenes are there in English history than those of the closing years of the reign of its first Protestant king. The Government was corrupt. The currency was ruined. The leading Reformers seemed making common cause with men whose motive was robbery rather than Reformation. Wealth that had been dedicated with good intent, though to superstitious use, instead of being applied to purposes of spiritual instruction, education, or relief of the poor, was squandered in the enriching of those whose lives brought disgrace on their Protestant profession. Of the universities, a Reformation preacher said, 'The two wells of this realm, Oxford and Cambridge, they are almost dried up.' The churches were many of them without incumbents, or badly served by quondam monks or chantry priests, appointed by patrons bound to pension them or provide them with preferment. Many of the clergy, notwithstanding their outward compliance, were papists at heart, ready, as they soon had the opportunity of showing, to apostatize from Protestantism. The unsettling of religious beliefs in the time of transition had its effect upon the social life. Some persons it drove to fanaticism, some to profligacy.

To cast the reproach of this deplorable time upon the leading Reformers would be as thoughtless as unjust. There was not a friend of the Reformation who did not raise his voice against the manifold abuses in the Church and nation. In their letters to one another the Reformers complained bitterly. No severer condemnation of the tyranny, the corruption, the sacrilege is to be found than in the discourses of Ridley and other leading Reformers, who kept up the honour of the Reformation by their lives, as they did afterwards by their deaths. In a sermon of Bernard Gilpin's, preached before the court at Greenwich in the year 1552, the courtiers upon whose estates large inclosures were being made and evictions effected are denounced as men 'so far from mercy, that their hearts will serve them to destroy whole towns; they would wish all the people destroyed, to have all the fields brought to a sheep pasture.'

The misgovernment denounced by the Reformers.

Latimer, after his wont, boldly protested against the rapaciousness of the chief men of the State in his sermons at court, and did not scruple to call upon the possessors of ill-gotten wealth to make restitution: 'If thou wilt not make restitution, thou shalt go to the devil for it. Choose then either restitution or else damnation.' Of the misappropriation of the chantry lands, he said, 'the king was disappointed,' 'the poor were spoiled,' 'learning decayed,' and the hangers-on upon the Council only 'enriched.'

No plunder of Church or Crown enriched the Protestant bishops; they themselves were sufferers in this time of misrule. There was not a bishopric but suffered, some to the extent of one-half of their manors and lordships. The names of Cranmer, Ridley, Hooper, Latimer, and other prominent Reformers are those of true-hearted, devoted men, who, whatever their mistakes and failures, are clear of any charge of enriching themselves in the days of spoliation, and who in the time of trial were not found wanting in steadfastness to the faith they taught in their days of power.

Not less to their honour is it to find there was little or no persecution on account of religion, certainly nothing to be compared with that in the succeeding reign.

The treatment of Catholic bishops. At the strong persuasions of Cranmer and Ridley, the Princess Mary, who held by the old religion, was allowed to have mass performed. Heath of Worcester, Daye of Chichester, were deprived of their sees, and committed, as we have seen, one to the friendly custody of the lord chancellor, and the other to Bishop Ridley. Tunstall's deprivation was solely a political matter. The character and influence of Bishop Gardiner's opposition caused him to be more severely dealt with. Nearly the whole of Edward's reign he was a prisoner in the Tower, and at times treated with such rigour that he was denied the use of pen, ink, and paper. It is to the discredit of the Protestant rulers that this eminent ecclesiastic in vain demanded 'to have an Englishman's liberty to hear what law or statute he had broken.' Bishop Bonner, for refusing to take the oath of supremacy, was sent to the Fleet, but released on promising obedience to the law. Two years later, 1549, he again incurred the displeasure of the Council, for refusing to enforce the use of the new Prayer-Book. After a long trial he was committed to the Marshalsea Prison, where he remained till the accession of Queen Mary.

Of Gardiner and Bonner.

Executions for heresy. Of the few instances of execution for heresy with which the English Reformers can be charged, two belong to this reign. For denying the human nature of Christ, a Kentish woman, Joan Bocher, was burned alive.

The oft-told story of the young king's tearfully yielding to Cranmer's persuasion to sign the death-warrant of the unfortunate creature vanishes in the light of historical research. The warrant never was signed by the king, and Cranmer was not present when it was determined upon by the Council. In the following year (1550) a Dutchman, Van Parre, who practised as a surgeon in London, was convicted of Arianism, and likewise committed to the flames. Remembering the temper of the times, the wonder is not that there were two executions for religious opinion in the course of Edward's reign, but that there were not more; for 'tolerance in religion,' says Hallam, 'was seldom considered as practicable, much less as a matter of right, during the period of the Reformation.'

Amidst the conflicts of selfish passion, the perplexity and despair of the people, scenes of spoliation in every parish church, and the reaction of sentiment that was setting in against the Reformation movement, it must have seemed to many that the cause of Reform was hopelessly lost. The transition from Romanism in England, as in every country in which it has been effected, was marked by manifest evils and perils. Yet amid the perils of that transition time real progress in the cause of Reform was made. Services wholly in the language of the people were substituted for those in a foreign tongue. The communion service took the place of the mass, with its dogmas of transubstantiation and propitiatory sacrifice. A liturgy was given to the nation that has become a prized inheritance. To the clergy were restored the sanctities of home life in all its influences for good, by the right of marriage that had been lost for centuries. The Edwardian days of the breaking up of old habits of thought and feeling in the restatement of doctrine, new formularies of faith, and the clearing away of extravagant superstitions, could not be other than days of struggle and exasperated party feeling. The days of Edward were those of chaos; but darker days were coming, and those whose faith failed amid them were to learn that even worse was the bondage of Rome. *Review of progress made.*

On July 6th, 1553, the young king, long weakened and emaciated by consumption, died, in the sixteenth year of his age, and the seventh of his reign.. All that was known of him, *Death of the young king, July, 1553.*

his stainless character, his devout bearing, made him beloved by the people, who called him Josiah and Edward the saint. The one hope of the nation had been that, when he was of age, he would set all things right. At what was considered his untimely death, 'the greatest moan was made for him as ever was heard or seen.' It was perhaps well that his reign came to an end when it did. It was well that his plan—to which he clung with such tenacity in his dying hours—to set aside Mary in favour of a Protestant successor, failed. There were lessons for England to learn under Catholic rule concerning Romanism that would never be forgotten in the interest of Protestant faith and freedom.

CHAPTER XIX.

REFORMATION LITURGIES AND MANUALS OF SPIRITUAL INSTRUCTION, 1534-53.

THE advancement of the Reformation through the reigns of Henry VIII. and of Edward VI. is strikingly illustrated in the successive editions of the authorized primers and public service books. Primers, or manuals of primary instruction in religious truth and practice, had been in use in England from the days of Langland and Chaucer, who both refer to them. Beginning, probably, with only the Creed, and the Lord's Prayer, and the Ten Commandments, 'the Prymer passed on,' says Mr. Maskell, 'gradually collecting now an office, and then a prayer; at one time the penitential psalms, at another the Litany, at another the dirge, until at last it arrived at the state in which, with little further alteration, it remained during the fifteenth and sixteenth centuries.'[1] At the Reformation nearly one half of the Primer was occupied by the offices called 'The Hours of the Blessed Virgin,' to be used in honour of the Virgin Mary at the seven canonical hours of daily worship. Hence the Latin editions of the Primer were usually called *Horæ*. According to Mr. Maskell, the titles, Horæ, Prymer, Enchiridion, Orarium, and others were used interchangeably for the manuals of devotion, intended for the instruction of the laity, and as aid to private devotion.

Pre-Reformation primers.

Before any alterations were made in the public service books, great changes had been effected in the primers. The first Reformed primer appeared in 1534, under the royal sanction. It is supposed that George Joye was the translator, under the direction of Cranmer. In it the invocation of saints is recognised; there are prayers for the departed, and a

Reformed primers.

[1] *Monumenta Ritualia Ecclesiæ Anglicanæ*, vol. ii. p. 49.

general recognition of Romanist doctrines, excepting, of course, those referring to the pope. A second and revised edition of this Primer was published in the following year, 'newly corrected and printed, with certain godly meditations and prayers added to the same for all them that right assuredly understand not the Latin and Greek tongues.' This was followed in 1539 by *The Manual of Prayers; or the Primer in English and Latin, by John [Hilsey], Bishop of Rochester, at Commandment of Lord Thomas Cromwell.* Others of minor importance preceded the famous Primer of 1545, 'set forth by the king's majesty and his clergy, to be taught, learned, and read, and none other to be used throughout his dominions.' ' A preface made by the king's most excellent majesty unto his Primer-book ' was prefixed, and ' for the better bringing up of youth in the knowledge of their duty towards God, their prince, and all other in their degree, every schoolmaster and bringer up of young beginners in learning, next after their A, B, C, now by us also set forth,' were commanded to ' teach this Primer or book of ordinary prayers unto them in English,' and were forbidden to buy, sell, use, or teach any other primer, either in Latin or English. Like its predecessor, it retained invocations of saints, and the angelic salutation, ' Hail, Mary.' The references to the ' A, B, C, now set forth,' is probably to a school manual, containing the alphabet, lessons in spelling, and a brief catechism, published by royal authority in 1539. Various Reformed versions of Romanist manuals were also in circulation at this time.

The changes in the public service of the Church began with the issue of an order in 1542, that on Sundays and holy days a chapter should be read out of the English Bible. A committee was also appointed for the revision of the ancient service books. Of these several forms were in use, the most ancient and the most general being *The Use of Sarum*. There were others, bearing the name of *The Hereford Use, The Use of Bangor, The Use of Lincoln,* and *of York.* These service or prayer-books were all modifications of the four books commonly used in the services of the Church of Rome: viz. (1) the *Missal*, containing the service for the celebration of the mass; (2) the *Breviary*,

Pre-Reformation service books.

containing the forms of devotion for the different hours of the day; (3) the *Manual*, setting forth the forms and services observed by priests at baptism, marriage, burial, extreme unction, etc.; (4) the *Pontifical*, containing the forms of service required to be performed by a bishop, such as confirmation, ordination, consecration, etc. In the revision of these service books 'all manner of mention of the Bishop of Rome's name' was to be expunged, also 'all apocryphas, feigned legends, and superstitions, and all names of saints not mentioned in the Scriptures or authentical doctors.' Such were the first steps towards the revision that resulted in the Book of Common Prayer.

It is interesting to note the fact that for public worship the first liturgical form published in English was the Litany. Translated from the Latin either by Archbishop Cranmer or by King Henry himself, it was issued in the summer of 1544, with 'An Exhortation unto Prayer, thought meet by the King's Majesty and his clergy to be read to the people in every church afore processions.' The Litany was to be said or sung at the time of such processions. In its earliest form it differed from that now in use only in its invocation of saints, and in a petition for deliverance 'from the tyranny of the Bishop of Rome, and all his abominable enormities.' In the year following, a collection of English prayers was added to the Litany, a service for morning and evening, and for the burial of the dead; and the king in a general proclamation directed that they should be used in all churches and chapels in place of the Breviary.[1] *The Litany published in English, 1544.*

For the purpose of popular instruction in a time when the need was great, and when many of the parish priests were too illiterate or disinclined to preach such doctrines as were desired, Erasmus' *Paraphrase of the New Testament* was translated into English, and a copy ordered to be set up in every parish church for persons to read at their will. For the 'staying of such errors,' it was said 'as were then sparkled among the people,' a volume of homilies was issued. These homilies, twelve in number, on the chief doctrines of Christianity, and on Christian practice, were pre- *The Book of Homilies, 1547.*

[1] *Primers put forth in the Reign of Henry VIII.* (Oxford, 1834).

pared under the direction of Cranmer, who was himself the author of three, those on 'Salvation,' 'Faith,' and 'Good Works.' The others were prepared probably by Ridley, Latimer, and Bucer. As illustrative of the doctrines of the Reformation at this period, the homilies are of special interest and value.

Another step in advance, taken in the reign of Henry, was seen on the Easter Sunday of 1548, when for the first time an English service for the administration of the Holy Communion was used, and the long-forbidden wine, in silver cups, was given to the laity. Cautiously the innovation was made. The old Latin service of the mass was retained up to the end of the prayer of consecration, but after the priest himself had partaken, then followed in English the Exhortation, Invitation, General Confession, Absolution, the Comfortable Words, the Prayer of Humble Access, and the sentences of administration. When all had partaken the Benediction of Peace was given. No change was made in the doctrine of the sacrament. 'The whole body of our Saviour Jesus Christ' was declared to be in each piece of sacramental bread; but there was a material alteration respecting confession: it hitherto had been required of all communicants, but was now left optional.

Communion Service in English, 1548.

In the summer of this year, 1548, was published Cranmer's Catechism, as it is commonly called. The Primate's connection with it is nominal. The work, originally written by a German, was translated into Latin by Justus Jonas, a Lutheran divine, and a guest at one time of Cranmer at Lambeth Palace. Under the archbishop's supervision an English translation was issued, entitled, *A Short Instruction to Christian Religion, for the Profit of Children and Young People*. The instruction, conveyed not in the form of question and answer, but in expositions of the Ten Commandments, the Creed, the Lord's Prayer, and the sacraments, is decidedly Lutheran. Its sacramental teaching represents the transition stage of Cranmer's opinions before abandoning the doctrine of transubstantiation, and accepting the medium position between Lutheranism and Zwinglianism soon afterwards set forth in his book on the sacrament of the Lord's supper.

Cranmer's first catechism, 1548.

With the full sanction of Church and State, the first complete English Prayer-Book was published in 1549, and solemnly used in old St. Paul's Cathedral on the Whitsunday of that year, the day of Pentecost being chosen as that on which all Englishmen should, not only hear, but worship 'in the tongue wherein they were born.'

The actual change introduced by the Reformed service was not so great as might at first be supposed. We must remember that for five years an English translation of the Litany had been in use, and that for a longer period a lesson from the Old or New Testament had been read from the 'Great Bible.' By a recent injunction the Epistle and Gospel at the mass were to be read in the vernacular. Already, as we have seen, the communion service had been celebrated in English. Translations also of portions of the old Latin services for matins and evensong had appeared in the king's Primer. But the Whitsunday of 1549 is memorable in the religious history of our country as that on which for the first time the *whole* service of the National Church was in the common language of the people.

The chief changes introduced by the publication of the Book of Common Prayer consisted—

1. In the use of one book instead of several: the Prayer-Book being a condensed reproduction in English of the old Latin service books, that of the *Use of Sarum* being principally followed.

2. In the substitution of two daily services, 'matins' and 'evensong,' for those of the seven hours, which, except in the monasteries, were rarely observed.

3. The removal from the services of a vast quantity of legendary matter, which was read in the form of lections, and of numerous litanies to and invocations of the saints, especially of the Virgin Mary.

4. In the increased use of Scripture by the lengthening of the lessons, which sometimes consisted of tiny portions of one or two verses, so 'that many times there was more business to find out what should be read, than to read it when it was found out.'

5. In the rearrangement of the reading of the Psalter for a monthly course, instead of a weekly.

6. In the omission of various offices for the souls of the departed, and numerous prayers which implied a belief in purgatory.

In looking through the various services of the first Reformed Prayer-Book, some of the old usages and the changes they have undergone at once arrest attention. The order appointed for morning and evening prayer began, not as now with sentences of Scripture, but with the Lord's Prayer. In none of the services was the Apostles' Creed used; its only appearance being in the Catechism. The form for the celebration of the communion, described as 'commonly called the mass,' was evidently intended to assuage as much as possible antagonistic feeling. Though referred to as 'the Lord's table' and 'God's board,' no changes were directed to be made in the altar, nor in the vestments of the ministering clergy. The priest who celebrated was to wear the usual vestments, an alb and a cope, and assistant priests or deacons who might be present were to have albs and tunicles, thus preserving to the eye what the worshipper had been accustomed to see. It is worthy of note, however, that there was to be no elevation of the sacrament in the sight of the people, but the minister was directed, when preparing the bread and the wine, to mix 'a little pure and clean water with the wine.' The solemn prayer of self-dedication, instead of being, as now, towards the close of the service, was part of the consecration prayer, emphasizing the truth that the sacrament is not offered by the priest for the people, but is the offering of the people by themselves: 'Here we offer and present unto Thee, O Lord, ourselves, our souls and bodies, to be a reasonable, holy, and lively sacrifice unto Thee.' Though the idea of a propitiatory sacrifice being offered in the service is carefully resisted, the doctrine of transubstantiation is prominent. Commemoration of the departed is retained, though in such language as wholly to exclude the notion of purgatory.

Turning to other offices, it is curious to find in that for baptism, that the rite was not to be deferred 'any longer than the Sunday or other holy day next after the child was born, unless upon a great and reasonable cause declared to the curate, and by him approved.' In the rite itself, a form of exorcism was pronounced over the child. At

Peculiarities of the first Reformed Prayer-Book.

the naming of the child three times it was dipped in the water. 'First dipping the right side; second, the left side; the third time dipping the face toward the font.' After this operation had been, as the rubric directs, 'discreetly and warily done,' the chrisom, or white robe in token of baptismal purity, was laid upon the child by the minister; and then came an anointing with oil, the whole concluding with an exhortation to the god-parents, as in the present service.

The Catechism in the first Reformed Prayer-Book forms part of the office for Confirmation. It is much shorter than the form now in familiar use. It consists of no more than thirteen questions concerning the Ten Commandments, the Creed, and the Lord's Prayer, and has no definition of doctrine respecting the Lord's supper. The Marriage Service is nearly the same as that now in use, except that at the loosing of hands the man was to give unto the woman 'a ring, *and other tokens of spousage*, as gold or silver, laying the same upon the book;' and then the words ran, 'With this ring I thee wed; this gold and silver I thee give,' etc. In the Order for the Visitation of the Sick, anointing with oil was permitted, if the sick person desired it. At the burial of the dead, the general custom was for the mourners to go direct to the grave, and after the interment into the church. Prayer for the departed was retained, and an office for communion at funerals provided.

These particulars show the caution with which the compilers of the First Prayer-Book of King Edward VI., as it is commonly called, moved, and how much was left for subsequent revision and excision.

Though in reference to doctrine and ritual the first Reformed Prayer-Book can be regarded only as an imperfect draft of that now in use, the Reformers were eminently successful in their rendering of the prayers into English, in the composition of the few they added, and in the exhortations, for which they alone were responsible. Instead of losing by translation, many of the prayers actually gained by the process. In the whole compass of English literature it would be in vain to look for any liturgical compositions equalling those found in the Book of Common Prayer.

Its excellences.

The chief share of the praise bestowed by writers of every school of thought belongs to Archbishop Cranmer. Mr. Froude has justly remarked, 'While the Church of England remains, the image of Cranmer will be ever reflected on the calm surface of the Liturgy.' As primate, Cranmer presided over the twelve commissioners appointed for its preparation. In its diction we have in perfected form the grave rhythmic melody of the *Institution*, in the authorship of which, beyond all question, Cranmer took a prominent part. Upon the whole there is the impress of his gentle, prudent mind, which, in spite of the wide chasm between the ancient and the Reformed Church, still in a measure belonged to both. The Prayer-Book itself occupied a middle position between Romanism and Protestantism. Cranmer's policy, nowhere more clearly seen than in the preparation of the Prayer-Book, was to change as little as possible the externals of worship, until such time as the people were able to bear the change. He did not want a religious revolution, but a gradual transformation. His was a position of compromise, varyingly estimated according to personal opinions and tendencies; but none can do other than admire the spirit that urged charity as the one thing needful, and 'exhorted every man to be satisfied with his own conscience, not judging other men's minds or consciences, whereas he hath no covenant of God's Word to the same.'

Thrust upon the people by an Act of Uniformity at a time when the country was in a most unsettled state, the new service book was protested against both by Reformers and Romanists. To large numbers of the people, who clung to the old forms of worship, the new liturgy was a grievance to be resisted with all possible zeal and energy. While some were assailing the new service book from dislike of any change in religious worship, others were its assailants because it did not go far enough. Hooper, one of the most learned and eloquent leaders of the Protestant Reformation in England, writing to his friend Bullinger, said: 'I am so much offended with the book, and that not without abundant reason, that if it be not corrected, I neither can nor will communicate with the

Church in the administration of the Lord's supper.' It is characteristic of the position Hooper took, that, when nominated to fill the vacant bishopric of Gloucester, he refused to wear the episcopal vestments, to which he objected as remnants of popery, and refused to take the oath required, regarding it as unscriptural, because in it saints and angels were adjured as well as God. [margin: Bp. Hooper.]

To such an extent did Hooper carry his resistance in the publication of his treatise a *Godly Confession and Protestation*, that he was actually committed to the Fleet Prison. At length a compromise was effected. The objectionable words in the oath were struck out, and he consented to wear the episcopal vestment on certain public occasions—at his consecration, before the king, and in his own cathedral. With the moderate and cautious spirit of Archbishop Cranmer Hooper had no sympathy. He was the leader of an agitation that, within two years of the authorization of the Reformed Prayer-Book, secured the appointment of a committee for its revision.

Consequently the first Prayer-Book of Edward VI., 'the book so much travailed for, and also sincerely set forth,' had only a short life of three years. It failed altogether to satisfy the growing Protestant sentiment of the country, largely influenced by the thought and writings of Continental Reformers. Growth there had also been in Cranmer's views on transubstantiation, and his long-cherished hope of seeing all the Reformed Churches at home and on the Continent united in one confession of faith inclined him to view more favourably than might have been supposed the early revision of a work upon which laborious pains had been taken. Early in the year 1551 a revision committee of bishops took the task in hand. The help of foreign divines was invited. Peter Martyr, an Italian, who had been appointed divinity professor at Oxford, and Martin Bucer, a German, who held like office at Cambridge, prepared annotations for the consideration of the revisers. Early in the spring of the following year, the result of the deliberation was submitted to Parliament, sanctioned, and what is known as the second Prayer-Book of Edward VI. was ordered to be taken into use on November 1st—All Saints' Day.

The changes effected in the work of revision enriched

the Liturgy by adding to the morning service the introductory sentences of Scripture, the exhortation, confession, and absolution. In this introductory portion of the service, not inserted in the order for evening prayer until the revision of 1661-2, the revisers followed the plan of Calvin's Liturgy and that used by John à Lasco, a learned Pole and friend of Cranmer, who ministered to a congregation of foreigners in London. Pollanus, another learned foreign divine, pastor of a church of French Protestants at Glastonbury, who published with additions of his own Calvin's Liturgy, is followed in the recital of the Ten Commandments at the Communion Service. In the same service an important change was made through the influence of the Presbyterian John Knox, in the rubric introduced to explain that, by the act of kneeling at reception, no adoration of the bread or wine was meant; 'for that were idolatry, to be abhorred of all faithful Christians.'

Changes introduced.

The commemorative character of the Communion Service was emphasized in the words of administration: 'Take and eat this, in remembrance that Christ died for thee, and feed on Him in thy heart by faith with thanksgiving;' 'Drink this in remembrance that Christ's blood was shed for thee, and be thankful,' substituted for those previously used, taken from the *Sarum Missal:* 'The body of our Lord Jesus Christ, which was given for thee, preserve thy body and soul unto everlasting life;' 'The blood of our Lord Jesus Christ, which was shed for thee, preserve thy body and soul unto everlasting life.' Subsequently, in the Elizabethan Prayer-Book, these two sentences, which each in turn ousted the other, were combined, as in the present service.

Other changes of doctrinal significance were made. Though not uniformly, yet in several places 'minister' is substituted for 'priest,' and 'table' or 'board' for 'altar.' The words, 'commonly called the mass,' used as a sub-title of the Communion Service in the former book, are left out in the second. In 1549 the sign of the cross was directed to be used in the consecration of the elements, in the services of Confirmation, Marriage, and Visitation of the Sick; in the book of 1552 no such directions occur. As already mentioned, exorcism, anointing with oil, and prayers for the souls of the departed are recognised in the book of 1549; but in that of 1552 they are omitted. Further signs of the anti-Roman views of the revisers are seen in the rubric respecting clerical vestments. A surplice was to be the only vestment worn by priest or deacon, and a rochet by archbishop or bishop. Albs and copes are expressly forbidden.

This most Protestant of all the Liturgies of the Church of England was first read by Ridley, as Bishop of London, in St. Paul's Cathedral on November 1st, 1552—All Saints' Day. The second Prayer-Book of Edward VI. was shorter-lived even than the first. Within eight months of its introduction the frail life of the boy-king ended, and a little later the Latin missal again took the place of the book that had been prepared with studious and anxious care.

In the intervening months between the publication of the second Reformed Prayer-Book and the death of the king the Reformers zealously went on in their work of educating the people. Provision having been made for the public services of the people, an endeavour was made to provide for their private devotions also, by the issue of a *Primer or Book of Private Prayers*, adapted for personal and household worship. [*A Book of Private Prayers, 1553.*] It was an attempt to meet a want in the spiritual life for which little real provision has been made in Protestant literature. The want is one that has caused many to turn to the devotional literature of Rome for its supply. The Reformers' *Book of Private Prayers* provides a short liturgical form of worship for every morning and evening of the week. There are numerous prayers for all ranks and conditions of men under almost every imaginable circumstance. The language and sentiments of some of the prayers are as appropriate for this century as for the sixteenth.

In the same year as the Forty-two Articles referred to in the previous chapter were approved by convocation and sanctioned by the king, there was set forth by authority *A Short Catechism*, as it was called, drawn up by Poynet, Gardiner's learned and virulent successor as Bishop of Winchester. This catechism, sometimes called Cranmer's, having been drawn up under his direction, was approved [*Cranmer's second, or Poynet's Catechism.*]

by other bishops and divines, and intended 'for all schoolmasters to teach.' It is written in the form of a dialogue between master and scholar, in which the master questions in paragraphs, and the unfortunate scholar replies in answers of a page or more in length. Faith is described as 'the mouth of the soul;' the sacrament of the Lord's supper as a 'thankful remembrance of the death of Christ; forasmuch as the bread representeth His body, betrayed to be crucified for us; the wine standeth in stead and place of His blood, plenteously shed for us.' Not much can be said in favour of this production. Two editions of it appeared, Latin and English, with the Forty-two Articles appended; but its cumbersome style, and the date of its publication, as the last work of the Reformers in the reign of Edward VI., must have prevented its rendering any effectual aid in the strengthening of the Reformation movement.

With the death of the young king in the July of 1553 came that of many plans of reforms, but probably none at the time more disappointing to Cranmer than that of his elaborate scheme for the remodelling or correcting of the canon law. Thirty-two persons, one half of whom were clergy, and the other members of one or other House of Parliament, had in the previous reign been appointed to examine and report upon all laws ecclesiastical. The commission was re-appointed with extended power in the time of Edward. Cranmer, to whom the task was a congenial one, prepared an elaborate scheme for reforming and reconstructing the canon law. The king's death prevented it receiving any authoritative sanction; had it not done so, the *Reformatio Legum Ecclesiasticarum*, as the code which was drawn up is called, would have changed the whole after course of the Church of England.

Cranmer's Reformatio Legum.

CHAPTER XX.

REFORMATION PREACHERS.

IN an age which was eminently a hearing and not a reading one the influence of such able and zealous preachers as Latimer, Knox, Ridley, Hooper, Bradford can scarcely be over-estimated. In preaching at its preachers rather than its rulers was the strength of the Reformation movement. Especially is this seen during the time of the Protectorate. It was a wise provision of the Council that, when the general visitation of the churches was made, a preacher was appointed to every district. It was also arranged that when not required at court, four out of the six appointed chaplains should itinerate in various districts of the country; but this scheme was never fully carried into effect. Important as preaching was regarded, there was no recognition of the 'liberty of prophesying' during the Protestant Protectorate. Unlicensed preachers were contrary to the proclamation of April 24th, 1548, 'that no man hereafter be permitted to preach except he be licensed thereunto by his Majesty, the Lord Protector, or the Archbishop of Canterbury, under his seal, the same to be shown to the parson and curate and two honest men of the parish before his preaching, upon pain of imprisonment, both of the preacher so preaching without license and of the curate or parson permitting him.' Unlicensed incumbents and curates were to confine their pulpit ministration to the use of the Homilies. Just before the introduction of the new service book, all preaching was prohibited, and afterwards, through certain complaints made by Lord Chancellor Rich, 'divers preachers in Essex' were forbidden to preach on week-days, as it drew the people from their work. Elsewhere certain bishops were found fault with for not keeping more preachers.

Influence of preaching at the time of the Reformation.

Itinerating preachers.

Proclamation against unlicensed preachers.

Cranmer, whose preaching power was small, recognised its worth in others; and while he wrote with the pen abundant liberty was given to Latimer, Knox, Taylor, Parker, Grindal, Bradford, and others to preach.

When men's minds were stirred by great religious questions, crowds of people gathered in front of the celebrated structure known as St. Paul's Cross. Mounted on stone steps was an hexagonal structure. From one side of the building projected a wooden pulpit, before which was an inclosed space for the mayor, aldermen, and other official and distinguished hearers, and beyond a broad area for the general congregation.[1] Throughout the conflict waged between the old and new beliefs great preachers made the time-honoured pulpit the place for defending or inveighing against the doctrines of the Reformation.

Preaching at St. Paul's Cross.

It was the preaching of Latimer more than the edicts of Henry that established the principles of the Reformation in the minds and hearts of the people, and the preaching that sustained them during the time of the Protectorate. In no disparaging sense it may be said, what Tindale wrote in secret Latimer proclaimed in public. Thousands who never saw a page of Tindale's *Obedience of a Christian Man* received its teaching from the lips of the great preacher. It was Latimer's famous Christmas sermon on the Card which awakened the controversy that excited Henry's curiosity to hear the preacher, and led to his being made a royal chaplain. The charm of Latimer's power was in the personal character of the man. It has been described as that of one 'of thoroughly English type, transparently and practical honest, simple to rudeness, outspoken to rashness, bubbling over with raciest, homeliest wit, open-hearted, he was just the man to draw thousands to Paul's Cross.' Of his style of preaching, Mr. Demaus, in his able biography, says: 'In the strictest sense of the term he was a practical preacher.' 'The practical abuses of the Romish faith, the lying miracles, the debasing superstitions of that Church, the perversion of justice, the disregard of the legal rights of

Influence of the preaching of Latimer.

The charm and practical nature of his discourses.

---

[1] The exact site has been recently ascertained, and is marked by an octagon on the pavement of the cathedral gardens, just to the north of the present east end of St. Paul's.

the poor, the corruption of morals, the tyranny of nobles, the dishonesty of the traders, the indolent pride and luxury of the dignitaries of the Church, were the chief subjects which Latimer handled in his discourse.' The humour of his sermons is eminently notable, pungent, homely, picturesque; sometimes in the form of personal reminiscences; sometimes in quaint colloquialisms; often appearing in the most unexpected way, and even in most solemn passages. His power of invective was at times in its earnestness almost terrible. Think of the impressiveness of such a preacher standing before the congregation massed at St. Paul's Cross, as he exclaimed in the midst of his famous 'Plough' sermon:

'O London, London, repent, repent; for I think God is more displeased with London than ever He was with Nebo. Repent, therefore; repent, London! and remember that the same God liveth now that punished Nebo, even the same God and none other; and He will punish sin as well now as He did then; and He will punish the iniquity of London as well as He did that of Nebo.'

Very different from Latimer was another of the famous St. Paul's Cross preachers—Bishop Hooper. Tall, thin, grave, ascetic-looking, reminding one of what he had been, a Cistercian monk, was the first Protestant Bishop of Gloucester. Hooper was a good biblical scholar, 'well skilled in Latin, Greek, and Hebrew; a little of his would go far in our day,' writes his biographer, Fuller. Hooper had not the racy humour, the genial cordiality, the fund of animal spirits of Bishop Latimer; but he had an indomitable power of work. In London, when chaplain to the protector, the Duke of Somerset, he generally preached twice a day, with such effect that the churches could not contain the crowds that flocked to hear him. To further the progress of the Reformation he was specially retained in London. *[marginalia: Hooper, Bishop of Gloucester. His learning. Chaplain to the protector.]*

In 1550 he preached before the court a course of Lent sermons on Jonah. Then came the miserable controversy with his fellow reformers, Cranmer and Ridley, about vestments, wasting nearly a year of his life. After his consecration to the bishopric of Gloucester, he began at once to preach throughout the diocese with such diligence,

that his wife wrote to his friend Bullinger to recommend
'Master Hooper to be more moderate in his labour. He
preaches four, or at least three times every day, and I am
afraid lest these over-abundant exertions should cause a
premature decay.' It is lamentable to think that Hooper's
most useful episcopal labours did not last longer than two
years.

In the eastern counties, first as Bishop of Rochester,
and then of London, Ridley was ably furthering the
advance of the Reformation. So far as scholarship may test a man, he was the greatest of
the reformers. He was Master of Pembroke College,
Cambridge, and his reputation great as a Greek
scholar. The general idea of his importance
to the cause of the Reformation may be estimated from the words of one of his most
distinguished adversaries: 'Latimer leaneth
to Cranmer; Cranmer leaneth to Ridley; and Ridley leaneth to his own singular wit.' That he was a theologian,
we know from his writings; that he was a preacher of
singular persuasive power, we learn from contemporaries.
He was of fine bodily presence, and of 'gentle nature and
kindly spirit.' 'Every holiday and Sunday he preached
in some place or other, unless hindered by weighty business. The people resorted to his sermons, swarming
about him like bees, and coveting the sweet flowers and
wholesome juice of the fruitful doctrine, which he did not
only preach, but showed the same by his life.'[1] Ridley
was one of the selected preachers appointed to accompany
the commissioners at the first general visitation of the
churches.

Bishop Ridley.

In scholarship the greatest of the Reformers.

Interesting associations are connected with a sermon
preached by Ridley in the palace of Whitehall, towards the
end of the troubled years of the Protectorate.
Ridley referred to the distress which the
spoliation of public charities had occasioned, and pleaded
for the poor in Christ's name. The preacher was sent for
by the young king, who received him at the great gallery
of the palace, told him he had been 'especially touched'
by the sermon, and inquired what should be done. The
result of the sermon and the interview that followed was

Sermon at Whitehall.

---

[1] Foxe, *Acts and Mon.*, vol. vii. p. 407.

the institution of the Blue Coat School for the education of poor children, of St. Thomas's Hospital, and a re-organization of St. Bartholomew's for the diseased poor, and of the royal palace of Bridewell, described by Ridley as 'a wide, large house of the king's majesty's called Bridewell, that would wonderfully well serve to lodge Christ in,' as a workhouse for able-bodied labourers out of employ. The most famous sermon of Ridley was the one fatal to himself, and that referred to events that have yet to be related. On the first Sunday of the reign of Lady Jane Grey he was the preacher at St. Paul's Cross. Impressed with the conviction that Romanism would be re-established should Mary succeed to the throne, he 'declared his mind to the people as touching the Lady Mary, and dissuaded them, alleging the incommodities and inconveniences which might arise by receiving her to be queen; prophesying as it were before that which after came to pass, that she would bring in foreign powers to reign over them, besides the subverting of all Christian religion then already established.'[1] *Sermon referring to Mary.*

On the following Sunday, Prebendary Rogers, the friend and literary executor of Tindale, 'made a godly and vehement sermon at St. Paul's Cross, confirming such true doctrine as he and others had taught there in King Edward's days, exhorting the people constantly to remain in the same, and to beware of all pestilent popery, idolatry, and superstition.'[2] It was the last sermon Rogers preached: the last Protestant sermon heard before the storm gathered, which in its violence swept away many leaders of the Reformation, and Rogers among the first. *Rogers at St. Paul's Cross.*

Well known at this time as that of a popular preacher, was the figure of John Bradford, tall, thin, of a ruddy complexion, and with auburn hair and beard. He also was of Pembroke College, Cambridge. *John Bradford.*
His great friend at Cambridge, Martin Bucer, urged him to become a preacher, and when Bradford pleaded inability, replied: 'If thou have not fine manchet bread, give the poor people barley bread.' Bishop Ridley ordained him, and made him a canon of St. Paul's. Then for the space

---

[1] Foxe, *Acts and Mon.*, vol. vi. p. 389.
[2] *Ibid.*, vi. p. 592.

of three years Bradford diligently laboured in many parts of England.

Another brave and and noble disciple of Ridley was Thomas Lever, Master of St. John's College, Cambridge.

Thomas Lever. He used to preach at St. Paul's Cross and before the court, and is said to have had a 'true tincture of the spirit of Latimer and Luther.' Strype in his *Memorials* quotes largely from Lever's sermons.

John Knox is so intimately associated with the work of the Reformation in Scotland, that his share in that of Preaching of England is often forgotten. Five years of his *John Knox.* eventful life were spent in this country. It was here he found an asylum after his release from the French galleys. Never robust, the hardships he had undergone must have told severely on the 'frail, weak little body' of the man of dauntless spirit. Archbishop Cranmer and the Council welcomed the exiled Scot, and appointed him preacher at Berwick. There, and over all the north, in which long-standing beliefs had been comparatively undisturbed, it was speedily recognised that a man whose word was with power had appeared. Tunstall, the old friend of Sir Thomas More and Erasmus, the buyer up *Bishop Tunstall and John Knox.* of Tindale's Testament, had been translated from the diocese of London to that of Durham. It can be no matter of surprise that Tunstall and Knox soon came into collision. The offending preacher was cited to appear before the bishop, and to give an account of his preaching. Accordingly Knox appeared before the Council of the North for Public Affairs, and with the utmost boldness vindicated his doctrine, beginning with the words, 'This day I do appear in your presence, Honourable Audience, to give a reason why so constantly I do affirm the mass to be, and at all times to have been, idolatry and abomination before God.'[1] According to Dr. Lorimer,[2] John Knox had at this time not only substituted common bread for wafer-bread, but sitting instead of kneeling at the communion service—daring innovations which might well excite Tunstall's ire.

From Berwick the bold reformer was transferred to

---

[1] *Works*, vol. iii. p. 33.
[2] *John Knox and the Church of England.*

Newcastle. Afterwards he was appointed one of the six
chaplains to the young king. The Duke of Northumberland, evidently not knowing his man, suggested Knox as a
bishop for the vacant see of Rochester, naïvely hinting that
he 'would be a whetstone to quicken and sharpen the Archbishop of Canterbury.' When, however, the Protector
met the Scotch chaplain, he found him 'neither grateful
nor pleasable.' As royal chaplain Knox took his turn with
his colleagues before the court. In his last discourse he
'made this affirmation, That commonly it was seen that
the most godly princes had officers and councillors most
ungodly, enemies to God's true religion and traitors to their
prince.' After illustrating his 'affirmation' by references
to the characters of Ahithophel, Shebnah, and Judas, he
went on to say: 'What wonder is it that a young and
innocent king be deceived by crafty, covetous, wicked, and
ungodly councillors! I am greatly afraid that Ahithophel
is councillor, that Judas bears the purse, and that Shebnah
is scribe, controller, and treasurer:' the allusion being to
the Protector as Ahithophel, and to Sir William Paulet,
successively comptroller, secretary, and lord treasurer.
And yet afterward the self-accusation of the preacher was,
'that he was not so fervent in rebuking manifest iniquity'
as he ought to have been, and that 'he had played the
faint heart and feeble soldier.'

A convert and fellow countryman of John Knox, John
Rough, was a well-known preacher in the North and other
parts of the country. He continued faithful
to the ministry of the Reformed faith amid *John Rough.*
the troubles of Mary's reign, and died a martyr's death.

Rowland Taylor was a vigorous preacher, not only at
Hadleigh, but as one of the six preachers in Canterbury
Cathedral.

Nor must Bernard Gilpin be forgotten, the Apostle of
the North, as he was sometimes called, from his life of
holy zeal in preaching and works of charity.
His is one of the most charming characters of *Bernard Gilpin.*
the age. Reference has already been made to
the courageous sermon he preached before the court of
Edward VI., the only sermon of his that survives. Fuller
somewhat plaintively says of him, 'he hated vice more
than error;' yet so far was Gilpin from being indifferent
to error, that at the time of Mary's death, he was on his

way to London as a prisoner, owing to a charge of heresy. It is a relief to think of him, not as alone, but as one of the few who, amid the great revolution in Church and State, was in mind and spirit tolerant: one in whom both parties saw the beauty of Christian charity.

MARY TUDOR.

CHAPTER XXI.

THE DARK DAYS OF MARY.

THE reign of Queen Mary was the trial, the fierce trial, of the Reformation movement in England. All at once it was as though the labours of many years, with their trials and sufferings, were to be as nothing, and that all had been done in vain. Northumberland's purpose to settle his daughter-in-law, Lady Jane Grey, upon the throne was utterly futile. The ambition of the scheme was discerned and resented. Northumberland was disliked by almost all. Strongly Protestant as London was, on the day that the Protector rode out at the head of the troops to uphold the claims of Lady Jane, he observed the ominous silence of the people; not one wished him or his cause 'God speed.' {Fierce trial.}

The popular sense of justice was in favour of Mary's right to reign. Though her rejection of the Reformed faith was well known, there was an eager desire to atone to her for her mother's wrongs. Many, too, were weary of the changes ordained by law or proclamation that had followed one another so rapidly in doctrine and ritual. No one, lay or clerical, knew what he might be called upon to believe or subscribe to next. There was also the natural re-action that follows a time of exciting change, and a general anticipation that under Mary's rule the country would find rest. It was assumed there would be no return to the tyranny of Rome, renounced by her father, and that there would be freedom also for Protestant belief and worship. So popular was the sentiment in favour of the Princess Mary, that a Protestant eye-witness of what he describes wrote concerning the day of her proclamation as queen (July 19th): 'Great was the triumph here at London; for my time I never saw the like, and by the report of others the like was never seen. The number of caps that were thrown {General feeling for Mary. Causes of the re-action.}

up at the proclamation was not to be told; the bonfires were without number; and what with shouting and crying of the people, and ringings of bells, there could no man hear almost what another said.'

While her prospects yet remained doubtful Mary had said that she would not alter the religion which had been settled and confirmed in the reign of her brother; but no sooner was her position secure, than it was clear she purposed to reverse absolutely the whole policy, not only of the Protectorate, but of her father's renunciation of Rome likewise.

Within three months of the tumultuous joy at Mary's accession, Bishops Gardiner, Bonner, Daye, and Tunstall were sitting in judgment upon their episcopal brethren of the Reformed faith. Gardiner, released from his captivity in the Tower, was at once made lord chancellor, with the supreme administration of affairs. A month had not elapsed before Ridley, for his sermon in which he had predicted that Mary's accession would be disastrous to the religious interest of the country, by royal order was deprived of the bishopric of London and committed to the Tower. Then shortly after brave old Latimer joined him, saying, as he journeyed up to London, 'I go as willingly to render a reckoning of my doctrine as ever I went to any place in the world.' Within a few weeks Cranmer followed. He might have fled the kingdom, opportunity of escape was his; but, with courage greater than is often accredited to him, he refused. 'It would be no way fitting for him,' he said, 'to go away, considering the post in which he was, and to show he was not afraid to own all the changes that were by his means made in religion in the last reign.'[1]

Reformers imprisoned.

John Bradford, the popular preaching prebendary of St. Paul's, was already there. The Sunday before his arrest a scene of tumult had occurred at St. Paul's Cross, occasioned by the preaching of Bourne, the chaplain of Bishop Bonner, Ridley's successor in the diocese of London. Murmurs arose as Bourne inveighed against the doctrines of the Reformation. Caps were thrown up and stones cast at the obnoxious preacher. The

---

[1] Strype, *Memorials of Cranmer*, p. 314. [1694].

lord mayor's calls for silence were unheeded. Bonner
appealed in vain to the people to be quiet. A dagger
was hurled at the preacher, and in fear of his life
he turned round and besought Bradford, who, as prebendary of St. Paul's, was sitting near him, to come forth
and befriend him. Bradford, standing up where he had
often been the preacher, was received with applause.
'Thou savest him that will help to burn thee!' shouted
some one, as Bradford quelled the tumult that Bonner's
presence only served to exasperate. Three days after he
was accused of having taken upon him 'to rule and lead
the people malapertly,' thereby declaring that he was the
author of the sedition. Bradford, Ridley, Latimer, and
Cranmer, for want of room imprisoned together, 'availed
themselves of the opportunity to read over their New
Testament with great delectation and peaceful study.'
The dungeons of the Marshalsea and the Tower were
crowded with prisoners, some 'upon the Lady Jane business, some upon the business of religion.'

Outside the prisons changes were everywhere being
made in public worship. Compliant clergy, taking their
cue from headquarters, without waiting for
legal authority, restored the old services. *Rapid changes.*
According to the prevailing local sentiment,
in some places the mass was welcomed with enthusiasm, in others the officiating priests were attacked
and their vestments torn off, and preachers who attacked
the Reformed religion were assailed, as Bourne was, with
showers of stones. In these early weeks of Mary's reign
the success of the Romanists was greatly accelerated by
the late Protector's recantation of his belief *Recantation
in the Reformed faith. The recantation of a of Northum-
man who made religion a cloak for ambition berland.*
may be taken for what it is worth; but for awhile it
silenced with a sense of shame all but the boldest Protestants. 'The shame of the apostasy,' observes Mr.
Froude, 'shook down the frail edifice of the Protestant
constitution, to be raised again in suffering, as the first
foundations of it had been laid by purer hands and nobler
spirits.'[1] Before the execution of Northumberland a
guard of soldiers was necessary for the protection of a

---

[1] *History*, vol. v. p. 246.

Romanist preacher at St. Paul's Cross; two days after so little was a guard necessary, that in the cathedral mass was publicly said in Latin, the crucifix replaced in the rood loft, and the high altar re-decorated.

Mary was crowned queen Oct. 1st, 1553. She was thirty-seven years of age; in appearance, short and thin, sallowed complexion, and with bright eyes; her voice was deep like that of a man. It was a matter of concern to her that a fresh supply of holy oil for the royal anointing should be obtained, she fearing that already on hand had lost its efficacy through the Pope's interdict. A new chair, sent by the Pope, was used in preference to the usual coronation chair, lest that had been polluted by her Protestant brother.

Coronation of Mary.

Another and significant sign of coming changes arrested the attention of all. There was no archbishop to perform the coronation rites; the Archbishops of Canterbury and of York were both prisoners in the Tower. Bishop Gardiner, of Winchester, the queen's chief minister of State, was therefore chosen to anoint and crown the new sovereign, and Bishop Daye, restored to the see of Chichester, preached the sermon.

Five days after the queen's coronation Parliament assembled, and with it, as usual, the Convocation of the clergy. The proceedings began by a mass of the Holy Ghost being solemnly performed, the members of both Houses attending. Already the number of Reforming bishops holding sees had been thinned down to two, Taylor of Lincoln and Harley of Hereford; these, refusing to attend the mass, were excluded from the deliberations of the house. It was an easy thing for Gardiner to get the new Parliament to annul the enactments which rendered the marriage of the queen's mother invalid, and to declare Mary 'born in lawful matrimony;' but even in this reactionary Parliament Protestant sentiment was sufficiently strong to withstand for eight days the passing of an Act for restoring throughout the queen's dominions 'all such divine service and administrations of the sacraments as were commonly used in the last year of King Henry the Eighth,' and prohibiting the use of 'any other kind or order of divine service or administration of sacraments.'

A strong minority of eighty in a house of four hundred

and thirty members resisted the passing of this Act, and obtained the concession that no punishment should be inflicted on those who declined to attend the Catholic services.

Meanwhile in Convocation the same work of re-action had been going on. In the absence of all the Reforming bishops appointed in the late reign, now either imprisoned or driven into ignoble seclusion, the doctrine of transubstantiation was re-affirmed; only a small minority of the clergy, led by one of the ablest of the Protestant disputants, Archdeacon Philpot, of Winchester, and by Archdeacon Aylmer, who had been the tutor of the accomplished Lady Jane Grey, resisted the change. Celibacy upon the part of the clergy was again required; those having wives were required either to put them away or resign their benefices. *Transubstantiation re-affirmed.* *Celibacy of clergy again required.*

Within three months of the death of the first Protestant King of England the whole conduct of public worship was again under the control of Romanists. The Prayer-book was abolished; the altars replaced; crosses and rood lofts, which had been pulled down, set up again; and the legends of the Church substituted once more for the Bible. Altar vessels and ecclesiastical vestures, that friendly hands had secreted, re-appeared. The completeness of the revolution, and the prompt return to the old ritual, is significantly shown in the carefully edited records of St. Michael's parish church, Bishop's Stortford, where we find the expenses of this reaction thus entered, under the date of the year of Mary's accession to the throne: *Changes in public worship.*

	s.	d.
Item for making up of the altar		xiiij
Item for meat and drink to his (the mason's) servant that wrought it		vj
Item to Mr. Vicar for a Mass Book	xij	
Item paid for a Pyx [1]	v	
Item paid for a Holy Water-Stoup [2]	iij	ii

[1] A metal box suspended over the altar, frequently shaped as a dove, in which the altar bread was reserved.
[2] A stone basin placed at the entrance of the c'urch for holy water.

		s.	d.
Item paid to John Turner for painting of the cross staff	...		iiij
Item to Burl for making of the Rood	...	xx	
Item paid to Burl for a cross	...		viij
Item paid to Thomas Barbore for a ship[1] for frankincense	...		xvj
Item paid to Tyre for two standards at the high altar	...		xij
Item paid to Tyre for the cross	...		iiij

So far the majority of the nation seemed willing to acquiesce in what was done and to return to the customs of the old religion. Had the time of the Romanist reaction from the violent Protestantism of the Protectorate been wisely turned to account, Romanism would have regained, for possibly a century or more, its former ascendancy in Great Britain. Mary, in her zeal to restore papal authority in England, defeated the purpose she had most at heart—first, by her determination to marry Philip, son of Charles V., Emperor of Germany and King of Spain, and subsequently by the policy of persecution, that, instead of putting down Protestantism, won for it the admiration of the nation.

The suggestion of the queen's marriage to Philip came from the emperor. He desired an alliance with England that would unite all Western Europe under the rule of one family, and make it one in policy, political and ecclesiastical. Mary, naturally influenced by one who had been her mother's best friend in adversity, and her own in the preceding reign, saw in the emperor's son one whose ultra-Romanism would strengthen and help her in bringing back her country to the Romanist faith. The very reasons, though, that favourably influenced the emperor and Mary in prospect of the proposed alliance made it positively hateful to Mary's subjects.

Unpopularity of Mary's proposed marriage to Philip of Spain. Romanists and Protestants saw in it a union that would interfere with national independence, and that would drag England helplessly in the wake of the powerful house of Austria.

For political reasons the Spanish marriage project was strongly resented. There were other reasons also. The English Romanists did not wish to bear the

---

[1] A vessel, in the shape of a boat, for incense.

bondage of Romanism as it was borne in Spain; while the English Protestants saw in the marriage, not only the overthrow of their religious hopes, but the horrors of the Inquisition.

The general opposition to the alliance found expression in a deputation from the House of Commons, who, with the speaker at their head, petitioned the queen not to marry a foreigner. Before the speaker had finished his address, she interrupted him, sharply rebuked the Commons for taking too much on themselves, and claimed for herself the liberty of a subject to marry whom she would. The fact that Gardiner and others wanted her to marry young Courtenay, Earl of Devon, strengthened her determination to have no other husband but Philip. She was eleven years his senior, and he had already been twice a widower; but Mary loved him with an admiration she never was favoured to enjoy in return. Her determination was made, but it at once nearly cost her her crown, and ultimately broke her heart. *Petition from the House of Commons against the marriage.*

The marriage being decided on, the treaty was drawn up, Gardiner taking care that on the English side it should be as stringent as possible. Philip was to have nothing more than the title of king in England. He was to have no right of succession, and no legal influence in English affairs. The treaty was agreed to early in the January of 1554, and before the Lent of that year Mary hoped to have Philip at her side. While she was impatiently awaiting dispensations from Rome—one for her to marry a cousin, and another permitting the ceremony to be performed by a bishop of a country still in a state of schism—the popular feeling of indignation against the marriage found expression in open rebellion. *Marriage Treaty.*

In the midland counties the Earl of Suffolk, in Devonshire and Cornwall Sir Peter Carew, in Kent Sir Thomas Wyatt, 'the Younger,' were the leaders of an uprising that would have dethroned Mary in favour of her sister, the Princess Elizabeth, or of Lady Jane Grey. Though nothing but the match with Spain ostensibly appeared as the cause of the rebellion, Protestant sympathies encouraged it, and the holders, both Protestant and Romanist, of church lands, fearing *Uprisings among the people.*

for their possessions, lent their aid. The queen was seen at her best in this her time of danger. Her Council was inactive and divided. Even Gardiner urged her to escape from London to Windsor. But with true Tudor courage she rallied the citizens of London to the cause of their sovereign, addressing them herself in the Guildhall. Young Wyatt, with his Kentishmen, marched up to London, expecting the citizens would rise in his favour. Finding London Bridge closed against him, he withdrew, and crossing the river at Kingston, rapidly made his way round to Brentford, Knightsbridge, and Piccadilly. For

State of London. five days London was as in a state of siege: mass was said by priests in armour; lawyers appeared at Westminster Hall fully armed; tradesmen had arms with them behind their counters. The queen had only the help of a wavering Council to guide her. On one point she was absolutely determined: 'Whatever happens,' she exclaimed, ' I am the wife of the Prince of Spain—crown, rank, life, all shall go before I will take any other husband!' Wyatt's troops fell away, and, bravely fighting, he was taken prisoner and sent to the Tower (Feb., 1554).

The collapse of the uprising was followed by the usual sickening butchery. Earliest amongst the victims was the unfortunate creature of circumstances Lady Jane Grey, barely seventeen years old. Elizabeth, hateful to Mary as the daughter of Anne Boleyn, narrowly escaped; she was sent to the Tower, but no evidence of complicity in the rebellion being forthcoming, the Council interposed on her behalf. For some days the headsman had a busy time in the Tower, and in London and in Kent more than a hundred gibbets had dangling from them the bodies of insurgents.

The armed revolt against Mary's marriage having miserably failed, the way was now clear for its accom-

Mary's marriage at Winchester. plishment. In July Philip landed at Southampton, having with him a fleet that in its number of ships rivalled his afterwards ill-fated Armada. On the 24th, St. James' Day (the patron saint of Spain), the marriage of the ill-matched pair was celebrated with all possible pomp in Winchester Cathedral. The misgivings of those who had opposed the Spanish alliance were soon to be verified. Virtually, with the queen's marriage, the government of England passed into the hands of Philip and his Spanish advisers. Within four months of Philip's arrival England made humble submission to the Pope, and sought his absolution; within two months later began the ghastly burnings which have for ever cast their lurid light upon the reign of Mary. The failure of the revolt that would have placed Elizabeth upon the throne is not, though, to be regretted. 'Elizabeth,' as Mr. Froude observes, 'would have ascended a throne under the shadow of treason. The Protestants would have come back to power in the thoughtless vindictiveness of exasperated and successful revolutionists, and the problem of the Reformation would have been farther than ever from a reasonable solution.'[1] By other and surer methods than by the sword of brave young Wyatt was the Reformation to be established in England.

The Spanish king made his first public appearance in London, with Mary, six weeks after their marriage. He did his best to please the people of this country, even to drinking their beer. He was profuse in his gifts, and in his own reserved way courted popularity. But as the staring crowds of people looked upon the young king—he was but twenty-six, fair-haired, small, and of fragile frame—they could not forget that he came from a land of crushing despotism, and may have felt more than they could describe the disposition of one who a few years later, in his own kingdom, condemned thirteen persons at once to the stake, as an expression of gratitude to Providence for the preservation of his life from shipwreck. *Philip's first appearance in London.*

Many distinguished Spaniards, already well known, or destined soon to become prominent, accompanied their prince. One, of kindred spirit with him, was the Duke of Alva, iron in will and heart; another was Count Egmont, who had before been in England to arrange for the marriage treaty, and to whom, as Philip's proxy, Mary had given her hand in a solemn service of betrothal. There also was Bartolomeo Carranza, great in reputation as a Romanist theologian. With Cardinal Pole and others of his time, he held *Distinguished Spaniards.*

---

[1] *History*, vol. v. p. 354.

Lutheran views on the doctrine of justification, and defended them at the Council of Trent, but was a stern persecutor of heretics. Zealously he laboured to restore the Roman faith in England; from his swarthy visage, he was known as 'the Black Friar.' Another present on this occasion was Pedro de Soto, who also had distinguished himself at the Council of Trent, and had the reputation of being one of the most profound scholastic theologians of his time. To counteract Peter Martyr's teaching at Oxford, Pedro de Soto was appointed his successor as Regius Professor.

Another who accompanied Philip, and one not likely to be forgotten, was his confessor, Alphonso de Castro, afterward famous for his sermon in which, with feigned honour, he tried to throw the odium of the persecution upon the English bishops, though, as the author of a book *On the Just Punishment of Heretics*, he had said 'they ought to be dealt with, not with words, but with clubs, and whips, and swords.' Clerks and servants swelled the retinue of Philip as he entered London, and friars, who were advised to put off their habits, for fear of popular vengeance.

As the procession passed over London Bridge—a long narrow street, guarded that day by the images of Gog and Magog—the guns from the Tower boomed forth, and all along the route there was the usual pomp and pageantry of a royal welcome. In Gracechurch Street the quick eye of Mary was offended by a decoration representing her father giving a Bible to her late brother and predecessor. The Lord Chancellor's attention was called to it, and he sending for the unfortunate draughtsman, caused the offending Bible to be struck out, and a harmless pair of gloves inserted in its place. To the relief of all, the dreaded day of Philip's first appearance in the capital passed off without disturbance.

So completely was the Protestant spirit at this time crushed, that in October, by a general election, the question was put before the country whether consent would be given to a formal and parliamentary reconciliation to Rome. Packing Parliament was too common an occurrence on the part of both parties in the sixteenth century for special attention to be called to the pressure on this occasion put upon the electors, who were directed to choose men 'of the wise, grave, and Catholic sort.' To allay the fears and secure the support of all proprietors who had received or purchased monastic and Church property, information was authoritatively and industriously circulated that 'no alteration was intended of any man's possessions.'

The returns were favourable to the Government policy. When the measure for which Parliament had been specially summoned was laid before the House, out of three hundred and sixty members present there were only two dissentients—'one, whose name is not mentioned, gave a silent negative vote, the other, Sir Ralph Bagenall, stood up alone to protest. 'Twenty years,' he said, 'that great and worthy prince, King Henry, laboured to expel the Pope from England. He for one had sworn to King Henry's laws, and he would keep his oath.'[1] In such a Parliament it was easy to repeal the attainder of Cardinal Pole, the queen's cousin, made against him for his bitter attack upon the king in his book on *The Unity of the Church*. With all the triumph of a conqueror, Pole had returned to his native country as papal legate, appointed to receive the submission of the realm.

Sir Ralph Bagenall's protest.

St. Andrew's Day, the 30th November, was chosen for the formal reconciliation to Rome, a day which it was desired and supposed would ever afterwards be observed as the Feast of Reconciliation. After high mass had been sung in Westminster Abbey, Philip being present, attended by an escort of six hundred courtiers, in white velvet costumes, striped with red, the Lords and Commons assembled in the great hall of Westminster. In the presence of the king and queen, and Cardinal Pole, the Pope's legate, they were asked by Lord Chancellor Gardiner whether they desired absolution and reunion with Rome. A shout of assent was taken for general consent. Thereupon their petition was read aloud, in which they declared themselves 'very sorry and repentant of the schism and disobedience committed,' and desired absolution from all such censure as they had incurred. Philip and Mary then went through their

The day of reconciliation.

[1] Froude, vol. v. p.457.

form of intercession, and the cardinal having responded, there came the supreme moment of all, when, 'amid the fast waning light' of that November afternoon, the whole assembly of bishops, nobles, and Commons knelt before the representative of Rome, as he, standing erect, pronounced the solemn words of absolution, received at the close with loud and emphatic Amens. As the assembly arose, some wept, some embraced each other with joy, 'Then the cardinal, leading the way into the chapel of the palace, king, queen, and Parliament following, *Te Deum* was sung in the presence of all the members, and the great day of reconciliation closed with a benediction from the altar.'

It was late in the evening before the public ceremonials of the day ended, but not too late for the joy and gladness of Romanist hearts to find expression in two letters, written that same night—one by Philip, the other by Pole —to the reigning pope, Julius III. Few nights in the weary life of Mary were happier than that which closed in upon the day that witnessed the formal act of her country's reconciliation to the Church at Rome.

The happiness thus gained was, though, short-lived. The submission so solemnly made was never ratified at Rome. Before the English ambassador arrived at Rome, Julius III. was dead; and his successor, Paul IV., hostile to Philip, and yet more hostile to Pole, repudiated a submission barren of any surrender of the Church lands.

The submission never ratified at Rome.

It can be no matter of surprise that the same Parliament that agreed to unite the English Church with the Church of Rome restored to the statute book the old laws against the Lollards, which had been done away in Somerset's Protectorate, and gave legislative power to the bishops to proceed against heretics. Means were thus prepared for the scenes of persecution that soon followed. In January the Reconciliation Parliament was dissolved, having made a clean sweep of the entire ecclesiastical legislation of Henry VIII. Two things only its members absolutely refused to do—one, to restore the abbey and other Church lands to the Romanists; the other, to set aside the succession of Elizabeth to the throne.

Laws against Lollards restored.

The coercive measures against Protestants provoked retaliations that gave great offence. Bishop Gardiner was greatly irritated by the reprinting of his celebrated book, *Of True Obedience*, denouncing the marriage of Mary's mother as incestuous, vindicating Henry's marriage with Anne Boleyn, and the repudiation of the Roman dominion. *[Protestant retaliation.]* Priests were teased by ballad singing, caricatures, and practical jokes expressive of contempt and abhorrence. An oft-told story is of a dead cat with a shaven crown, and with a piece of paper like a sacramental wafer tied between its fore-paws, that was found hanging on the post of a gallows in Cheapside. Such importance was attached to this act that the animal was carried to Bonner, who caused it to be exhibited that day during a sermon at St. Paul's Cross. Newly erected statues of saints mysteriously lost their fingers, heads, and arms, or, Dagon-like, were found prostrate. Even into the palace and royal apartments offensive bills and exasperating pamphlets made their way, to the queen's annoyance. But in no such acts can there be found the occasion of the cruel atrocities that have made so notorious the reign of Mary.

Who was their instigator? Gardiner, nicknamed Wily Winchester, has long borne the opprobrium of being the chief adviser of the persecutions. That he was a conscientious Romanist, and the determined opponent of Cranmer, at whose hands he had in some degree suffered unjustly, is well known. *[The instigator of the persecution.]* As a minister of the crown he was stanchly loyal to his country. None more than he opposed the Spanish alliance. Finding it inevitable, he used his high position of influence to exclude all Spaniards from offices of government in this country, and took care that no innovation should be made in the laws of succession. Though he never lost the queen's favour, his influence manifestly declined after her marriage and the coming of Cardinal Pole. As a matter of course, Bishop Gardiner was one of the commissioners of bishops for the trial of heretics. But being placed on a commission does not necessarily imply assent to all done in its name. His connection with the commission lasted for only nine months, and during part of this time he was away at the Calais peace conference. It was after, and not before, this great prelate's death that the persecution raged in its greatest vehemence.

Bonner, Bishop of London, was a man of altogether coarser nature than Bishop Gardiner. Though not the originator, there is no evidence to resist the popular testimony that he was the chief instrument of the persecutions. Bonner was a canonist, quick-witted and ready in argument, but a merciless persecutor. He had suffered under the Protestant Protectorate, but more than took his revenge in the death of the two hundred Protestants he is said to have condemned to the flames. But behind Bonner there was a power that more than once admonished him to proceed more expeditiously with the prosecution for heresy. In his own day, and in his own diocese, Bonner was so hated that men would say of any ill-favoured, fat fellow in the street—that was Bonner; a hatred that in after years neither his fallen fortunes nor death could assuage. For fear of disturbance, he was buried in secret and at midnight.

Bonner and the other persecuting bishops were the instruments, not of an English, but Spanish, policy of persecution. That, rather than the will of any English statesman or bishop, kindled and fanned the fires of Smithfield. The queen, half Spanish by birth, and more so in sympathy by marriage, was under the influence of Spanish statesmen and Spanish confessors, who hated the English because they were heretics, and hated them more because they were Englishmen.

Carranza took the place of Gardiner as Mary's confessor, and 'on his counsel and disposal,' says a Spanish historian, 'depended the major part of the spiritual government of the kingdom.' There is no need to look farther for the instigators of the Marian martyrdoms, when we think of the dominating influence over the lonely, sad heart of Mary of Spanish friars, confessors, and of a husband who was a born persecutor.

CHAPTER XXII.

THE TRIUMPH OF SPANISH POLICY, 1555–1558.

It was in the beginning of the year 1555, four months after the coming of the Spanish king with his train of priests and theologians, that the triumph of Spanish policy showed itself in the methods adopted to destroy the Reformation movement in England. Cardinal Pole, to whom, as pope's legate, supreme power in all ecclesiastical matters had been given, appointed a commission of bishops —Gardiner, Bonner, Tunstall, Capon, Thirlby, and Aldridge—to proceed against heretics. The commissioners held their court in the diocese of Gardiner, in the church of St. Mary Overy (*i.e.* St. Mary 'over-the-water'), the fine old church known now in its altered condition as St. Saviour's, Southwark, seen by every passer over London Bridge who looks towards the western side of the Borough High Street. In its beautiful Lady-chapel, still remaining, Gardiner and his fellow commissioners had brought before them John Rogers, a prebendary of St. Paul's, whom we remember as the intimate friend of Tindale, and as the editor of the famous Matthew's Bible; Bishop Hooper, a champion of the extreme reformers, of austere and saintly life; Laurence Saunders, Rector of All Hallow's, Bread Street, and popular preacher of the reformers' faith; John Bradford, another such preacher, and a prebendary of St. Paul's; Rowland Taylor, the learned and devoted Rector of Hadleigh; and six others, whose zeal as reformers had caused their imprisonment. Five of the twelve were condemned to the fire as obstinate heretics; and the more effectually to strike terror into the hearts of Protestants throughout the country, it was ordered that the sentence should be carried out at the places where each had ministered. Rogers was to be a wholesome terror to the

Marian martyrs.

The Southwark Commission, 1555.

Trial of Rogers, Hooper, Saunders, Taylor, and six others.

Protestants of London; into the midland counties, to the ancient city of Coventry, then third in point of importance of all the principal towns of England, Saunders was sent; Hooper was sent into the west, to be burned in his cathedral city of Gloucester, and Rowland Taylor into the eastern counties, to suffer at Hadleigh. The execution of the fifth who was condemned, John Bradford, was deferred for some months.

Of John Rogers, the first of the Marian martyrs, there exists an interesting memorial. It is an account of his examination and defence before the commissioners, written by himself in such snatches of time and with such poor ink and paper as he could command as a prisoner in Newgate. With little of the dignity of a judicial court, sentence of death was passed upon him for not believing that the bread and wine in the Lord's Supper are 'really and substantially the body and blood of Christ.' As a condemned man, he asked of Gardiner a single favour—permission to speak with his wife, a German, that he might 'counsel her what were best for her to do.' 'No,' was the reply; 'she is not thy wife.' And he did not see her until the day of his execution, when she, with his family of ten children, the youngest of them in her arms, awaited him in the crowd, as he was on his way from Newgate to Smithfield. As the martyr passed on his way, full of faith and heroism, the people gazed with wondering admiration. The French ambassador, who happened to be an onlooker, writing the same day of what he had seen, said of Rogers, 'He went to be burnt as if he had been going to a marriage.' At the stake, when asked if he would revoke 'his evil opinion of the sacrament of the altar,' he replied, 'That which I have preached I will seal with my blood.' Even the poor wife exulted in the courage of her husband, who seemed to be above pain, and died 'bathing his hands in the flame, as if it had been in cold water.' Altogether, the death scene of the first of the Marian martyrs was a triumph in the cause of Protestantism, rather than the defeat desired and expected.

In the midland counties the influence of Laurence Saunders was considerable. He had successively ministered at Fotheringay, Lichfield, and Northampton.

[margin: A week of martyrdoms, Feb. 4–9, 1555, of John Rogers.]

Like Rogers, he was married; and when he was in prison 'his wife came to the prison gate with her young child in her arms to visit her husband. The keeper durst not suffer her to come into the prison, yet did he take the little babe out of her arms and brought him unto his father. Saunders, seeing him, rejoiced greatly, saying that he rejoiced more to have such a boy than he should if two thousand pounds were given him.' Saunders was the second of the Protestant martyrs in the reign of Queen Mary. Coventry, for the reason already noted, was selected for the place of his execution. There he died nobly, four days after the martyrdom of Rogers. He embraced the stake to which he was about to be chained, kissed it, saying, 'Welcome, the cross of Christ! Welcome, everlasting life!' *Laurence Saunders.*

To the West of England was sent Bishop Hooper, to be publicly burned in his own cathedral city. For eighteen months this godly prelate had been immured in a filthy, poisonous cell of the Fleet Prison, part of the time with only 'a little pad of straw and a rotten covering with a tick and a few feathers therein' for his bedding, and compelled to endure the presence of 'a wicked man and woman.' Three times he was examined before the commissioners, by turns insulted, reviled, entreated and begged to recant, and finally condemned for denying the doctrine of transubstantiation, and for holding the right of priests to marry. The popular esteem in which Bishop Hooper was held was such that, to avoid tumult and any attempt at rescue, he was taken to Newgate, not only under charge of a strong escort, with 'bills and weapons,' but through darkened streets, sergeants going on before to put out the costermongers' candles, then the principal source of light in the London streets. With a hood over his face, to prevent recognition, he went the three days' journey to Gloucester. At Cirencester he was recognised. From there to his destination the road was thronged with persons loud in their expressions of lamentation. The guard that attended him throughout the journey had treated him with becoming respect, and the mayor and the aldermen of Gloucester showed such consideration as was possible. The place chosen for the burning was an *Bishop Hooper.*

open space before the cathedral. There the stake—the stump of which, charred and blackened by the fire, was some years since dug up—was driven deep into the earth. The morning of the long-remembered Saturday, the day of the execution, was 'lowering and cold.' The crowd which had gathered together to gaze upon the scene was immense. Every spot from which a glimpse of the tall, gaunt figure of the beloved bishop could be caught had its occupant; it was remembered that even the leafless elms bore a living load of onlookers. On the evening of that day, in a thousand West of England homes, a ghastly story was being told and re-told. Through the grossest of blundering or brutality, the faggots supplied for the burning were green and damp: three times the fire had to be rekindled, while scorched and partially consumed the old man had lived on in the agonies of death, praying, till his scorched and blackened lips could move no longer, 'Lord Jesus, receive my soul!'

On the same day, in the eastern counties, at Hadleigh in Suffolk, the flames were burning Dr. Rowland Taylor.

Rowland Taylor. Unlike the grave, ascetic-looking martyr of the west, Taylor was tall and burly, and full of humour. To quote the words of Fuller, he had 'the merriest and pleasantest wit of all the martyrs.' He had been at one time Cranmer's chaplain, and assisted him in preparing the revised edition of the Book of Common Prayer. For resisting the innovations of Mary's reign he was deprived of his living and ordered to the King's Bench Prison, where he was kept for two years. With others, as already described, he was brought before Gardiner and the commission, and was one of the five appointed for death. Few scenes in the history of martyrdoms are more touching than Taylor's farewell to his wife and children. She, with one, an adopted child, named Elizabeth, and another named Mary, had kept watch in the porch of St. Botolph's, Aldgate, on the night it was thought he would be removed from London. In the coldness and stillness of a winter's night they waited till two o'clock in the morning. The darkness was such that one could not well see the other, when the elder child, hearing the sound of passers-by, exclaimed, 'Oh, my dear father! Mother! mother! here is father led away.' Then cried the wife in the darkness, 'Rowland, Rowland, where art thou?' The guards were for passing on, but the sheriff, with kindlier heart, said, 'Stay a little, I pray you, and let him speak to his wife.' 'Then came she to him, and he took his daughter Mary in his arms, and he, his wife, and Elizabeth, kneeled down and said the Lord's Prayer. After they had prayed he rose up and kissed his wife, and shook her by the hand, and said, " Farewell, my dear wife; be of good comfort."' Then he kissed his daughter Mary, and said, 'God bless thee, and make thee His servant;' and kissing Elizabeth, the adopted orphan child, he said, 'God bless you. I pray you all stand strong and steadfast unto Christ and His word.' His not less noble wife's reply was, 'God be with thee, dear Rowland. I will, with God's grace, meet thee at Hadleigh.' So they parted in the cold and darkness of the winter's night.

Through Brentwood, as a prisoner, set on horseback, closely hooded, 'with two holes for his eyes to look out, and a slit for his mouth to breathe at,' Taylor was taken on his way to Hadleigh. Yet the heart of the hooded figure was calm, and even cheerful. At Chelmsford some of his friends, Romanist and Protestant, drank his health, to which he responded with grim humour. When within two miles of his own town, he obtained permission to dismount. Asked by some one, 'How do you now?' his reply was, 'Never better; for now I know I am almost at home. I lack not two stiles over, and I am at my Father's house.' Passing through the broad High Street of the little town, as his parishioners thronged him and bemoaned his fate, he said, 'I have preached to you God's word and truth, and am come this day to seal it with my blood.' His sufferings were less than those of Hooper. While singing in the midst of the flames, some bystander struck him on the head with a halbert, and the body fell dead into the fire.

Taylor's journey to Hadleigh.

The effect of this almost simultaneous lighting of martyr fires in the western and eastern counties, in London, and in Coventry, was the opposite to that desired by the queen and her advisers: it ennobled the cause it was meant to crush.

The campaign of persecution, sickening in its details to the nineteenth-century reader, continued with occasional intermission as long as Mary's reign lasted. On the same day that Hooper and Taylor suffered, six others received, from the same commission, sentence to be burnt. Five out of the six were from the county of Essex. The fires were kindled for their burning in the towns and villages where they had lived. At Brentwood a granite obelisk is the memorial of a youth of nineteen, William Hunter, a weaver's apprentice, faithful unto death. On the same day, 26th March, in the neighbouring village of Horndon-on-the-Hill, and at Rayleigh, within ten miles, two gentlemen were burned in sight of their homes. Three days after, a like ghastly scene was witnessed in the town of Braintree, where William Pigott suffered, and in Maldon, where Stephen Knight witnessed a good confession. At Colchester a priest, weakened by the severities of long imprisonment, could not walk, but was carried to the stake in a chair. As he sat there, the dying martyr's heart was cheered by the prayers of a group of children, who, amid the horrors of the scene, cried to him, 'God strengthen you! God strengthen you! good Master Lawrence.' Wales had a martyr-bishop in Ferrar, of St. David's, condemned by his successor, and martyred in the market-place of Caermarthen.

The Essex martyrs, March, 1555.

The martyr-bishop of Wales.

After the condemnation of the Essex martyrs, the aged Bishop Gardiner, either from increasing bodily infirmity, or, as may be charitably hoped, as a dissentient from the policy pursued, withdrew from the commission. From that time, Bonner figures above all others as active in the Marian persecution. In his diocese, as might be expected, both from his Catholic zeal and its Protestant character, the burnings were the most frequent. In the open tournament ground of Smithfield as many as seven persons were sometimes burned together. At Stratford thirteen were burned on one occasion, and five others in the immediate neighbourhood. At Colchester, in all, twenty-three suffered; of these five men and five women on one day were burned in the courtyard of Colchester Castle. In the diocese of Canterbury, where Cardinal Pole was Cranmer's successor, and Harpsfield was his energetic archdeacon, eighteen persons were burnt in the place long remembered as the Martyrs' Field, where the London,

Gardiner's retirement from the Southwark Commission.

Chatham, and Dover Railway station now stands. In the neighbouring diocese of Chichester twenty-seven persons suffered, ten at one time at Lewes. It would be unjust to suppose that the English bishops were actuated by special motives of cruelty in their work of bloodshedding. They were often the unwilling instrument of laws they were loth to execute. In a circular letter from Philip and Mary they were rebuked for their tardiness; and it was under pressure of royal authority that the Spanish policy to burn out Protestantism in England was pursued.

Meanwhile, the three most illustrious of the Reforming bishops—Cranmer, Ridley, and Latimer—remained in the common gaol at Oxford. Their death had long been determined on, and the plan of their prosecution arranged by Carranza. Some hesitancy at the execution of men so illustrious may have been felt. Even their imprisonment was beginning to recoil upon their persecutors. Sir Henry Bedingfield, under whose surveillance was the Princess Elizabeth, writing to the Council on 4th July, 1555, said 'that the remaining of Cranmer, Ridley, and Latimer at Oxford in sort as they do, hath done no small hurt in these parts, even among those that were known to be good before.'

On 7th September, 1555, about a year and a half after his first condemnation, Cranmer was brought up for trial before a commission, appointed by Cardinal Pole. At St. Mary's, the University church, famous from the days of Wycliffe down to our own for its associations with the ecclesiastical and religious life of the nation, the commissioners met. The venerable archbishop was brought into their presence 'under the custody of the city guard, in a black gown, and leaning on a stick.' To the representatives present, on behalf of the crown, he uncovered his head, and deferentially bowed; then, putting on his cap again, he refused to acknowledge the authority of the papal commissioner, courteously saying he meant no personal disrespect, but had sworn never to admit 'the authority of the Pope of Rome in England.' The accusations against him were read. He was charged with being married, with having written heretical books, with having publicly maintained various heresies, and with having violated his consecration oaths. An official

Charges against Cranmer.

report of his replies was prepared for transmission to Rome. Formally he was cited to appear before the Pope himself within eighty days; in reality he was sent back to his cell in Bocardo, the Newgate of Oxford, there to await the Pope's decision.

<small>Trial of Ridley.</small> A few days later the trial of Bishop Ridley and of Latimer was proceeded with. The court sat in the Divinity School, White, Bishop of Lincoln, presiding. Ridley, as Cranmer had done, formally refused to acknowledge the authority of the Bishop of Rome. The charges against him were those of denying transubstantiation and the propitiatory sacrifice of the mass. Ably, as a scholar and divine, Ridley defended himself. His position with regard to the sacrament of the altar was that as 'in baptism the body is washed with visible water, and the soul is cleansed from all filth by the invisible Holy Ghost, and yet the water ceaseth not to be water, but keepeth the nature of water still, in like manner in the Lord's supper the bread ceaseth not to be bread.' Such was the doctrine that, with all possible earnestness and with becoming respect, the Bishop of Lincoln, as president of the court, urged Ridley to recant.

<small>Of Latimer.</small> Bishop Ridley dismissed, aged Latimer, now eighty years old, was brought in, 'wearing an old threadbare frieze gown, girded with a common leathern girdle, to which were fastened his Testament and spectacles.' The old man's humour had not been crushed out of him, though he had been kept, as he said, with 'bare walls for a library and without book, or pen and ink.' He caused laughter in the court, by turning against the Bishop of Gloucester, one of the commissioners, what he had said, in a sermon at St. Paul's Cross, about the 'clipping of God's coin,' meaning the Scriptures; not knowing at the time, through his weakness of sight, that the bishop was present. 'Was it yours, my lord?' said Latimer to the Bishop of Gloucester, upon discovering what he had done. 'Indeed, I knew not your lordship; neither ever did I see you before, neither yet see you now, through the brightness of the sun shining betwixt you and me.'

With Latimer, as with Ridley, the testing point was transubstantiation. 'Did he believe that the bread and the wine are, after consecration, neither more nor less than the body and blood that was crucified on Calvary?' His reply is significant: 'I do not deny that in the sacrament by spirit and grace is the very body and blood of Christ, because that every man by receiving bodily that bread and wine spiritually receiveth the body and blood of Christ, and is made partaker thereby of the merits of Christ's passion. But I deny that the body and the blood of Christ is in such sort in the sacrament as you would have it.' The examination of Latimer ended about one o'clock, and the court adjourned till the next morning, when it met in St. Mary's Church, and sentence of condemnation was passed upon the two noble-minded reformers.

On October 15th the sentence was put into execution. The place selected was opposite the south front of Balliol College, now marked by a cross in the roadway, and within sight of Bocardo, where Cranmer still remained imprisoned. For some days Ridley and Latimer had been separated. On their way to the scene of their suffering, Ridley, looking round, caught sight of Latimer limping after him, burdened with fourscore years, and somewhat lame. 'Oh, be ye there?' was Ridley's exclamation. 'Yes,' replied the cheery old man; 'I am after you as I can follow.' Within a few minutes the two companions, not in tribulation only, but in triumph also, were together at the halting-place. There they embraced each other, kissed the stake prepared for their burning, and prayed together. Ridley, exhorting Latimer, said, 'Be of good heart, brother; for God will either assuage the fury of the flame or else strengthen us to abide it.'

With unconscious irony a Romanist priest, himself a renegade Protestant, then preached a sermon on charity. The controversial spirit in Ridley would fain have replied to the discourse, but was repressed. When the two bishops removed their clothes, it was seen that Latimer had put on a shroud; and as he stood in it before all the people, it was noted and long remembered that, whereas he had before appeared stooping and feeble, he now 'stood bolt upright, as comely a father as one might behold.' At the awful moment, when the faggots were kindled and blazed up at Ridley's feet, Latimer cheered his fellow sufferer with the now historic words : ' Be of good comfort, Master Ridley, and play the man; we shall this day light such a candle, by God's grace, in England, as I trust shall never be put out.' Latimer's sufferings were shorter than those of his friend; he was seen to put forth his hand, as if embracing the flames, and to stroke his aged face with them, and was heard to say, ' Father of heaven, receive my soul!' So died brave old Latimer. Bishop Ridley's sufferings were more prolonged; great anguish was his, until the fire did its work, and the charred, lifeless body of the greatest scholar of the Reformation fell over its chain at the feet of the lifeless body of its greatest preacher.

From the roof of the Bocardo prison it is said Cranmer saw the dense crowd that thronged the place of burning, and the ascending smoke that told of what was going on, and falling on his knees prayed God to strengthen the martyrs in their agony, and to prepare him for his own.

The executioner's costs for this ghastly business was xxvs. iid.; but Mr. Demaus forcibly observes, when giving the items of the 'bill of charges for burning Ridley and Latimer,' 'It appears to have cost the Government of Mary, one pound five shillings and twopence to burn the two martyrs. Such was the money value of the transaction; but the real price paid was the overthrow of the Romish religion in England.'

Cost of the burning.

In this time of fiery trial no one can wonder that persons should have been found unequal to the task of maintaining their faith with their lives. Many, as before stated, welcomed the return to the old ceremonial of the papal Church; others complied externally, willing to keep their sentiments to themselves, so long as they were not challenged; some were so favourably situated that they held fast their faith without inquisition and without compromise; many of strong reforming views escaped from England to Switzerland, and to the free cities on the Rhine.

In individual cases of persecution the triumphs of the Romanists were not such as to occasion great boasting. The recantations of these times were far fewer than those of the Lollards in the preceding century, whose faith oftentimes flickered.

Of the Reforming bishops, only one recanted, Scory of Chichester, who, after having been removed from his see, was absolved by Bonner. But even he after- *Of the* wards repented, for we find him acting in *Bishop of* concert with the English Reformers abroad. *Chichester.* Another person, of whom better things were expected, was West, at one time Bishop Ridley's chaplain. *West.* Having recanted, he wrote to Ridley when in prison, urging him to save his life by doing the same. The bishop's answer showed he was of sterner stuff. An Essex rector recanted before the bullying Bonner, but, overwhelmed with shame and horror at what he had done, he sought out the bishop's registrar, recovered his recantation, tore the paper into pieces, and 'after was as joyful as any might be,' though the cost of the act was death at Smithfield. A more prominent instance of retraction than any of these was that of Sir John Cheke, who *Sir John* had been the tutor of the young King. At the *Cheke.* time of the Northumberland conspiracy he had fled from the country, but was arrested in Flanders, by Philip's order, and brought back to England. Under Cardinal Pole's persuasion he recanted, and so for a brief while preserved his life. Bonner, it is said, sought to make use of the old man's example by compelling him to sit with him at the trial of Protestants, but it was not for long: the sense of shame so preyed upon him that he soon afterwards died, it is said, brokenhearted. John Jewel, afterwards Bishop of Salisbury, was *Jewel.* another whose courage yielded to the fury of the storm. Speedily he repented of his faithlessness to his convictions, and in order to escape the penalties of retraction, fled to Frankfort, where he publicly abjured his recantation. Jewel lived to render distinguished service as a defender of the doctrines of the Reformed faith.

Saddest and most conspicuous of all the recantations was that of the long recognised leader of the Reformation in England—Archbishop Cranmer. His *Archbishop* sentence of condemnation was received in *Cranmer's* February, 1556. As a follower of the teach- *successive* ings of John Wycliffe and Martin Luther, 'of *recantations.* accursed memory,' as one who had published books containing matters of heresy, and still obstinately persisted in his erroneous opinions, Cranmer was to be degraded, excommunicated, and delivered over to the secular powers.

The sentence of degradation was carried out in all the humiliating minutiæ of its detail in Christ Church, the the cathedral church of the diocese. Bonner was brutally exultant, glorying over his fallen adversary. As he stood in old canvas garments, representing his robes of office, defenceless before him, Bonner declaimed to the assembly: 'This is the man that hath ever despised the pope's holiness, and now is to be judged by him. This is the man that hath pulled down so many churches, and now is come to be judged in a church. This is the man that contemned the blessed sacrament of the altar, and is now come to be condemned before that altar.' Bonner was the Jeffreys of his day in his disregard of all reason and right.

The ceremony of Cranmer's degradation from the office of archbishop successively down to that of a doorkeeper, or sexton, was then gone through. Last of all, they put upon him a poor yeoman-beadle's gown, 'full bare and nearly worn, and as evil-favouredly made as one might commonly see, and a townsman's cap on his head.' 'And now,' said Bonner with brutal scorn, as he gazed at Cranmer, 'you are "my lord" no longer.' As a layman, the fallen primate was then handed over to the secular power for burning.

The saddest scenes of Cranmer's life were yet to come —not in those of his burning, but in those of his shame, through successive recantations, six in all, according to current report. Cranmer was not a man of the stuff of which martyrs are made. 'The temperaments of men,' it has been truly remarked, 'are unequally constituted, and a subtle intellect and a sensitive organization are not qualifications which make martyrdom easy.' It was so with Cranmer. We have seen him all along a man of compromise, true to his convictions, but liable to have those convictions varied by the force of circumstances or the arguments of others. It was so in the days of Henry VIII.; it is seen in the reluctant assent he gave to the unconstitutional will of Edward VI.; again it is seen in his last days, in his first scanty recantation and its aggravated repetitions. Yet all true-hearted men will regard with ndignation the crafty wiles of the deans and friars by whom the recantations were extorted.

No intimation was given to Cranmer when the final sentence was to be put into execution. After three years' imprisonment, apparent kindness and earnest persuasions took the place of insults and threatenings. From the wretchedness, filth, and vile companionship of the common debtors' prison, he was taken to the house of the Dean of Christchurch; his former rank, his learning and seniority were courteously acknowledged. He was allowed to walk abroad, invited to genial dinners, and shared in pleasant games at bowls. One of the most skilful controversialists of his age, John de Villa Garcia, a friend of Carranza, the queen's confessor, was told off to aid in the scheme of inducing Cranmer to recant. All the natural clinging to life and liberty was worked upon to induce him to abjure. The result desired was achieved, but at a cost worse than a defeat. Whatever shame belongs to the vanquished greater belongs to the victors. At the very time the archbishop's recantations were being received, under the delusive promises of life and liberty, Dr. Cole, the Provost of Eton, had Cranmer's funeral sermon in preparation. Blind to the shame of burning one who had purged himself of the offence with which he was charged, the intention was to triumph openly over their enemy by compelling him in public to reaffirm his recantation, and then, as nothing less than his death would satisfy the vindictive feelings of the queen, to allow the papal sentence to take its course.

Cranmer was taken back to his old quarters in Bocardo, left in absolute uncertainty as to the fate that awaited him. Early in the morning of the 21st March, Dr. Cole, who had visited him the previous evening, and said nothing of the sentence that was to be put into execution, again called upon him. As one not having the courage to tell the message on which he had come, Cole inquired of Cranmer if he had any money, and placed fifteen crown pieces in his hand. The prisoner read aright the ominous sign. It was customary for one about to be executed to distribute alms. Cole left him with exhortations to steadfastness in his recent professions of faith. A little later, between the hour of nine and ten, he was summoned

The day of martyrdom.

from his cell. It was for the last time. A procession was formed, the mayor and aldermen leading the way, followed by Crammer between two friars, who as the procession made its way through the crowded High Street alternately recited verses of certain psalms. It being a 'foul and rainy day,' it was arranged for the sermon to be preached in the University Church, instead of at the place of burning. In front of the pulpit a platform had been erected. There the old man stood the observed of all, short in stature, with bald head, and white flowing beard, 'his countenance sorrowful, his face bedewed with tears, sometimes lifting his eyes to heaven in hope, sometimes casting them down to earth for shame—an image of sorrow, the dolour of his heart bursting out of his eyes, retaining ever a quiet and grave behaviour, which increased the pity in men's hearts.' Such is the description preserved by the pen of a sympathetic Romanist of the deposed archbishop as watched while Dr. Cole proceeded with his sermon. That ended, the preacher called upon Cranmer to make a public confession of his faith. 'I *will* do it, and that with a good will,' was the reply. It was not, though, the expected confession that was heard, and which it had been so taken for granted would be read that it was actually printed as having been made; but one utterly renouncing his late recantations. Many celebrated utterances have been made in the far-famed church of St. Mary's, but none more memorable than that of Cranmer, as amid breathless silence he proceeded to say:—

Confession in St. Mary's Church.

'And now I come to the great thing, which so much troubleth my conscience, more than anything ever I did or said in my whole life, and that is the setting abroad of a writing contrary to the truth, which now I here renounce and refuse, as things written with my hand contrary to the truth which I thought in my heart, and written for fear of death, and to save my life if it might be, and that is, all such bills which I have written or signed with my own hand, since my degradation, wherein I have written many things untrue. And forasmuch as my hand offended in writing contrary to my heart, therefore my hand shall first be punished. For if I may come to the fire it shall be first burned.'

Then, as one whose spirit was renewed, and whose

weakness was a thing of the past, he exclaimed, amidst the suppressed excitement around him :—

'As for the pope, I refuse him as Christ's enemy, and antichrist, with all his false doctrine. As for the sacraments, I believe as I have taught in my book against the Bishop of Winchester.'

A few words more, then the pent-up feelings of the assembly burst forth: some applauded, others cried, 'Pull him down!' 'Away with him!' From the pulpit Dr. Cole shouted, 'Stop the heretic's mouth!' Hurried amid the uproar to the place of execution, the same as that where Bishops Ridley and Latimer had made their bold confession, the deposed archbishop was chained to the stake. The flames made quick work of their prey. Imperishable in the history of the English Reformation is the picture of the martyr holding his right hand in the flame,

> 'Crying in his deep voice more than once,
> "This hath offended, this unworthy hand."'

Till it dropped off in the scalding heat.

Three centuries after the event, it is easy for critics at their ease to sit in condemnation upon one who wavered; but 'the worth of a man must be measured by his life, not by his failure under a single and peculiar trial.' If the erring hand was that of one lacking the decision of purpose and the high courage of Hooper, Ridley, Latimer, and others less known to fame, it must not be forgotten that it was that of a man sincerely devout and a diligent student, of one distinguished above most, amid the harsh tempers of those times, for moderation and forbearance, and of the man who more than any one else helped to formulate the faith of the Protestant Church of England.

It belongs to the general historian to describe the troubles that were now thickening round the unhappy queen. Philip, weary of the English people, and with scarcely veiled contempt and indifference for Mary, who clung to him with passionate devotion, had returned to Spain in the August of the previous year. Cardinal Pole, who was solemnly consecrated Archbishop of Canterbury on the day following Cranmer's awful death, and who had been the queen's chief adviser since the death of

Bishop Gardiner, was in ill favour at Rome with the new pope.

Petty conspiracies, for which scarcely a month passed in which executions did not take place, harassed Mary, as showing the revulsion of popular feeling that was setting in against her. She feared to appear in public, and in private 'dreaded every moment that her life might be attempted by her own attendants.' Outside the palace there was misery also, for in thousands of homes there was scarcity through famine prices, occasioned by a disastrous harvest. And still the ghastly burnings went on.

Protestantism, though suppressed in England, was not crushed. During the whole of these troublous and perilous times private congregations of those who remained steadfast to the Reformed faith met in different parts of the country, and ministers, some of them laymen, were travelling from county to county, visiting, comforting, and exhorting these assemblies of the faithful. Bishop Harley, to whom reference has been made as one of the bishops who attempted to take their seats in the House of Lords at the beginning of the reign, in woods and secret places preached and administered the sacraments, and at last 'died like an exile in his own country.' In London one of these suppressed assemblies, which though 'often dispersed by the attacks of its enemies,' yet kept together an attendance of from forty to two hundred persons, was led by a succession of pastors—

<small>Congregations of the Reformed faith.</small>

> 'Each stepping where his comrade stood,
> The instant that he fell.'

Five successively ministered in this period of peril. Edward Scambler,—afterwards Bishop of Peterborough,—Thomas Foule, John Rough, a Scotchman, who was betrayed by one of the members, and burnt, together with one of his flock. He was succeeded by Latimer's faithful Swiss friend and servant, Augustine Bernher, after whom Thomas Bentham, subsequently Bishop of Lichfield, bravely held office. It is recorded concerning this congregation of the faithful that as opportunity presented it was their custom to meet in private houses, or at inns, where a room would be engaged for a dinner, or even for a play, and there

<small>Places of meeting.</small>

spend two or three hours in worship, the Reformed liturgy being used, a sermon preached, the Lord's supper commemorated; after which there was consultation on the affairs of their afflicted church, and contributing alms for the relief of their brethren, an account of the receipts and disbursements of which were regularly presented. Sometimes, as convenience or safety suggested, these meetings were held in an empty warehouse, or in a ship known by the trusted as 'Jesus Ship,' or in secluded suburbs. The martyrologist Foxe gives many instances of marvellous escapes this congregation had, which, nevertheless, in the later years of Mary's reign, greatly increased.

The fear of persecution drove numbers of persons of rank, learning, and piety abroad. It is commonly stated that no fewer than eight hundred fled from England during the reign of terror. Many of them were the ejected married clergy whom Bonner's Visitation Articles required to bring their wives to be divorced, or to resign their benefices. Three were bishops: Barlow of Bath and Wells, Coverdale of Exeter, Bale of Ossory. Others, whose names were already or subsequently prominent in ecclesiastical affairs, were Knox, Lever, Jewel, Grindal, Nowel, Whittingham, Foxe. Some were persons of distinction among the laity—the Duchess of Suffolk, Sir Richard Morrison, Sir Anthony Cook, and Sir John Cheke. The exiles went, some into France, and Flanders, and Geneva, and others into those parts of Germany and Switzerland where the Reformation had taken place. *Exiled Protestants.*

The fame of Calvin drew many of the exiles to Geneva, where the bold experiment was being tried of establishing an ideal theocracy, in which God should reign over every detail and circumstance of life. There the refugees formed a congregation, of which John Knox was for a time the pastor. In the famous city of Frankfort the English refugees received a cordial welcome. Prominent among them was Whittingham, who had married the sister of Calvin's wife, and afterwards became Dean of Durham, a scholarly man, and a Reformer of advanced type. It would be beside our purpose to enter on the details of the 'troubles at Frankfort,' to which may be traced the origin of the Puritans, *'Troubles at Frankfort.'*

and that nonconformity to the Church of England which continues to this day. The French Protestants generously granted the use of their church for worship to the English exiles, but questions of polity and ritual divided them as to the form of worship to be observed. Some wanted a full conformity to the English Prayer-book, others, largely influenced by Whittingham, wished to have the worship conducted somewhat after the model of Geneva, without the use of the surplice, and without audible responses. The latter party prevailed, and invited John Knox to come from Geneva, with some others of like sentiments; and the celebrated Reformer was elected minister of the church at Frankfort. A compromise was arrived at, in which it was agreed that a liturgical form, adopted partly from the Geneva service and partly from the English Prayer-book, should be observed. Other exiles at Strassburg, amongst whom was Grindal, subsequently made Archbishop of Canterbury, were communicated with, and invited to come and strengthen the church at Frankfort; but they were loyal to the English service, and, possibly, not knowing that Knox was already in authority, recommended that Bishop Scory, then at Emden, should be asked to take charge of the church. Lever and other refugees at Zurich were equally loyal to the English Prayer-book, and declared themselves 'fully determined to admit and use no other than the order last taken in the Church of England.' Many will think that the Frankfort church might have been left to pursue its own course. Dean Cox, who had been one of the three tutors of Edward VI., and a compiler of the English Service-book, and who afterwards rose to be Bishop of Ely, thought otherwise. He, with others of like opinion, appeared in the congregation one Sunday morning, and interrupted the service by following aloud the minister, according to the rubrics of the English Prayer-book; and the next Sunday one of his party ascended the pulpit and read the Litany. John Knox was not a man to take such opposition quietly. In the afternoon, in unmistakable language, as his habit was, he told the congregation what he thought of the English Liturgy, and declared that one cause of the present affliction of the English Church was the half-measures taken for its reformation. His opponents in this dispute, in the heat of the passion of the hour, denounced

Knox before the magistrates for having declared in a published sermon of his, preached in England against the Spanish alliance, that the emperor—the father of Philip of Spain—'was no less enemy to Christ than was antichrist.' The author of such a saying could no longer be permitted to remain in a city subject to the emperor. Knox, therefore, in the March of 1555, returned to Geneva, and again became pastor of the English congregation. Others also left Frankfort, among them Whittingham and Gilby, who went to Geneva, and Foxe to Basle. After this the English service was restored.

It is a relief to turn from these pitiable dissensions among those who were fellow sufferers in tribulation to the laudable endeavour of Whittingham and others to perfect the English version of the Scriptures. Whittingham was a man of considerable learning, and published in 1557 a revised translation of the New Testament, in which, for the first time in an English version, the chapters were divided into verses, and italics used to denote words not in the original. The work appeared with a preface written by John Calvin. In the materials collected by Foxe for his martyrology reference to the 'New Testament of Geneva' shows that it soon found its way into England, and was welcomed by the persecuted adherents to the Reformed faith. Though we are anticipating events, it may be conveniently stated here that the Geneva Testament was followed by a revision of the whole Bible, a work in which many of the Geneva refugees shared, Coverdale and Knox amongst others, and John Bodley, the father of the famous founder of the Bodleian Library. The chief credit, though, is due to Whittingham and two fellow exiles—Thomas Sampson and Anthony Gilby. 'For the space of two years and more, day and night,' they toiled at their task. Early in the next reign (1560) the result of their labours appeared in what is known as the Geneva Bible, from the place where it was prepared and printed, familiarly known also as the 'Breeches Bible,' from its translation of the last clause of Genesis iii. 7: 'They sewed fig-tree leaves together, and made themselves breeches'; a rendering nevertheless as old as the days of Wycliffe.

Whittingham's revision of the New Testament, 1557.

Geneva Bible, 1560.

The Protestants beyond sea were busy, not only in their

biblical studies and in controversies among themselves
on questions of church polity, but also in the
production of books and pamphlets giving
free expression to their indignation, stirred by
the tidings which reached them of the atrocious cruelties
perpetrated under the rule of Queen Mary. 'We see our
country set forth for a prey to foreign nations; we hear
the blood of our brethren, the members of Christ Jesus,
most cruelly to be shed; and the monstrous empire of a
cruel woman we know to be the only occasion of all these
miseries.' So wrote John Knox in his famous *First
Blast of the Trumpet against the Monstrous Regiment*
[government] *of Women*, a little book of 112 pages, provoked by the iniquities of the times, but one that itself
wrought great mischief. The stern Reformer wrote as
he felt against Mary, the 'cursed Jezebel of England,
with the pestilent and detestable generation of papists.'
He thought also of Mary Stuart, Queen of France and
Queen-Regent of Scotland, and of her hostility to the
Reformed faith; and with such specimens of feminine
government before him he declared the rule of women to
be against the law of Nature and of God. 'To promote
a woman to bear rule, superiority, dominion, or empire
above any realm, nation, or citie is repugnant to Nature,
contumely to God, a thing most contrarious to His
revealed will and approved ordinance, and finally, it is
the subversion of good order, of all equity and justice.'
The writer seemingly forgot in his exile, possibly failed
altogether to realize, how tenderly and hopefully at the
very time he wrote the eyes of Englishmen were turned
toward a princess—a Protestant and a sufferer for
Protestantism—as heir to the English throne. The ill-
timed blast not only exposed the author to the resentment
of two queens, during whose reign it was his lot to live
—a matter of little moment to one who 'neither feared
nor flattered any flesh '—but it hindered his subsequent
work; enemies of the Reformation did not fail to make
capital out of the book written against female sovereignty
when Elizabeth came to the throne. Another book of the
same class, written by the exiled Bishop of Winchester
—Poynet—argued the right of tyrannicide. In his
Politic Power Poynet heads a chapter, 'Whether it be
lawful to depose an evil governor and kill a tyrant,' and

Writings of the exiles.

leaves no doubt as to the answer in his own mind. In
the judgment of Hallam the book is 'closely and vigor-
ously written, deserving in many parts a high place
among the English prose of that age, though not entirely
free from the usual faults, vulgar and ribaldous invective.'
Another exile, Christopher Goodman, wrote on *How
Superior Powers ought to be obeyed of their subjects, and
wherein they may lawfully by God's Words be disobeyed
and resisted. Wherein also is declared the cause of all the
present misery in England, and the only way to remedy
the same.* The remedy is thus suggested: 'If your
Jezebel, though she be an unlawful governor, and ought
not by God's word and your own laws to rule, would seek
your peace and protection, . . . then might you be
quiet and pray for her life. But because her doings
all tend to the contrary, . . . what cloak have you to
permit this wickedness?' It is true, as Lingard says,
'Tracts filled with libellous and treasonable matter were
transmitted from the exiles in Germany, and successive
insurrections were planned by the fugitives in France.'
But it is idle to pretend that such provocations were the
occasion of the persecutions; they gave the Government,
though, cause for complaint, and afforded excuse for
increasing the severity of the persecutions.

Too often the Reformers in exile fell to the level of
their opponents in virulence of spirit and coarseness of
style. Their writings teem with expressions so offensive
to the taste of a more refined age that they are now in a
great part unreadable. They wrote in the free, blunt,
plain speech of the early days of Shakespeare and Marlow,
and must be judged accordingly. If the spirit of some
of the Protestants was more that of the Hebrew psalmists
than of the saintly Stephen, the causes of their indignation
must be remembered. Banished from their country,
themselves beyond the reach of harm, they could not forget friends, kindred, and fellow countrymen, who, either
because they were unable, or because they scrupled to fly,
were being put to death for their belief, and therefore—
in words of Becon's *Humble Supplication to God*, they
prayed:—

'Let them be confounded and put to shame that seek
after the lives of the faithful. Oh, let them be turned back
and brought to confusion that imagine mischief against

them. Let them be as dust before the wind, and the angel of the Lord scatter them. Let their way be dark and slippery, and let Thy angel, O Lord, persecute them. Let the swords they draw out go through their own hearts, and the bows they have bended slay themselves.'

For two and a half years longer, after the burning of Archbishop Cranmer, this reign of terror lasted. The queen, in the sincerity of her devotion to Romanism, by example and encouragement, did all she could to satisfy the unyielding demand of Pope Paul IV. With great difficulty the consent of Parliament was obtained to a restoration of whatever abbey lands had been attached to the Crown, but the proportion was small compared with that which had passed into the possession of forty thousand owners, some of whom declared 'they would never part from their abbey lands as long as they were able to wear a sword by their side.'

Restoration of the abbey lands formerly held by the Crown.

Monks and Friars were again to be seen in some of the places from which they had been driven. Westminster was again an abbey, with Feckenham, the last to hold the office, as abbot over a small company of monks. In Smithfield and at Greenwich the houses of the Dominicans and Franciscans were restored. Here and there a few chantries were founded for the masses for the dead. Bishops who were becoming slack were urged on in the work of persecution. It was all of no avail. The curse of Heaven seemed to rest upon the land.

To the religious troubles of the times were added that of famine, quickly followed by those of pestilence, 'the sweating sickness' desolating the land. The harvest of 1556 was no better than that of the previous summer. Corn was too dear for the poor to buy, and many were 'driven of hunger to grind acorns for bread meal, and to drink water instead of ale.' Children were forsaken and cast upon the chance charity of those who might be willing to undertake their support. To Mary's sorrow and dismay, Philip was at war with the papacy, and his general, the Duke of Alva, with 12,000 men, had entered the States of the Church, while the French, in league with the pope, were preparing to invade Spain.

Famine and pestilence.

Philip at war with the papacy.

Philip, notwithstanding the careful proviso made by Gardiner in the marriage treaty, by a personal visit to Mary in the spring of 1557, prevailed upon her Council to assist him against France. So the very marriage that was to confirm England in the old religion led to a war against the occupant of the see of Rome. The pope in retaliation cancelled Cardinal Pole's commission as legate, and threatened him with a charge of heresy. Such was the queen's reward—her husband accused of schism; her cousin and chief adviser dishonoured and suspected of heresy by the power in whose support he spent his life. In heaviness and sorrow Mary's heart was breaking. And still the burnings went on.

The beginning of the year 1558 was darkened by the calamity which brought to an ignoble end the English power in France. Calais, called the 'brightest ewel in the English crown,' after being upwards of two hundred years in the possession of the English, was taken, after an eight days' siege. *Loss of Calais.* So heavy at heart was England at this time, by reason of war, and famine, and pestilence, that no attempt was made to recover the lost possession. It was humiliatingly declared that the country was too poor to afford equipment for a fleet. The utmost that could be obtained was a subsidy towards strengthening the sorry defences of the island against possible invasion.

During the sitting of Parliament at the beginning of 1558 there was a brief respite in the burnings; but the session closed in March, and in the same month the Smithfield fires were rekindled. Proclamations against the distribution or possession of anti-Romanist and seditious books were in force, but proving ineffectual in the summer of 1558, the year in which Knox's famous *First Blast* was issued, it was enacted that 'any person possessing such books shall be reported and taken for a rebel, and shall without delay be executed for that offence according to the order of martial law.' *Brief respite in the burnings. Act against seditious books, 1558.* No wonder Sir Thomas Smith said of such a time, 'My countrymen went about their matters as men amazed, they wist not where to begin or end; here was nothing but firing, heading, hanging, quartering and burning, taxing and levying.'

In the same summer, an important arrest was made of the members of one of the suppressed congregations of the Reformed faith, who had met for worship in a field near Islington. Out of forty men and women, twenty-two of them were secured and committed to Newgate. There for seven weeks they were kept without being once called up for examination. Two died amid the fever, depression, and misery of their dungeon life. Of the remaining twenty, thirteen were condemned to perish at the stake. To check the demonstrations of sympathy with which the martyrs were greeted, a proclamation had been issued, 'that no man should either pray for or speak to the condemned or say, "God help them."' Royal proclamations, though, were powerless to restrain the sympathy of the crowd for those who bravely and calmly suffered death for their belief's sake. On the day appointed for the death of the seven, a vast concourse stood awaiting their arrival at Smithfield. Thomas Bentham, afterwards Bishop of Lichfield, was then the pastor of the church to which the martyrs belonged. He too was there, to encourage and bid them farewell. The royal proclamation enjoining silence, that had already been once read at the starting of the procession from Newgate, was again read at the place of execution. Bentham, then stepped forward into the open space that immediately surrounded the just kindled fire, and turning his face to the pressing crowd of onlookers, calmly, distinctly said of those about to die, 'We know they are the people of God, and therefore we cannot choose but wish well to them, and say, "God strengthen them."' Then, in a still louder voice, he added, 'Almighty God, for Christ's sake, strengthen them!' Officers with their halberts and swords were near, but not a hand was put forth to touch him, as there rose from the dense crowd a solemn and loud 'Amen! Amen!' to the pastor's prayer.

Marginalia: Arrest of the members of a congregation near Islington.

The last of the martyr fires of the Marian persecution was in the diocese of Cardinal-Archbishop Pole, where, on 10th November five suffered at Canterbury. It was a place where many had suffered before, but on that day, with a confidence possibly strengthened by a general anticipation of the queen's approaching death, one of the sufferers made a great

Marginalia: The last of the Marian martyrs, 10th Nov., 1558.

impression by saying, 'After this day, in this place there shall no more be put to the trial of fire and faggot.'

Seven days after, in the grey twilight of dawn, Mary, the most miserable, the most unfortunate of England's queens, died. Within a few hours her cousin and chief adviser, Cardinal Pole, the last Romanist Archbishop of Canterbury, was also numbered with the dead. He was buried in his own cathedral in St. Thomas's Chapel. His memorial, a plain brick and plastered monument, stands in suggestive contrast to the pomp of the solemn scene when, with the British Parliament kneeling before him, England was supposed to be restored to its ancient state of union with the Roman see.

Of the cost in human life and suffering of the last three and a half years of Mary's reign no estimate can be made. Perfect accuracy as to the number of actual martyrdoms is unimportant, when it is remembered martyr- *Sufferings of* dom was often a relief from more barbarous *Protestants* atrocities. Men and women untried, uncon- *in Mary's* demned, were crowded into the prisons. 'They *reign.* were beaten, they were starved, they were flung into dark, fetid dens, where rotting straw was their bed; their feet were fettered in the stocks, and their clothes were their only covering, while the wretches who died in their misery were flung out into the fields, where none might bury them.' There is not a sentence in these words of Mr. Froude that does not admit of verification. The horrors of the Lollards' Tower in old St. Paul's, and of Bishop Bonner's coal-house, anticipated the horrors of the Black Hole of Calcutta, and were even more prolonged. To many of the nearly three hundred who were burned alive it was indeed the day of release when from dark, dank dungeons and vile companions they were led forth into the fresh air and golden sunshine, even though it was to undergo the dread ordeal that awaited them. Of those who thus suffered there were five bishops; twenty-one clergymen; eight laymen of independent means; eighty-four artisans; one hundred farmers and labourers; fifty-five women; two boys; two infants.

It is a matter of interest to observe, as illustrated in the accompanying map, that it was in the *The area of* eastern counties and in London, where Lol- *the persecu-* lardy had most flourished, that the Reformed *tions.*

faith was most strenuously held. No fewer than one hundred and twelve persons suffered in the diocese of Bonner, Essex, then part of the London diocese, contributing fifty-two of the number. In the counties of Norfolk and Suffolk, forming the diocese of Norwich, Hopton, at one time the queen's confessor, being bishop, thirty-two men and women were burnt at the stake, twelve at Bury St. Edmunds, eight at Norwich, five at Ipswich, three at Beccles, and one each at Thetford, Walsingham, Hadleigh, Yoxford. On the south side of the Thames, in Cardinal Pole's diocese of Canterbury, fifty-two suffered—forty-one in the cathedral city, seven at Maidstone, two at Ashford, and the same number at Wye. In the small diocese of Rochester six persons were sent to the flames—five at Rochester, one at Dartford. In that of Chichester, where Daye and Christopherson successively held sway, twenty-seven were executed—seventeen on different occasions at Lewes, three at East Gumstead, two in the cathedral town, one at Steyning, four at Mayfield. In the diocese of Winchester, where for the most part the people were Catholics, none suffered during Gardiner's episcopate, but afterwards, in that of White, a gentleman of position was burned at Winchester; and in part of the diocese adjoining London, St. George's Fields, Southwark, four persons were burnt, for 'the nearer London the more the heat.' In the island of Guernsey three poor women were burned, and a newly-born babe cast into the flames with its mother. In the midland counties, where the personal influence of the queen was not so great, there were fewer persecutions unto death. In the diocese of Ely, the episcopate of Thirlby, only three suffered—two at Ely, one at Cambridge. Bishop King of Oxford has the honourable reputation of 'not caring to have anything to do with those who were called heretics.' Remembering the hold Lollardy had in Oxfordshire, it is to the credit of his clemency that, excepting a martyrdom at Banbury, none other occurred for which he can be held personally responsible. In affixing his seal of office to the commissional letters by which Cranmer, Ridley, and Latimer were tried, he is to be considered the mere instrument of a government prosecution. Baine of Lichfield and Coventry, was a zealous Romanist. His diocese contributed seven sufferers to the list—one at

Map of the Dioceses of England and Wales in the time of Mary Tudor, showing the area of the Persecutions, the places where Martyrs suffered, and the number of Sufferers.

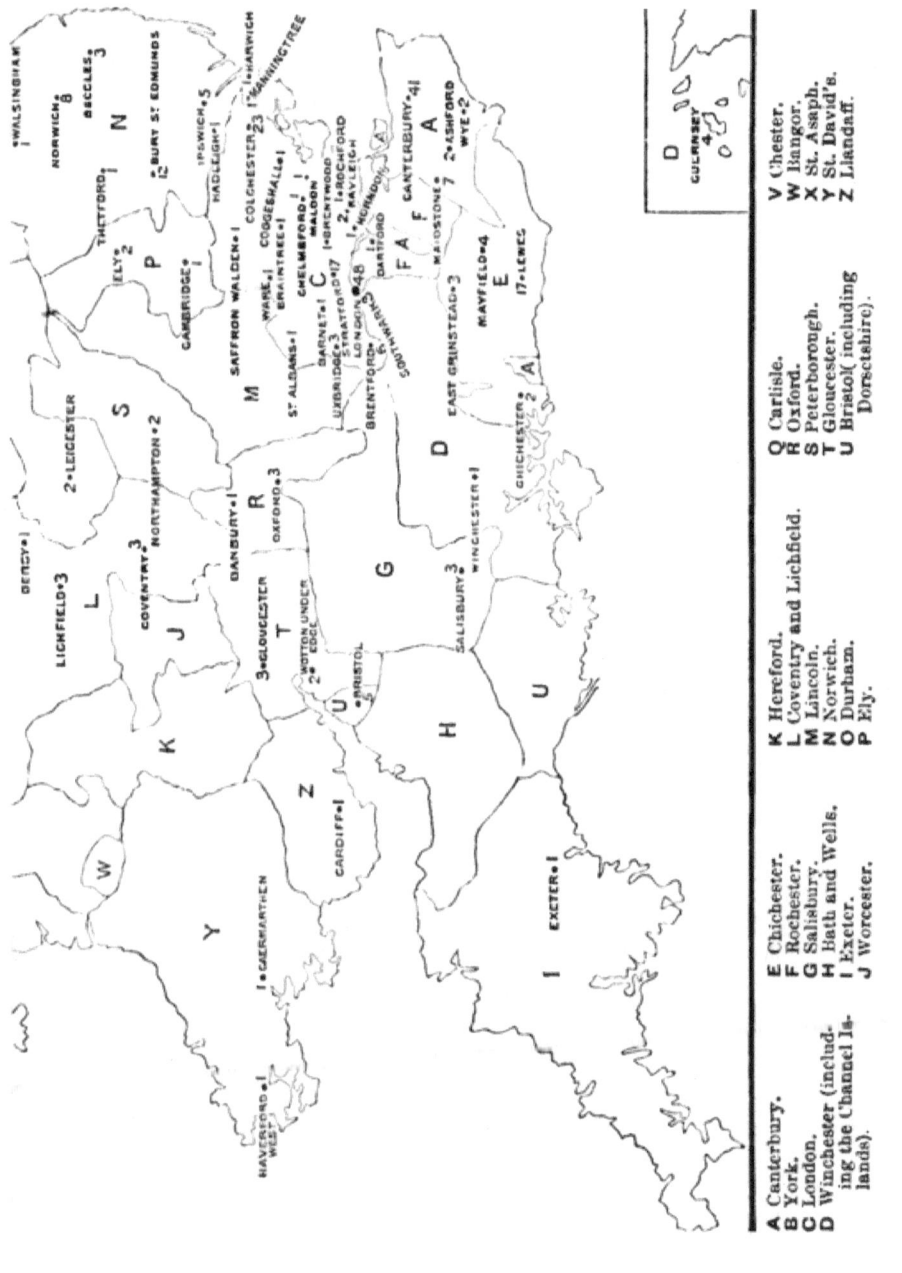

Derby, a poor blind woman, who, 'having by her labour gotten and saved a New Testament, . . . would give a penny or two to such persons as would read to her;' three suffered at Lichfield, one a niece of Bishop Latimer, led to prison by her husband, three at Coventry, one of whom was Saunders, to whom we have before referred.

In the large diocese of Lincoln, the bishopric of Watson, there were only two executions—both at Leicester, the same number as at Northampton, in Daniel Pole's diocese of Peterborough. In Chester, where Cotes and Scot were successively bishops, four persons suffered—two at Bedale, and two in the cathedral town. To the northern dioceses of York, Durham, and Carlisle, the storm of persecution that raged so fiercely in those of the south-eastern parts of the country did not reach. Westward, the dioceses of Hereford, Worcester, Bath and Wells, were, as Heylyn observes, 'like the land of Goshen, where there was nothing but fair weather, when there was so much thunder and lightning in the rest of Egypt.' In the four dioceses of Wales little was seen of the atrocities of the stake and faggot: three executions are recorded—one at Haverfordwest, another at Caermarthen, that of Bishop Ferrar, the third at Cardiff. But in the south-west persecution was severer; there seventeen suffered. Capon, or Salcot, the pliable Bishop of Salisbury, who held his episcopate through all the changes from the close of the reign of Henry VIII. to the early years of Elizabeth, sent six victims to the stake—three at Salisbury, three at Newbury. One suffered at Exeter, the diocese of Tuberville; five in Bishop Brooke's diocese of Gloucester—three in the cathedral city, two at Wotton-under-Edge; five more at Bristol, where Bishop Holyman held sway.

Of the failure of this policy of persecution we have already spoken. Instead of putting down Protestantism, it won sympathy for the sufferers, converts to its principles, and purified its followers. 'You have lost the hearts of twenty thousand that were rank papists within these twelve months,' wrote a Protestant triumphantly to Bonner. Modern English Roman Catholic writers frankly admit the mistake that was made. 'No allowances can relieve the horror,' says Tierney, 'no palliatives can remove the infamy, that must ever attach to these proceedings.' Mary's reign began in hope for the restoration of Romanism, but its end was in disappointment and defeat. Her death, like Edward's, came at a time fortunate for herself—when a revolution was preparing to sweep away all that she held most dear.

CHAPTER XXIII.

THE ELIZABETHAN COMPROMISE.

WITH Elizabeth's accession to the throne there opened a new era for England. While Mary had been straining every nerve to restore the ancient faith, and rebuild the ruined altars, Princess Elizabeth, her half-sister, daughter of the unfortunate Anne Boleyn, had been kept in retirement at Woodstock, under care of Sir Henry Bedingfield, a strict Romanist. With extreme wariness Elizabeth had baffled every effort to entrap her, and had lived as though unconscious of how all eyes turned towards her. In outward observance of religion Elizabeth conformed to the Roman ritual, having in her chapel an altar with lighted candles and a crucifix. Not unnaturally, this conformity has been ascribed to dissimulation; but part was probably real. It has been regarded as in accord with the Lutheranism that influenced her mind, the sacramental doctrine of which was scarcely distinguishable from the Roman. To the end of her life she disliked all preaching and controversy on the subject of the real presence. *[Elizabeth's life in Mary's reign.]*

Elizabeth was in her twenty-fifth year when her sister died. She was strong-minded; she had acquired a degree of learning not so rare among women then as in later times; with Latin and Greek she was familiar, and could speak French and Italian with fluency. In self-will and haughty temper, in love of courtly pomp and magnificence, she resembled her father. Though not the beautiful creature admiring courtiers represent, she had the personal charms of a profusion of auburn hair—'hair more reddish than yellow' is the statement of a contemporary—clear complexion and broad, commanding brow. With years her vanity grew. At thirty, by proclamation, it was ordered that none but a 'special cunning painter' was permitted to draw her likeness; and the time came when the mirrors that could not flatter were removed from rooms through which she was *[Her appearance and character.]*

about to pass. With enthusiasm Elizabeth was welcomed to the throne. As Protestants had forgotten their prejudices in the prospect of relief from the terrible oligarchy of the Protectorate when Mary ascended the throne, so now Romanists, wearied by the troubles of her reign, joined in the welcome to her successor.

With the sagacity and resolution which have rendered her reign remarkable, the young queen appointed as members of her Council Romanists who had served under her sister, among them being Heath, Archbishop of York and Lord Chancellor; but with these she associated seven others of broader sympathies, the most eminent being Sir William Cecil, under whose guiding hand, as Secretary of State, the destinies of England for forty eventful years were placed. The position the queen took with regard to the great religious difficulty of the times was one of studied compromise. For the first ten years of her reign Elizabeth's endeavour was to conciliate both parties. Gradually, by reason of Romanist conspiracies, she was drawn into a more and more decided support of the new and opposition to the old faith, until at last Elizabeth was recognised throughout Europe as the head of the Protestants. Her accession was announced to the pope in the usual way, and she continued to attend mass, as she had done during Mary's reign, but a proclamation was issued forbidding preaching, but directing that in all churches the Gospel and the Epistle of the day, the Ten Commandments, Creed, and Litany be read in English; otherwise the Romanist form of service was not to be altered.[1]

Sir William Cecil.

Her religious policy of compromise.

Proclamation concerning religious services, 1558.

To check the vehemence of religious controversy, by the same proclamation all preaching was forbidden; an injunction observed with such strictness that from Christmas to Easter no preacher appeared in the famous pulpit of St. Paul's Cross. This being only a temporary arrangement, a small committee of divines—made small, no doubt, that it might not attract too much attention—was appointed to revise the Prayer-Book, and so modify it as to make it more conformable to Romanist sentiment.

The occasion of the queen's coronation (15th January,

---

[1] Cardwell, *Documentary Annals*, vol. i., pp. 208-210.

1559) was one of quaint and gorgeous pageantry. Protestant expectations found expression in the presentation of an English Bible, let down from one of the pageants by a child representing Truth. Fervently the new queen clasped the book to her bosom, saying she would 'diligently read therein;' but the coronation service itself was according to the Romish ritual, Feckenham, the last mitred abbot, taking part in the ceremony. Coming changes, though, made themselves felt, for the Litany was read in English, and as a yet more significant sign of compromise, the Gospel and Epistle in both Latin and English. According to some authorities, only one bishop was present,—Oglethorp, Bishop of Carlisle,[1]—who, it is said, performed the ceremony of the coronation in Bonner's robes, borrowed for the occasion; the rest absenting themselves either on account of the queen having forbidden the elevation of the host in the service of the mass, or because of the pope's reply to the notification of her accession, he having declared that Elizabeth was illegitimate, and could not inherit the crown, and demanded that her claims should be submitted to the judgment of Rome—a demand met with the disdain her father would have shown. Neither the pope's displeasure nor the bishops' absence affected the general congratulations that attended the queen's coronation.

Queen's coronation, 15th January, 1559.

Within a fortnight of the coronation day Parliament met. High mass was celebrated; but a returned exile, Dean Cox, preached the opening sermon. In the Commons there was a strong Protestant majority. In the House of Lords the Romanists had the ascendancy; but they were powerless to successfully resist the great Protestant reaction. In defiance of the pope's refusal to recognise Elizabeth's claims, within a few days an Act was passed, recognising the queen's title to the crown, and another restoring to the Crown the 'firstfruits' of ecclesiastical benefices which Mary had given back to the priests. But long and strenuous opposition met the bill to re-establish the royal supremacy 'in all causes, ecclesiastical as well as civil.' Henry VIII.

New Acts.

Act of Supremacy.

[1] Heylyn, *Hist. Ref.*, ii. 275; Aikin, *Elizabeth*, i. 252; followed by Stanley; Gairdner, *Dict. Nat. Biog.*

had called himself 'the only supreme head on earth of the Church of England,' a title odious to Romanists, and even Protestants who had any worthier thought of the Church than as an appanage of the Crown felt its inappropriateness. Adroitly to the pleasing both Romanists and Protestants, Elizabeth, while preserving the power claimed, dropped the offending title, 'supreme head of the Church,' and by her direction was declared to be 'the only supreme governor of the realm, as well in all spiritual or ecclesiastical things or causes, as temporal.' To carry out the authority of the Crown in ecclesiastical matters, a body of commissioners was appointed, afterwards known as the

High Commission Court appointed, 1559. High Commission Court. The action of this court, often arbitrary and high-handed, and notorious in the time of the Stuarts as the Court of Star Chamber, was yet a decided improvement upon the bishops' and archbishops' courts. All holding office under the Crown were required to take the oath of supremacy, but instead of refusal being, as in the days of Henry, punishable by death, as treason, on the part of the clergy deprivation of office alone was to follow. A remarkable feature of this Act, as a great and beneficial precaution in times of bitter religious controversy, was its enactment forbidding any expression of religious belief to be determined as heresy, unless already so adjudged by any of the first four general councils in the express and plain words of the canonical Scripture, and so determined by the joint assent of Parliament and

Statutes against heresy repealed. Convocation. The statutes against heresy, revived by Mary, were again repealed. In the matter of the election of bishops, instead of renewing the Act of Edward VI. for their appointment by the Crown, the older method was revived of a *congé d'élire* for their election, which still remains

Manner of election of bishops. the law of the land, and preserves the memory of ancient custom with regard to episcopal elections.

In April, the results of the revision of the Prayer-Book by the appointed committee were laid before Parliament in 'An Act for the Uniformity of

Act of Uniformity of Common Prayer ac- Common Prayer, and Service in the Church, and Administration of the Sacraments.' It prohibited the use of any other 'order' or form of service in public or private, and made who did not attend the Protestant services on Sundays and holy days liable to a fine. In three days the Act was passed, notwithstanding the united opposition of the Romanist bishops and members of the House of Lords. *[According to the Elizabethan Prayer-Book, 1559.]*

Substantially the book thus authorized was the same as the second book of Edward VI. According to the Act, it is the same, 'with one alteration or addition of certain lessons, to be used on every Sunday in the year, and the form of Litany altered and corrected, and two sentences only added in the delivery of the sacrament to the communicants, and none other, or otherwise.'[1] But when the book appeared, it was *[Points of difference between the Elizabethan Prayer-Book and those of Edward VI.'s reign.]* found that subsequent alterations that weakened its Protestant character had been made. Upon these alterations Dr. Cardwell observes: 'It is supposed by some that these changes were introduced during its progress through Parliament; but it is more probable, from the known sentiments and subsequent conduct of the queen, that they were inserted previously by herself and her Council. This, however, is certain, that the committee of divines disapproved of any distinction, as to the use of vestments, between the celebration of the communion and the other services of the Church; and by a still bolder act of concession, left it to every man's choice to communicate either standing or kneeling. Both these changes, however, were withdrawn before the book was eventually published.'[2] The revisers justified standing as an optional attitude in receiving the sacrament, as symbolical of resurrection, and quoted patristic authorities for its sanction.

It is important to observe the principal points of difference between the Elizabethan Prayer-Book of 1559 and the second Prayer-Book of Edward VI., 1552, as they will clearly show the endeavours made to conciliate the Romanists.

I. OMISSIONS.

1. Of the strong denial of the 'real and essential

[1] *Liturgical Services of Queen Elizabeth*, p. 28 (Parker Soc.).
[2] *Hist. of Conferences on Book of Common Prayer*, pp. 21, 22 (1840).

presence,'—contained in the 'Black Rubric,'—appended as a declaration at the end of the Communion Service—concerning the posture of kneeling: 'We do declare that it is not meant thereby that any adoration is done or ought to be done either unto the sacramental bread and wine there bodily received, or unto any real and essential presence there being of Christ's natural flesh and blood.' [This was restored in the revision of 1661.]

2. From the Litany a prayer for deliverance, 'From the tyranny of the Bishop of Rome, and all his detestable enormities.'

II. ALTERATIONS.

Second Prayer-Book of Edward VI.	Prayer-Book of Queen Elizabeth.
1. The morning and evening prayer shall be used in such places of the church, chapel, or chancel, and the minister shall turn him, as the people may best hear: and if there be any controversy therein, the matter shall be referred to the ordinary, and he or his deputy shall appoint the place.	The morning and evening prayer shall be used in the accustomed place of the church, chapel, or chancel, except it shall be otherwise determined by the ordinary of the place. And the chancels shall remain as they have done in times past.
2. 'Here it is to be noted that the minister at the time of the communion, and all other times in his ministration, shall use neither alb, vestment, nor cope; but being archbishop or bishop, shall have and wear a rochet; and being a priest or deacon, he shall have and wear a surplice only.'	'Here it is to be noted that the minister at the time of the communion, and at all other times in his ministration, shall use such ornaments in the church as were in use by authority of Parliament in the second year in the reign of King Edward VI., according to the Act of Parliament, set forth in the beginning of this book.'

III. MODIFICATION OF THE OATH OF SUPREMACY.

The Oath of the King's Supremacy.	The Oath of the Queen's Sovereignty.
'I, from henceforth shall utterly renounce, refuse, relinquish, and forsake the Bishop of Rome, and his authority, power, and jurisdiction. And I shall never consent nor agree that	'I, A.B., do utterly testify and declare in my conscience that the Queen's Highness is the only supreme governor of this realm, and of all other her Highness' dominions and countries, as well

the Bishop of Rome shall practise, exercise, or have any manner of authority, jurisdiction, or power within this realm, or any other of the King's dominions, but shall resist the same at all times, to the uttermost of my power. And I from henceforth will accept, repute, and take the King's Majesty to be the only supreme head in earth of the Church of England: and to my cunning, wit, and uttermost of my power, without guile, fraud, or other undue means, I will observe, keep, maintain, and defend the whole effects and contents of all and singular Acts and Statutes made, and to be made, in confirmation and corroboration of the King's power, of the supreme head in earth of the Church of England: and this I will do against all manner of persons, of what estate, dignity, or condition they be. . . . And in case any oath be made, or hath been made by me to any person or persons in maintenance, defence, or favour of the Bishop of Rome, or his authority, jurisdiction, or power, I repute the same as vain and annihilate; so help me God, through Jesus Christ.

in all spiritual or ecclesiastical things or causes, as temporal; and that no foreign prince, person, prelate, state, or potentate, hath or ought to have any jurisdiction, power, superiority, pre-eminence, or authority, ecclesiastical or spiritual, within this realm: and therefore I do utterly renounce and forsake all foreign jurisdictions, powers, superiorities and authorities, and do promise that from henceforth I shall bear faith and true allegiance to the Queen's Highness, her heirs and lawful successors, and to my power shall assist and defend all jurisdictions, privileges, pre-eminences, and authorities granted or belonging to the Queen's Highness, her heirs and successors, or united and annexed to the imperial crown of this realm; so help me God, and the contents of this book.'

3. The alteration in the words of delivery in the Communion Service is especially suggestive of the compromising spirit of the Elizabethan revision. In the first Prayer-Book of Edward VI., which retained as much as possible of the ancient forms, the words were almost the same as now used in the Roman Church, and as in the Sarum Missal:—

> 'The body of our Lord Jesus Christ, which was given for thee, preserve thy body and soul unto everlasting life.'

In the second and more Protestant Prayer-Book of 1552 these words were substituted:—

'Take and eat this in remembrance that Christ died for thee, and feed on Him in thy heart by faith, with thanksgiving.'

In the Elizabethan Prayer-Book these two forms appear together, as they have remained ever since:—

'The body of our Lord Jesus Christ, which was given for thee, preserve thy body and soul unto everlasting life. Take and eat this in remembrance that Christ died for thee, and feed on Him in thy heart by faith with thanksgiving.'

Similar alteration was made in regard to the delivery of the wine.

First Prayer-Book of Edward VI.	*Second Prayer-Book of Edward VI.*
'The blood of our Lord Jesus Christ, which was shed for thee, preserve thy body and soul unto everlasting life.'	'Drink this in remembrance that Christ's blood was shed for thee, and be thankful.'

Elizabethan Prayer-Book.

'The blood of our Lord Jesus Christ, which was shed for thee, preserve thy body and soul unto everlasting life. Drink this in remembrance that Christ's blood was shed for thee, and be thankful.'

Every one of these alterations, it will be observed, was a concession to the Romanists.

On the other hand, to those of the Protestant faith there was the immense satisfaction of having restored to public use in every cathedral and parish church of England and Wales their banished Liturgy: the Liturgy that, except perhaps in a score of lines, was as Cranmer had left it, and that was more Protestant than the first Prayer-Book of Edward VI. A satisfaction, as subsequent pages will show, seriously lessened to many by the prefatory rubric authorizing the use of before prohibited ornaments and vestments. Thus adroitly Elizabeth and her Council played off one against the other Romanists and Protestants.

One of the last Acts of this Parliament of reaction from the Roman system restored by Mary was for the dissolution of the few monasteries just recently refounded. On the 8th May, 1559, the work of the first Parliament of the famous reign of Elizabeth was declared finished. In the words of Mr. Froude : ' The vessel of the state, though heaving dangerously in the after-roll, was again on her right course, and began slowly to draw away out of the breakers.'[1]

While Parliament had been in session the bishops and clergy had met in Convocation, and shown that, had it been left to them, Romanism would have been confirmed as the national religion. They passed resolutions in which they declared their belief in the doctrine of transubstantiation, 'That in the mass is offered the true body of Christ and His true blood, a propitiatory sacrifice for the living and the dead,' and maintained that the clergy alone have authority to determine points of faith and matters ecclesiastical.[2]

Clerical opposition to Reformation doctrine.

Warned by these signs of hostility, and by the great influence of the Romanists in the country before the passing of the Act of Uniformity, it was determined by the Council that a conference of leading Romanists and Reformers should be held in Westminster Abbey for the guidance and instruction of Parliament. The following were the points proposed for discussion :

Conference of Romanists and Reformers in Westminster Abbey, 1559.

1. That it is against the Word of God and the custom of the ancient Church to use a tongue unknown to the people in common prayer and the administration of the sacraments.
2. That every Church has authority to appoint, take away, and change ceremonies and ecclesiastical rites, so the same be done to edification.
3. That it cannot be proved by the Word of God that there is in the mass offered up a sacrifice propitiatory for the living and the dead.

Priority in the debate was given to the Romanists, and the conditions agreed to on their behalf by Archbishop Heath. Face to face the opposing divines sat. 'This,' says Dean Stanley, ' was the last fight face to face between the Church of Rome and the Church of England.'[3] On

---
[1] *History*, vi. p. 195.
[2] Cardwell, *Synodalia*, ii. pp. 490–494.
Memorials of Westminster Abbey, p. 405.

the side of the Romanists were White, Watson, Baynes, and Scot, bishops of Winchester, Lincoln, Lichfield, and Chester, and four other divines, two of whom were Harpsfield, Pole's persecuting archdeacon, and Cole, who had distinguished himself by preaching at Cranmer's martyrdom. On the side of the Reformers were Scorey, late Bishop of Chichester, Cox, the opponent of Knox at Frankfort, Horne, Aylmer, Grindal, and Jewel, all likewise returned exiles. The result of the conference was such as might have been anticipated. In the words of Heylyn, it 'ended before it had been well begun.' Not later than the second or third day it came to an abrupt conclusion, the Romanists refusing to comply with the prescribed order of debate. Forthwith they were told the discussion was ended, the Lord Keeper, Nicholas Bacon, adding, 'Since you are not willing that we should hear *you*, you shall very shortly hear from *us*.'[1] The threat was fulfilled. Two of the Romish bishops, White and Watson, for contempt were sent to the Tower, with orders that they should be treated with becoming respect.

Abrupt termination of the debate.

On the 15th May the steadfastness of the bishops and the patience of the queen were put to the test. It was the day appointed for the bishops to take the oath of supremacy, and they were summoned to appear before the queen. For some unknown reason many bishoprics had been left untenanted in the preceding reign, and since the accession of Elizabeth others through death had become vacant.

The bishops, all but one, refuse the oath of supremacy.

There were but fourteen of the Marian bishops to obey the command. As priests or bishops, they had all taken the oath of supremacy in its baldest form[2] in the reign of one or other of the last two kings; but now, though conciliatory in expression, with one exception they all refused to swear to the oath of sovereignty. Kitchin, of Llandaff, a prototype of the famous Vicar of Bray, was the only one who conformed. Time was given to the others to reconsider their decision. As might have been anticipated, their refusal was followed by deprivations, but by none of the hardships to which the deprived

[1] Heylyn, *Eccl. Rest.*, ii., p. 290.
[2] See p. 266.

bishops of the previous reign had been subjected. They were all treated with respect. Their confine- ment was nominal rather than real. Arch- bishop Heath retired to his own estate at Cobham in Surrey, where on more than one occasion he was honoured by a royal visit. Tunstall, who had seen all the momentous changes from the days of Henry VIII., lived in friendly intimacy with Archbishop Parker at Lambeth. Some suffered short imprisonments, but Bonner was the only one treated with anything approaching severity. From the first Elizabeth had shown her aversion to him: she had refused him her hand to kiss when he with the other bishops went out to meet her at Highgate upon her accession to the throne. He was now imprisoned in the Marshalsea, where he had a 'room befitting his condition,' and liberty within the gates. The opinion of Heylyn may be taken for what it is worth, that prison to Bonner was his safest sanctuary from the fury of the people.[1] Bonner's steadfastness to his Church in Edward's and in Elizabeth's reigns is the one redeeming feature of his character. To the credit of the deprived Marian bishops it ought to be added, that, with a single exception, they showed due recognition of the clemency of Elizabeth and her counsellors by never making any attempt to set up a rival succession of bishops, or to take part in any of the plots against the queen, which in after years became so frequent.

Refusal followed by deprivation.

Bonner only one treated with severity.

The same policy of conciliation was shown towards the general clergy. Commissioners were appointed in the two provinces of Canterbury and York to administer the oath of sovereignty, also 'to reserve pensions for such as resigned their benefices, and to restore such as had been unlawfully put out in the late reign.' The general clergy were compliant where their bishops had been unyielding. Many in obscure parishes may have left the commissioners' summons altogether unheeded; others may have resigned rather than run any risk by refusing the oath; but the remarkable fact remains, that out of the whole body of the clergy, numbering between nine and ten thousand, only one hundred and eighty-nine refused the oath.

Conciliatory policy towards Romanist clergy.

[1] *Eccl. Rest.*, ii. p. 295.

The Revised Prayer-Book was ordered to be taken into general use on the Midsummer Day of 1559. It met with general acceptance. Probably the return to an English service after the Latin services of the past five years was more acceptable to the people than it had been on its first introduction. Protestants accepted the Revised Liturgy with thankfulness that they had got much of what they wanted; Romanists with thankfulness that so much was preserved to them, especially in what met the eye in public worship, by the enactment of the 'Ornaments Rubric.' According to Heylyn, the new Prayer-Book 'was so passable among the Papists that for ten years they generally repaired to their parish churches without doubt or scruple.' With more or less of connivance from Government, where priests had the sympathy of their congregation, they were allowed for a time to continue unchanged the old form of service. We have it upon Romanist authority,[1] that in some places the spirit of compromise was carried to such an extent, that the priest having celebrated mass at home, would take with him to church wafers consecrated according to the Romish rite, to give to rigid Romanist communicants, at the very time he was giving to others the bread prepared according to the Reformed Liturgy. On the other hand, there were churches in which the form of worship was devoid of all such observances as bore any resemblance to those of the Roman ritual. In some country towns and villages there was no service at all, the priests having resigned rather than accept the Protestant Liturgy. Thomas Lever, writing to Bullinger in the second year of Elizabeth, says: 'Many of our parishes have no clergyman. And out of that very small number who administer the sacrament throughout this great country, there is hardly one in a hundred who is both able and willing to preach the Word of God.'[2]

In such a state of disorganization little or nothing could be done until the appointment of bishops. All the dioceses being vacant, with the single exception of Llandaff, an almost absolutely new episcopate was required. Anxious care was taken,

The Revised Prayer-Book favourably received.

Disorganized state of public worship.

New episcopate.

[1] Rishton, in Sanders' *Anglican Schism*, Bk. iv. ch. iv. p. 267 (1877).
[2] Zurich Letters, 1st Ser., No. 35.

under such critical circumstances, to preserve the episcopal succession. Matthew Parker, an honoured friend of the queen, to whose charge she had been commended at her mother's death, was chosen to be Archbishop of Canterbury. He, during all the troubles of Mary's reign, had remained with his family in England, in such strict seclusion that his place of concealment was never discovered. His residence in England, while so many of the Reformed party were on the Continent, is deserving of note, as accounting in no small measure for the ecclesiastical policy he supported as archbishop. *[Parker made Archbishop of Canterbury, 1559.]*

He was duly consecrated at Lambeth, Dec. 17th, 1559, the consecrators being Bishop Barlow, formerly Bishop of Bath and Wells, Scorey, formerly Bishop of Chichester, Miles Coverdale, who had been Bishop of Exeter, and John Hodgkin, who had been suffragan Bishop of Bedford. These four bishops were all out of office; but it was argued they held their sees by the law of the Church, though deprived of them in the late reign by the law of the State. Forty years after, the Romanist party sought to throw discredit on Parker's consecration by circulating a story that the ceremony was performed in a tavern in Cheapside, called the Nag's Head, and that a chaplain of Bonner, peeping through a keyhole, had seen Scorey lay a Bible upon Parker's head, saying, 'Take thou authority to preach the Word of God.' And this was declared to be all the ordination he ever had. The utter absurdity of this oft-repeated story is well exposed in Dean Hook's life of the archbishop. *[Consecration of Parker.]*

After the consecration of Parker the filling up of the vacant bishoprics proceeded rapidly. Grindal, formerly a chaplain of Ridley, and a gifted preacher, was consecrated Bishop of London; Cox became Bishop of Ely; Sandys, whose ecclesiastical views were rather those of the German than of the English Reformers, was made Bishop of Worcester; and Jewel, also of the Continental school, was appointed Bishop of Salisbury. Barlow was translated from St. Asaph to Chester, and Scorey from Chester to Hereford. More consecrations soon followed. *[Appointment of bishops.]*

Ordinations of priests and deacons speedily followed the appointment of the Reformed bishops. To meet the pressing need of the many vacant benefices a temporary order of ordained readers was instituted. They 'readers' were to serve in small livings, where there was no minister, and to supply till they were filled. Their duties were to read the appointed services and the homilies, but not to administer the sacraments. The readers were under the oversight of one of the regular clergy, who went the round of a certain number of parishes, preaching and administering the sacraments. Subsequently the readers were not ordained, but simply appointed with consent of the bishop. It was long before the vacant benefices were efficiently served. In the province of Canterbury fourteen years after the accession of Elizabeth thirty-four important parishes were without resident clergy; many churches had only occasional services. The rarity of preaching was such that in some parishes only three sermons were preached in the course of twelve months, in others only two, in some but one, in some none.

An order of 'readers' instituted.

Eminent service to the cause of the Reformation was rendered by Bishop Jewel in his *Apology for the Church of England*, vindicating its separation from Rome. It grew out of a St. Paul's Cross sermon preached by him in November, 1559, and afterwards before the queen, in which he openly challenged the Romanists to prove twenty-seven tenets, which he enumerated as held by them. Among the points he called upon them to prove from the authority of Scripture, or of any general council or patristic writer during the first six hundred years, were these:

Bishop Jewel's challenge, 1559.

'That there was at that time any private mass in the world. Or that there was then any communion ministered to the people under one kind. Or that the people had their common prayer in a strange tongue, that the people understood not. Or that the Bishop of Rome was then called an universal bishop, or the head of the Universal Church. Or that the people were then taught to believe that Christ's body is really, substantially, corporeally, carnally, or naturally in the sacrament. Or that His body is or may be in a thousand places or more at one time. Or that the priest did then hold up the sacrament over his head. Or that whosoever had said the sacrament is a figure, a pledge, a token, or a remembrance of

Christ's body had therefor been judged for a heretic. Or that the lay people were then forbidden to read the Word of God in their own tongue.'[1]

Published originally in Latin, it was soon circulated among the learned, not only in England, but on the Continent. At the Council of Trent, then sitting, two divines were appointed to reply to its arguments. The work was translated into English by Lady Anna Bacon, the mother of the celebrated Lord Bacon, and such was the value attached to its controversial power, that Elizabeth ordered a copy of it to be chained in every parish church in England.

The challenge of Jewel was not left unaccepted. Thomas Harding, who had at one time been chaplain of the Duke of Suffolk, took it up, and published in 1565 a *Confutation of the Apology*, to which Jewel replied in 1567 by a *Defence of the Apology*.

Not less popular, and more lasting in its value, was another work likewise ordered to be placed in every parish church, Foxe's famous *Book of Martyrs*. Foxe was a man of considerable scholarship, a fellow of Magdalen College, Oxford, and at one time a prebendary of Salisbury Cathedral. *Foxe's Book of Martyrs, 1563.* It was at Lady Jane Grey's suggestion he began his laborious work, of which Professor Burrows says it 'has been as much undervalued in modern times as it was originally overvalued.' Written at a time when the people's minds were maddened by the cruelties inflicted upon some of the noblest men of the age, conciliatory language can scarcely be expected in its pages. Its material is often heaped together rather than arranged, but to its general accuracy and the integrity of the writer's purpose there is abounding testimony. 'I trust Foxe,' says Mr. Froude, 'when he produces documentary evidence, because I have invariably found his documents accurate.' His friendship with Archbishops Parker, Grindal, and others gave him access to the most valuable sources of information. In his *Acts and Monuments* a mass of valuable information, of original letters, records of judicial processes, and other documentary evidence, is presented to the reader, often with a dramatic power that is very affecting.

[1] Cardwell, *Documentary Annals*, i. 287-289.

With larger intentions than success Archbishop Parker arranged for a fresh revision of the authorized version known as the Great Bible of 1539. The archbishop's desire was to supplant in popular favour the Geneva version, the marginal notes and comments being of a pronounced controversial character. The work of revision was shared in and superintended by Parker and eleven other bishops and learned men. The principles on which the revision was made were admirable in spirit. The labours of previous translations were to be respected, so that the new version should vary as little as need be from the last authorized version. No 'bitter notes' were to be made upon any texts, or any 'determination in places of controversy.' As was fitting in a work of national importance, the revisers were men of different shades of opinion—Grindal, Sandys, Cox, Bentham, and others. The work of revision extended over four years. In the autumn of 1568 the result appeared in a large and elaborately got-up folio volume, printed in black letter, illustrated with wood engravings, and, following the precedent of the Great Bible, embellished with portraits of the queen, Leicester, and Burleigh. With the copy sent to the queen, humble petition was made that the new Bishops' Bible might receive the royal sanction as the authorized version; but for reasons never explained the favour besought was left ungranted. The Bishops' Bible was never authorized by other than ecclesiastical authority. 'Of all the English versions,' writes Prof. Plumptre, 'the Bishops' Bible had probably the least success.' The inconvenience of its size was met by the issue of a quarto edition in 1569, and of a revised version of both Old and New Testaments published in 1572. Practically the use of the Bishops' Bible was confined to public reading in church.

Bishops' Bible, 1568.

The first act of the royal supremacy was to issue, on the same day (June 24th, 1559) as the Revised Liturgy was ordered to be taken into use, Injunctions relative to religions.[1] For the most part they are literally the same as those issued in the first year of the Protectorate. They differ in some particulars, where they are modified to

The Queen's Injunctions and the 'Advertisements.'

[1] Cardwell, *Docum. Ann.*, i. pp. 210-231.

conciliate the Romanists, and in others according to the personal wishes of the queen. Especially stringent were the new Injunctions concerning the marriage of the clergy, against which Elizabeth was strongly prejudiced. Unable wholly to prevent it, she made its conditions as humiliating as possible. According to Injunction XXXIX., no priest was to be allowed to marry without the advice and permission of the bishop of his diocese, and of two justices of the peace 'dwelling next to the place where the woman hath made her most abode.' The clergy were also required to wear the ecclesiastical garments that had been laid aside in Edward's reign, 'not thereby meaning to attribute any holiness or special worthiness to the said garment, but, as St. Paul writeth, "Let all things be done decently and in order."' It was also considered necessary to enjoin 'that all ministers and readers of public prayers, chapters, and homilies be charged to read leisurely, plainly, and distinctly; and also such as are mean readers shall peruse over before, once or twice, the chapters and homilies, to the intent that they may read to the better understanding of the people and more encouragement to godliness.' *(Concerning marriage of the clergy. Vestments. Public reading.)*

One of the new Injunctions is of special interest, from its reference to the musical service in public worship. After directing that 'there be a modest and distinct song, so used in all parts of the common prayers, that the same may be as plainly understood as if it were read without singing,' it is added, nevertheless, 'for the comforting of such as delight in music,' permission was given 'that in the beginning or in the end of common prayer there may be sung a hymn, or such like song, to the praise of Almighty God, in the best sort of melody and music that may be conveniently devised, having respect that the sentence of the hymn may be understanded and perceived.' The hymns here referred to must have been the metrical version of the Psalms, commonly known as the 'Old Version,' begun by Sternhold and Hopkins in the time of Edward, and carried on by Whittingham, the editor of the Geneva New Testament, and Kethe, Marian exiles. Hymns, in the general acceptance of the term, there were next to none to sing. The English Reformation was characterized by no such *(Church music and hymns.)*

outburst of song as that of Germany. Not one of its leaders was ever inspired to move the hearts of the people, as the great Reformer of the German Church moved those of his land. Either through the influence of the reaction from the ornate musical service of the Roman ritual, or through an unfortunate lack of the hymnic faculty, little progress was made in hymnology during the earlier times of the Reformation. What may be called the Reformation Hymn-Book, published in 1562, according to Lord Selborne, was a very meagre production. It contained, besides the versified Psalms, several versions of the *Te Deum* and Lord's Prayer, a rendering of one of Luther's hymns, and two original hymns of praise, to be sung before Morning and Evening Prayer. The Book of Psalms was the real hymn-book of the English Reformation. Bishop Jewel, in a letter to Bullinger, refers to the impressiveness of the singing in the St. Paul's Cross services, where he had seen five thousand persons singing a psalm together. At Exeter public protest was made against the dean and chapter, for hindering the people from assembling to sing psalms in their cathedral before Divine service. It was not, therefore, deficiency in popular love of music and song, but ecclesiastical prejudice, which quenched its spontaneous utterance.

<small>Reformation Hymn-Book.</small>

Added to the Injunctions were certain 'Admonitions.' Concerning the material and position of the communion table, it was stated that where altars had not been removed, 'saving for uniformity,' it was a matter of no great moment, so that the sacrament be duly and reverently administered. Where a communion table had been substituted for a stone structure, it was directed that it should be 'set in the place where the altar stood, and there commonly covered, as thereto belongeth, as should be appointed by the visitors, and so to stand, saving when the communion of the sacrament is to be distributed; at which time the same shall be so placed within the chancel . . . as whereby the minister may be more conveniently heard of the communicants, . . . and the communicants also more conveniently and in more numbers communicate with the said minister. And after communion done, from time to time, the same holy table to be placed where

<small>'Admonitions' concerning communion tables.</small>

it stood before.' The bread directed to be used for the sacrament was to have no figure on it, and to be somewhat 'bigger in compass and thickness' than the usual wafer-bread.

Whatever may have been Elizabeth's expectations of a uniform order in all external rites and ceremonies in worship, she soon found, even among the bishops, conformity was only partial, and that among the clergy and laity there was a large and strong party that regarded with abhorrence many things which she, with her love of ritual and Lutheran bias, wished to have retained. Stanch Protestants, relatives, friends, and neighbours of those who had died in prison or been burnt alive for denying the doctrine of transubstantiation, resented all that pertained to the ritual and service of the dark Romish times. Their position was greatly strengthened by the number of returned exiles, who, during their absence from England, had become great admirers of the simplicity of worship in the Reformed Churches abroad. Eminent among the leaders of the stanchly Protestant party was Thomas Cartwright, Professor of Divinity at Cambridge, a man of learning and of high character, of whom Beza wrote that the 'sun never shone upon a more learned man.' Among them also was Laurence Humphrey. He had been at Zurich during the exile. Soon after his return to England he was appointed Master of Magdalen College, Oxford, and Regius Professor of Divinity in that university. He was a man of great piety and learning. Thomas Sampson, one of the Strassburg exiles, was not less distinguished. The extent to which the influence of the more advanced Reformers prevailed was strikingly shown in the year 1562, in a debate on ceremonies in the Lower House of Convocation. A series of resolutions was drawn up by them proposing[1]:—

Conformity only partial.

Thomas Cartwright.

Laurence Humphrey.

Thomas Sampson.

1. That all holy days, except Sundays and the festivals relating to Christ, be abrogated.

2. That the minister in common prayer turn his face towards the people, that he may be heard and they edified.

[1] Cardwell.

3. That in the sacrament of baptism the sign of the cross be omitted, as tending to superstition.

4. That kneeling at communion should not be compulsory.

5. That it be sufficient for the minister in time of Divine service and ministering the sacraments to wear a surplice.

6. That the use of organs be removed.

On these points of ceremonial the debate was very warm, ecclesiastical opinion being so equally divided that the resolutions were rejected by a majority of only *one*— fifty-eight voting for, fifty-nine against. The contest soon became embittered. The 'troubles of Frankfort' were transferred to England. At this stage no question of doctrine was involved; it was at first wholly one of Church order and discipline. The bishops would have devised some plan of compromise, or have connived at the irregularities. Several of the queen's Council, Leicester, Burleigh, and others, were disposed to favour the wishes of the advanced Reformers; but Elizabeth withstood all. Making use of the power that the royal supremacy gave, she addressed peremptory letters to Archbishop Parker, requiring him to repress the irregularities prevailing, and to exercise stricter methods of discipline for the future. Under royal pressure, Parker and other bishops prepared to exact obedience unto the law. Supplementary rules and orders to the Injunctions were issued, entitled 'Advertisements, partly for due order in the public administration of Common Prayers, and using the Holy Sacraments, and partly for the apparel of all persons ecclesiastical, by virtue of the Queen's Majesty letters commanding the same.'[1] The influence of the vestment controversy appears in the restriction of the use of the cope to the clergy of cathedral and collegiate churches; there 'in ministration of the holy communion . . . the principal minister shall use a cope with gospeller and epistles agreeably,' and 'at all other prayers to be said at the communion table to use no copes, but surplices.' In other churches the requirement made is 'that every minister saying any public prayers,

The 'Advertisements,' 1564.

Further regulations concerning vestments.

---

[1] Cardwell, *Docum. Ann.*, i. p. 321.

or ministering of the sacrament, shall wear a comely surplice with sleeves.' This was the only concession made to the German school of Reformers. It was still required of the clergy that they should never appear out of doors but in their square caps, gowns, or canonical coats. The *Advertisements* directed against the ultra-Reformers occasioned the first open separation of the Nonconformists from the Church of England.

<small>First open separation of Nonconformists.</small>

To compel the London clergy, who were especially unconformable, to wear the appointed habits they were summoned to Lambeth Palace. There, on the 25th March, Archbishop Parker met them, and presented before them a clergyman arrayed in the required vestments. Each minister was asked if he were willing to be so attired. Sixty-one promised to conform, thirty-seven absolutely refused. Those who refused were suspended, with intimation that if they did not conform within three months they were to be deprived.

It is beside our purpose to trace the course of the embittered conflict that ensued between the thorough-going Reformers, who soon obtained the name of *Puritans*, and the more conservative Reformers, content with the prescribed form of teaching and ceremonial. It is impossible to say whether any concessions would have retained the Puritan party; but the course that was adopted had the effect of precipitating a separation which was, perhaps, inevitable, at the same time that it seemed to afford a justification to those who were the immediate sufferers.

CHAPTER XXIV.

DOCTRINES OF THE ENGLISH REFORMATION.

THE doctrines of the English Reformation bear the impress of no one dominant mind. There was no master-intellect, no one profound theologian whose influence moulded the form of religious belief in England, as that of Luther in Germany, Calvin in Geneva, John Knox in Scotland. If Wycliffe, the great forerunner of the Reformation, had lived one hundred and thirty years later, his commanding intellect might have stamped upon the religious thought of England the peculiarities of his great intellectual and spiritual power. The prominent feature of the English Reformation theology is its eclecticism. The English Reformers did not attempt to develop a creed out of their own internal consciousness. Their inconsistencies, their variations, their controversies, their very retractations, witness to the gradualness with which the new light dawned upon them, and dispelled the old darkness. From research into Christian antiquity many of their old beliefs were corrected; from the Reformers abroad, who had advanced before them in the new faith, from Luther, from Zwingli, from Calvin, they received much; but the overruling sentiment was that the battle of Reform was to be fought and won, not by appeal to ancient opinions, but from the authority of the Scriptures. Patient, earnest study of the Scriptures was an eminent characteristic of Tindale, Cranmer, Ridley, Latimer, Hooper. By them all traditional authority was regarded as insufficient for the establishment of the faith. As expressed in one of the Articles of their belief, 'Things ordained as necessary for salvation have neither strength nor authority, unless it may be declared that they are taken out of Holy Scripture.'

In the Reformation principle of biblical interpretation

Eclecticism prominent feature of the English Reformation theology.

Authority of the Scriptures paramount.

there was a strong reaction from the scholastic system. Tindale, speaking of the scholastic divines, says: 'They divide the Scriptures in four senses—the literal, tropological, allegorical, and anagogical. The literal sense is become nothing at all.'[1] The Reformers contended for the original and literal sense of the Scriptures. Profoundly reverencing the Bible as a revelation of God to awaken men to a new life, they regarded the message as one to be interpreted by itself. The Reformers in all their discussions maintained the fact of inspiration, without binding themselves to any precise theory.

Principles of biblical interpretation.

Another sign of the reaction from the over-speculation of scholastic divines on the nature and being of God is seen in the prominence given by the Reformers to the manifestation of God in redemption. Melanchthon said: 'There is no reason why we should devote ourselves much to these most lofty subjects—the doctrine of God, of the unity of God, of the trinity of God.' Luther wished theology to begin at once with Christ Jesus. 'True Christian divinity,' he said, 'commandeth us not to search out the nature of God, but to know His will set out to us in Christ.' Again: 'I let pass all curious speculation touching the Divine Majesty, and stay myself in the humanity of Christ; and so I learn truly to know the will of God.'[2]

Prominence given to the manifestation of God in redemption.

The Reformers had no questioning as to the being of God. They were content to accept the doctrine of the Trinity as set forth in the] three Creeds—the Apostles', the Nicene, and the Athanasian. Their theology turned on the questions, What shall a man do to be saved? and, How shall a sinner be justified before a holy and a righteous God? To this the New Testament, and especially the Epistles to the Romans and Galatians, returned the answer. In them Luther found a revelation of God which stirred the heart of Christendom. To read Luther's famous *Commentary on the Epistle to the Galatians* is to feel that the great doctrine of God's free pardoning love, revealed in the person and

Justification by faith.

[1] *Obedience of a Christian Man*, 'The Four Senses of Scripture,' p. 265 (R.T.S. ed.).
[2] *Commentary on Galatians*, Introduction.

work of Christ, received through faith, was a fresh declaration to the hearts of sin-burdened men. It was infinitely more than a mere dogma. It was a gospel of 'grace, peace, and victory in the Lord Jesus Christ,' to thousands and tens of thousands of persons who in fear trembled before God as an exactor and judge. It was 'new doctrine' to hear that 'Christ is no Moses, no exactor, no giver of laws, but a giver of grace, a Saviour, and one that is full of mercy and goodness freely given, and bountifully giving unto us.'[1]

In such teaching there was an unveiling of the thought and heart of God that met its response in the belief, the gratitude of those who had all their life long been subject to the bondage of the teaching, penances, ceremonies of the Romish Church. Before the gospel of pardon, that waits for nothing but acceptance on the part of the soul, as the gloom of night before the rising sun, away from the heart of men went the necessity for purchased indulgences to defend one from the anger of God, or of saints to intercede with Him who beseeches us to be reconciled, and of painful penances to wring forgiveness of sins from Him who died that they might be forgiven.

The charge of Antinomianism against the Reformers' doctrine of justification by faith is opposed to the constant stress laid by them on holiness and good works, as the necessary manifestation of justifying faith. That Luther and other Reformers often spoke contemptuously of the law and of works is true, but never in a manner that may not be reasonably explained as due to the reaction from Roman teaching. Luther calls faith 'a living, busy, active, mighty thing,' and declares that it is as impossible to separate works from faith as heat from fire. 'Faith,' he elsewhere says, 'embraceth and wrappeth itself in Christ Jesus, the Son of God, who being apprehended by faith, giveth unto us righteousness and life.' The sentence inscribed on the bronze pedestal of Luther's statue at Worms, 'Faith is but the right and true life in God,' indicates that the Reformer's doctrine of 'faith in the free forgiveness of God is the fountain of a new life of holiness which depends not on fear and homage to law, but on gratitude and on filial sentiments.'

On the mysterious questions of predestination, election,

[1] Luther, *Comm. Gal.*, ii. 20.

and reprobation, the Reformers generally were united in opinion. Their teaching was Calvinistic, or more properly Augustinianism. The prominence given to these subjects in the Reformation theology is a sign of the reaction against the papal doctrine of human merit. *Doctrines of predestination, election, and reprobation.*

The great topic of doctrinal controversy among Protestants in the early history of the Reformation was concerning the sacraments. Luther, in most points the boldest, the most spiritual of the Reformers, on the subject of the sacraments was most hesitant and superstitious. In the water of baptism he believed an actual change to be wrought, so that 'it was no longer water, but had the power of the blood of Christ.' In the bread and the wine of the Lord's supper he taught, under the name of 'consubstantiation,' a corporeal real presence of the body and blood of Christ, thus giving, as has been observed, 'a fresh lease of life' to the old dogma of transubstantiation. *The great point of controversy the sacraments. Lutheran doctrine.*

To the 'clear-headed and intrepid Zwingli,' more than to any other of the Reformers, is the Protestant Church indebted for a doctrine at once more rational and spiritual. 'In language perhaps too austerely exact, but transparently clear,' says an eminent ecclesiastical historian of the Church of England, 'Zwingli recognised the full biblical truth that the operation of the Divine Spirit on the soul can only be through moral means, and that the moral influence of the sacrament is chiefly or solely through the potency of its unique commemoration of the most touching and transcendent event in history. This is the view which in substance became the doctrine of all the Reformed Churches; viz., the Swiss, South German, French, and English Churches.'[1] The cautious, slow-moving mind of Cranmer, after abandoning the doctrine of transubstantiation, halted for a while in the Lutheran doctrine; but Ridley held the Swiss doctrine, and Cranmer afterwards avowed himself of the same mind. Traheron, writing to Bullinger in 1548, after a public disputation on the subject of the eucharist, said: 'The Archbishop of Canterbury openly, firmly, and *Zwinglian. The Swiss doctrine that of the English Church.*

[1] Stanley, *Christian Institutions*, p. 97.

learnedly maintained your opinions on the subject. Next followed the Bishop of Rochester [Ridley]. I perceive,' adds the writer, 'that it is all over with Lutheranism, now those who were considered its principal and almost only supporters have altogether come over to our side.' Bishop Hooper, two years later, in his *Brief and Clear Confession of the Christian Faith*, says, 'I believe that the holy supper of the Lord is not a sacrifice, but only a remembrance and commemoration of the holy sacrifice of Jesus Christ.'[1] With this agrees a memorable statement of Hooker: 'The real presence of Christ's most blessed body and blood is not to be sought for in the sacrament, but in the worthy receiver of the sacrament.'[2]

On the question of the future life, the Reformers unanimously rejected the doctrine of purgatory and prayers for the dead, with its gross superstitions and abuses. Without discussion, the Reformers accepted the Augustinian teaching concerning the future of the impenitent and the blessedness of the righteous.

Teaching concerning the future life.

In the Thirty-nine Articles of the Church of England we have a summary of what was generally believed and taught by the leading Reformers, before the open separation of the Puritan party. For a long time Elizabeth withstood the desire of the bishops to issue an authoritative statement of doctrine. Whether it was her spirit of compromise and conciliation towards those who had been brought up in the Roman doctrine, or personal dislike to the issue of a dogmatic confession of faith in such a transition time of belief, for nine years she refused her sanction to a revision of the old Articles, prepared by Parker, and sanctioned by the Convocation of 1562. In that revision the number of articles was reduced from forty-two to thirty-nine. Four new articles were introduced; viz:

The Thirty-nine Articles represent the doctrines of the leading Reformers.

Revision of the Forty-two Articles.

Article V. *Of the Holy Ghost.*
Article XII. *Of Good Works.*
Article XXIX. *Of the Wicked which eat not the Body of Christ in the use of the Lord's Supper.* Obviously meant to

---

[1] Article XXVIII.   [2] *Eccl. Pol.*, v. 67, 6.

condemn the doctrine that there is any reception but a spiritual reception.

Article XXX. *On administering the sacrament in both kinds.*

The omissions through the growing influence of Calvin's views are significant. A clause concerning Christ's preaching to the spirits in prison originally belonging to Article III. was struck out; an article on Grace, favouring freewill;[1] another on Blasphemy against the Holy Ghost,[2] and one on the Moral Commandments of the Law.[3] And the four specially referred to in the account previously given of the Forty-two Articles. Twenty-two of the Articles were altered, in more or less important omissions or substitutions. In this revision, some of the changes introduced were Lutheran in tendency, several clauses being taken direct from the Wurtemberg Confession. The Articles, now thirty-nine in number, were submitted to the queen.

Elizabeth's treatment of the Articles was eminently characteristic. She 'diligently read and sifted them.' On her own authority she struck out one of the newly inserted Articles, and one of the most strongly Protestant in its declaration of the doctrine of the Lord's supper, and introduced into Article XX. the clause: 'The Church hath power to decree rites or ceremonies, and authority in controversies on faith.' After nearly a year's delay the Articles appeared, as authorized by the queen, thirty-eight in number, and with an insertion not approved by Convocation. The bishops resented the alteration, issued an English version of the Articles, ignored the clause inserted by the queen, but yielded to the rejection of Article XXIX. *Elizabeth's treatment of the Articles. Thirty-eight Articles, 1562.*

Eight years after (1571), the Articles, finally revised by Bishop Jewel, received the sanction of both Convocations, and were issued in their present form. By a curious oversight, the Articles as published in Latin omitted the queen's clause concerning Church authority, but retained it in the English version. Both contained the Twenty ninth *Thirty-nine Articles issued in 1571.*

---

[1] Art. X. of 1552.
[2] Art. XVI. of 1552.
[3] Art. XIX. of 1552.

Article, concerning the wicked not eating the body of Christ. A law was passed, in the same year, ordering that 'the clergy should subscribe to all the Articles, which only concern the confession of a true Christian faith and the doctrine of the sacraments.' In this final revision, it was Bishop Jewel's opinion that the Anglican Church was brought into accord with the Protestant Churches on the Continent. Writing to Peter Martyr, he said, 'As to matters of doctrine, we do not differ from you by a nail's breadth.'

Further expression of Reformation doctrine is found in the Second Book of Homilies, sanctioned by the Convocation of 1562. The queen's aversion to identifying herself with doctrinal teaching was again seen in the reluctant assent given to their authorization 'to be read in every parish church.' The number of homilies in this series is nearly double that of the first. Bishop Cox was the editor, and his fellow bishops, Parker, Grindal, and Pilkington, the contributors.

Second Book of Homilies, 1562.

By the authority of the same Convocation that issued the homilies, a larger catechism than that contained in the Prayer-Book was provided for the use of schools and the instruction of communicants. It was written by Nowell, Dean of St. Paul's. He was among the exiles of Strassburg in the reign of Queen Mary. It is of him the story is told, that, when preaching at St. Paul's, he spoke in a way displeasing to the queen, who was favourable to the use of crosses and crucifixes, concerning the sign of the cross. To show her authority in these things in the presence of the congregation, she called aloud to the preacher, 'Leave that alone.' Unheeding the interruption, he proceeded. 'To your text, Mr. Dean,' shouted the queen. 'To your text. Leave that. We have heard enough of that. To your subject.'[1] It is a characteristic incident of how in all matters of faith, discipline, and doctrine she sought, not always with success, to lay down the law for her clergy.

Nowell's Catechism. Prepared 1562, sanctioned 1571.

[1] Froude, vol. vii. p. 256.

CHAPTER XXV.

'THE ROMANIST MARTYRS.'

It is a humiliating fact that in the Protestant struggle with the papacy a considerable number of Roman Catholics were executed, and others grievously oppressed. Romanists are fully justified in calling attention to the 'troubles of their Catholic forefathers,' whose nonconformity was treated as a political offence, and as such dealt with by the Government. Queen Elizabeth exercised her supremacy as 'supreme governor' of the Church with thorough Tudor vigour, alike towards those who held puritanical objection to the Reformed Liturgy and those who clung to Roman doctrine and practice. That the Romanists suffered more severely than the Puritans was because their allegiance to the pope conflicted with their loyalty to the Crown. In the days of Elizabeth Romanism was not merely a religious question, it was a national question as to who was to rule in England—the pope or the queen. No Romanist writer can disprove the fact that the Roman Catholic Church, as represented by Pope Pius V., aimed at the deposition and even death of the queen, to whom the hearts of the mass of the people were loyally attached.

The quiet of the first eleven years of Elizabeth's reign was broken in 1569 by the Romanist rebellion in the North, the story of which has been graphically told by Mr. Froude. The leaders of the revolt were the greatest nobles of Northern England, the Earls of Northumberland and Westmoreland; their purpose was to subvert the government of Elizabeth in the interests of Mary Queen of Scots, and to re-establish the ancient faith. The insurgents began by taking possession of the city of Durham and the cathedral, where the Protestant Bible and Prayer-Book were torn to pieces, the communion table thrown down, and mass again triumphantly celebrated. Protestantism had

The Romanist rebellion, 1569.

gained little or no footing in the North of England. It was officially reported to Elizabeth that 'there were not ten gentlemen that favoured her majesty's proceedings,' and that among the people the 'old popish doctrine' prevailed. Had the Romanist lords of the North received help from Spain, as they hoped, the issue of the revolt might have proved calamitous to the Reformation movement; as it was, the same fate attended it as befel the half-Protestant rising in Mary's days. Confiscations and executions followed in a stern and ruthless policy of repression.

This rebellion was immediately followed by the pope's bull of excommunication, published in February, 1570, excommunicating Elizabeth by name, and absolving her subjects from any oath of allegiance that might have been taken, and forbidding her people to obey her, on pain of being themselves excommunicated. The news was soon known in England. A copy of the bull was found one morning nailed in defiance upon the door of the Bishop of London's palace, the deed of an enthusiast, who soon suffered death for his daring.

The bull of excommunication and deposition, 1570.

In self-defence against the power that had secretly stirred the rising in the North, and then openly in a bull of deposition sought to rouse a general insurrection throughout the realm, the Parliament of 1571 passed a statute forbidding the recognition of any bull, brief, or papal enactment, or of any person claiming to act under the authority of the Bishop of Rome. Offenders against this enactment were to be deemed guilty of high treason, and to suffer death as traitors. At the same time it was made high treason for any priest to absolve any one from heresy, or to reconcile any one to the Church of Rome, or for any one to receive such absolution at his hand.

How real the danger was that threatened the queen's life is seen in the Ridolfi plot of the same year, a deliberate attempt for the capture or assassination of the queen, and which led to the execution of the Duke of Norfolk for high treason. In the August of the following year came the horrible tidings of the massacre of St. Bartholomew. A thrill of horror went through the country. The court went into mourning. The queen's Council spoke of it as 'the most heinous act since the crucifixion of Jesus

Christ.' Among the people a report was current that the massacre was only part of a more general plan for the extirpation of Protestantism everywhere. This combination of circumstances did much to increase the fears of English Protestants, and to arouse a sense of detestation against Rome and all her ways.

Protestant convictions cannot lessen admiration for the courage and zeal of the young Roman Catholic missioners, chiefly priests, who in a time of persecution came to strengthen the faith of their co-religionists, and to minister to them the rites of their religion. <small>The seminary priests.</small> They came in companies from English seminaries on the Continent founded by William Allen, afterwards Cardinal Allen. Their leader was Edmund Campian, an Englishman, a member of the new religious order of the Jesuits, and the first of that order to set foot in England. The presence of these seminary priests is hopelessly mixed up with the religious and political disputes of the times. As missioners, the priests claimed to have no ulterior purpose than this spiritual ministry. In popular estimation they were conspirators against the queen's life, who could not be allowed to escape on any pretence of religious duty: a suspicion sustained by the number of publications industriously disseminated at this time in defence of the old religion and against a 'female papacy, unlawfully begotten, and lawfully deposed by the pope.' A Romanist writer asserts that in 1584 there were not less than three hundred seminary priests in England.

Against the Romanist missioners severe enactments were passed. It was enacted in the Parliament of 1581 that any person who persuaded another to forsake the religion of the Reformed faith was guilty of high treason. <small>Laws against Romanists.</small> Any priest saying mass was to forfeit two hundred marks, and be imprisoned for a year, and any person willingly hearing mass was to forfeit a sum of one hundred marks, in addition to a year's imprisonment. Finally an edict of expulsion was passed against the seminary priests, who in the January of 1585 were commanded to leave the country within forty days: any remaining were to be regarded as traitors, and suffer accordingly. 'No persons were to receive, relieve, or maintain them; those who did so were to be treated as felons, and suffer death and forfeiture, as in cases of felony.'

Under these Acts, enforced by the action of the Court of High Commission, a long succession of revolting cruelties and barbarities upon priests, laymen, and even women ensued. It is an oversight upon the part of Mr. Green, when he says that under the Act of 1581 'no layman was brought to the block,' and that the work of 'bloodshed was reserved wholly for priests.' According to the Romanist estimate, two hundred and sixty persons were put to death for saying mass and hearing mass; of these, seventy-three were laymen, and three were women. The priests, under sentence of treason, were 'hanged, bowelled, and quartered;' the laymen, for giving shelter and sustenance to the ministers of their faith, shared the ghastly accompaniments of a traitor's death—were hanged as felons. Few will be so ungenerous as to deny to these sufferers the honour due to those whose crime was faithfulness to their religion, and who met their end with courage and patience. Others of like faith suffered imprisonment; some, not having the means to pay the fines laid upon them for refusing to attend Protestant services, were stripped of their clothes, and whipped through the streets of the town where they dwelt. The story of the sufferings of the English Romanists in the days of Elizabeth is a salutary warning to mutual forbearance, when we read instances as piteous and as heroic as in the times of her predecessor. It is not a story to be shirked, nor glossed over in its ghastly details. The strongest Protestant will most honour those who in the cause of their religion were faithful unto death.

Yet, in comparing the number of victims in Queen Mary's reign with those put to death by her successor, it must not be forgotten that Mary reigned only five years, while Elizabeth reigned forty-five. Nor must the fact be overlooked that about the Marian martyrs no suspicion of treason gathers. Their offences were wholly ecclesiastical, concerning matters of spiritual belief, mainly concerning the sacrament of the Lord's supper. The Marian martyrs died in defence of what they believed to be the doctrines of Scripture as opposed to those of the Church of Rome. The sufferers in Elizabeth's reign died as those who perished in the Wyatt rebellion, who would have dethroned Mary for Lady Jane Grey or the Princess

Elizabeth; they were executed under what was regarded as proof of disloyalty to the sovereign. Elizabeth had worked hard to conciliate the Romanists during the early years of her reign; but after the pope's bull of deposition, and after the repeated endeavour of the Romanists at his instigation to dethrone her, it was difficult to see how those who recognised the sovereignty of the pope as superior to the authority of the Crown could be loyal to one whom he had declared deposed.

Happily, we live in days when the triumph of Protestant principles is seen in political liberty, in religious light and freedom. The principles of the Protestant faith make intolerance of another's religious belief impossible. But the same principles compel those who hold them to make it clear that tolerance is not indifference. Tolerance has been well defined as, 'The willing consent that other men should hold and express opinions with which we disagree, until they are convinced by reason that these opinions are untrue.' Amid the significant signs of the revival of Romanism in the present day, and of the active endeavour to un-Protestantize, as far as possible, the doctrine and ritual of the National Episcopal Church of our country, it is only by the establishment of the truth of God in the faith and love of the people that the true principles of Protestantism can be maintained, and the dominance of Romanism prevented.

In unswerving loyalty to Jesus Christ, and by personal faith in Him, through the saving power of the Holy Spirit of God, as 'the one Mediator between God and man, the man Christ Jesus, who gave Himself a ransom for all,' the Reformers of old bore their witness as confessors and martyrs.

In these truths, full of mighty inspirations, there is the assurance of life eternal to every one that believeth, and the fundamental principles of the English Protestantism, which has done so much to win for our country liberty and blessedness in freedom of faith.

CHRONOLOGICAL SUMMARY.

INTRODUCTORY.

Date.	Event.	Reign.	Archbishop of Canterbury.	Pope.	Contemporary Events.
1164	Constitutions of Clarendon restrict the power of the clergy.	Henry II.	Thomas Beckett.	Alexander III.	
1165	Council at Oxford condemns a company of Germans found teaching heretical doctrine.				
1166	Assize of Clarendon orders all heretics to be treated as outlaws.				
1170	Assassination of Archbishop Thomas at Canterbury.				Peter Waldo begins preaching at Lyons about this time. 1202 Death of Abbot Joachim.
1174	Henry II. does penance at the tomb of St. Thomas of Canterbury.				
1208	England placed under an Interdict.	John.	Stephen Langton.	Innocent III.	1209-29 Crusade against the Albigenses.
1213	John receives his kingdom as a papal fief.	Henry III.		Honorius III.	
1221	Dominican Friars land in England.				Albert the Great joins the Dominicans.
1224	Arrival of Franciscan Friars.		Edmund Rich.	Gregory IX.	1222 Alexander of Hales joins the Franciscans.
1235	Robert Grossetete Bishop of Lincoln.		Boniface.	Innocent IV.	
1250	Roger Bacon teaching at Oxford.		Robert Winchelsey.	Boniface VIII.	1274 Bonaventura and Thomas Aquinas died. 1282 The Sicilian Vespers.
1302	Duns Scotus teaching at Oxford.				
1322	William of Occam leading the revolt of the Franciscans against the pope.	Edward II.	Simon Meopham	John XXII.	1294 Roger Bacon died.
1324	John Wycliffe born about this time.				
1325	Thomas Bradwardine at Oxford.	Edward III.	John Straford.	Clement VI.	
1347	Fitzralph, Archbishop of Armagh, preaching against the Friars.		Thomas Bradwardine.		
1348-'50	First of successive visitations of 'the Black Death.'				
1349	The Statute of Labourers passed.		Simon Islip.		
1356	Death of Richard Rolle of Hampole, author of The Pricke of Conscience. Anonymous publication of The Last Age of the Church.			Innocent VI.	
1362	Longland's Piers the Ploreman.			Urban V.	

Wycliffan Reformation.

Year	Event	Monarch	Archbishop	Pope	
1366	Wycliffe opposes papal exactions.				
1368	Wycliffe's treatise *De Dominio* appears.				
1370	About this time Wycliffe first sent forth his 'Poor Priests.'				1369 Birth of John Huss.
1377	Wycliffe cited before the Bishop of London. Papal bulls against Wycliffe.	Richard II.	Simon Sudbury.	Gregory XI.	1378-1409 The Papal Schism.
1381	Wycliffe's declarations against Transubstantiation. Poll Tax levied upon all persons above 15 years of age. Revolt of peasantry, and monasteries attacked.		William Courtenay.	{ Urban VI. { Clement VII.	
1382	Wycliffe and Hereford's translation of the Bible finished.				
1384	Death of Wycliffe, 31st December.				
1387	Chaucer writes his *Canterbury Tales*.				
1388	Revised Version of Wycliffe and Hereford's Bible by John Purvey.				
1395	Lollard petition to Parliament.				
1399	Abdication of Richard II. and the accession of the House of Lancaster to the throne in the person of Henry IV.	Henry IV.	Thomas Arundel.	{ Boniface IX. { Benedict, 1394.	
1401	The Statute of Heretics (*De Haeretico Comburendo*) passed. The first Lollard martyr, Sawtre, burnt.				
1409	Council at Oxford for suppression of Lollardy.			Alexander V.	1410 Burning of Wycliffe's book by the Archbishop of Prague.
1413	Sir John Oldcastle, condemned as a heretic, escapes from the Tower.	Henry V.		John XXIII.	1414-18 Council of Constance.
1414	Persecution of Lollards. Rumoured Lollard conspiracy.		Henry Chichely.		1415 Martyrdom of John Huss. 1416 Martyrdom of Jerome of Prague.
1416	Archbishop Chichely's persecution of Lollards.			Martin V.	
1428	Burning of Wycliffe's bones.	Henry VI.			1452 Birth of Savonarola.
1450	Bishop Pecock's *Repressor* published.		John Stafford. Thomas Bourgchier.	Nicholas V.	
1455	Wars of the Roses begin.			Calixtus III.	
1457	Condemnation and recantation of Bishop Pecock.				
1476	Caxton sets up his printing press at Westminster.	Edward IV. Henry VII.		Sextus IV.	1480 The Spanish Inquisition established by Ferdinand and Isabella.
1485	Union of the Houses of York and Lancaster in Henry VII., first of the House of Tudor. Renewal of persecution of Lollards.			Innocent VIII.	

THE GREAT REFORMATION.

Date	Event	Reign	Archbishop Canterbury	Pope	Contemporary Events
1493	Colet leader of new movement for reform at Oxford.	Henry VII.	Morton.	Alexander VI.	
1503-32	Persecution and martyrdom of Lollards in various parts of the country.				
1516	Erasmus' Greek Testament published.	Henry VIII.	Warham.	Leo X.	1517 Luther's *Theses* published. 1518 Zwingli preaching at Zurich. 1520 Luther publishes *Babylonish Captivity of the Church*. 1521 Luther at the Diet of Worms.
1521	Henry VIII. writes against Luther, and receives title, Defender of Faith.				
1523	Suppression of monasteries begun by Wolsey.				
1525	Tindale's English New Testament published.			Clement VII.	The Peasants' War.
1527	Application of Henry VIII. to the pope to examine the lawfulness of his marriage.				
1529	Wolsey dismissed from office. Sir Thomas More chancellor.				1530 Confession of Augsburg.
1531	Submission of the clergy.				
1533	Cranmer and Gardiner pronounce Henry's marriage with Catherine (Charles V.'s aunt) null and void.		Cranmer.		1534 Society of Jesus founded by Loyola.
1534	First Reformed *Primer* published.				
1535	Thomas Cromwell appointed vicar-general. First complete printed English Bible published (Coverdale's). Visitation of the monasteries.			Paul II.	Calvin's *Institutes* published.
1536	Suppression of the lesser monasteries.				Tindale strangled and burnt at Vilvorde.
1537	'Pilgrimage of Grace.' Royal licence given to the printing of Matthew's Bible.				
1538	The pope excommunicates and deposes Henry VIII.				
1539	The Great Bible published. Suppression of all monasteries in England. Law of the Six Articles.				
1540	Cromwell died on the scaffold.				1542 Calvin's ecclesiastical polity in Geneva.
1543	Tindale's translations forbidden.				
1544	Introduction of English Litany.				
1545	The king's *Primer*.				Council of Trent opened. Death of Luther.
1546	Anne Askewe and others burnt for denying transubstantiation.				

The Protestant Protectorate, 1547-53.

1547	Duke of Somerset Protector. Visitation of churches and Injunctions issued. First Book of Homilies. Preaching of Latimer, Hooper, Ridley, Knox, Bradford, 1547-53. Peter Martyr at Oxford, Martin Bucer and Paul Fagius at Cambridge.	Edward VI.			

1548	Introduction of English Communion Service.			
1549	First Prayer-Book of Edward VI. and Act of Uniformity passed. Northumberland protector.			
1552	Execution of Somerset. Second Prayer-Book of Edward VI. and Act of Uniformity. Suppression of chantries, guilds, etc.		Julius III.	
1553	XLII. Articles.			

The Catholic Reaction, 1553–8.

		Mary.		
1554	Wyatt's insurrection (June). Marriage of Mary with Philip of Spain (July). Reconciliation with Rome (November).			
1555	The Southwark Commission (January). The martyrdoms begin (February). Ridley and Latimer burnt at Oxford (October). Troubles at Frankfort.			Marcellus III., pope 3 weeks. Paul IV.
1556	Archbishop Cranmer burnt at Oxford (March 21st). Exasperating and seditious writings of Protestant exiles.		Cardinal Pole (Mar. 22nd).	
1557	Geneva Testament. Famine and pestilence in England.			Charles V. retires to a monastery.
1558	Death of Mary (November 17th). Death of Cardinal Pole (November 18th).			Death of Charles V.

Protestantism Re-established, 1558.

		Elizabeth.	Parker.	Pius IV.
1559	The royal supremacy restored. Second revision of Book of Common Prayer issued with Act of Uniformity. High Commission Court appointed. Statutes against heresy repealed.			
1560				1560 Death of Melanchthon.
1562	Jewel's Apology for the Church of England published. Second Book of Homilies.			
1563	Foxe's Book of Martyrs published.			Council of Trent closed.
1564	Advertisements concerning Vestments. Thirty-seven of the London clergy refuse to conform to clerical vestments.			1565 Beza's Latin Testament published. English College at Douai founded. Persecution of Protestants in the Netherlands, 18,000 slain.
1568	Bishops' Bible published.			
1569	Catholic revolt in North of England.			
1570	The pope excommunicates Elizabeth. Thomas Cartwright expelled from Cambridge.			Pius V.
1571	Severe laws against the Catholics. Queen sanctions XXXIX. Articles.			

APPENDIX I.

LIST OF ABBEYS, PRIORIES, AND FRIARIES OF ENGLAND.

NORTHUMBERLAND:
 Lindisfarne (Benedictine).
 Tynemouth ,,
 Newcastle ,,
 Newminster (Cistercian).
 Brinkburn (Augustinian).
 Hexham ,,

CUMBERLAND:
 St. Bees (Benedictine).
 Carlisle (Augustinian).

DURHAM:
 Durham (Benedictine).
 Jarrow ,,
 Wearmouth ,,

YORKSHIRE:
 Grosmont (Benedictine).
 Handale ,,
 Richmond (Benedictine, Præmonstratensian)
 Rosedale (Benedictine).
 Selby ,,
 Whitby ,,
 York ,,
 Mount Grace (Carthusian).
 Hull ,,
 Bylau (Cistercian).
 Fountains ,,
 Jervaux ,,
 Kirkstall ,,
 Rievaulx ,,
 Sawley ,,
 Monk Bretton (Cluniac).
 Pontefract ,,
 Bolton (Augustinian).
 Bridlington ,,
 Guisbrough ,,
 Kirkham ,,
 Newburgh ,,
 Egglestone (Præmonstratensian.

YORKSHIRE (*continued*):
 Coverham (Præmonstratensian).
 Knaresborough (Trinitarian Friary).

LANCASHIRE:
 Lytham (Benedictine).
 Lancaster (Benedictine, Augustinian, Black Friars, Grey Friars.
 Penwortham (Benedictine).
 Upholland ,,
 Burscough (Augustinian).
 Cockersand ,,
 Preston (Gilbertine Friars).

CHESHIRE:
 Birkenhead (Benedictine).
 Chester ,,
 Combermere (Cistercian).
 Norton (Augustinian).

STAFFORDSHIRE:
 Brewood (Benedictine).
 Dudley (Cluniac).
 Stafford (Augustinian).
 Trentham ,,
 Stone ,,

DERBYSHIRE:
 Derby (Benedictine, Black Friars).
 Darley (Augustinian).
 Repton ,,
 Beauchief (Præmonstratensian).
 Dale (Præmonstratensian).

LEICESTERSHIRE:
 Hinckley (Benedictine).
 Langley ,,
 Leicester (Grey Friars, Austin Friars).

LEICESTERSHIRE (continued):
  Breedon (Augustinian).
  Launde   ,,
RUTLANDSHIRE:
  Brooke (Augustinian).
NOTTINGHAMSHIRE:
  Blyth (Benedictine).
  Beauvale (Carthusian).
  Rufford (Cistercian).
  Lenton (Cluniac).
  Newstead (Augustinian).
  Worksop   ,,
  Thurgarton   ,,
  Welbeck (Cluniac).
LINCOLNSHIRE:
  Bardney (Benedictine).
  Crowland   ,,
  Lincoln (Benedictine, Gilbertines).
  Spalding (Benedictine).
  Stamford   ,,
  Grimsby   ,,
  Humberstone ,,
  Stamford   ,,
  Epworth (Carthusian).
  Swineshead   ,,
  Kirkstead (Cistercian).
  Revesby   ,,
  Louth   ,,
  Elsham (Augustinian).
  Kyme   ,,
  Nocton   ,,
  Thornton   ,,
  Barlings (Præmonstratensian).
  Tupholm   ,,
NORTHAMPTONSHIRE:
  Peterborough (Benedictine).
  Pipewell (Cistercian).
  Northampton (Cluniac).
  Daventry   ,,
BEDFORDSHIRE:
  Elstow (Benedictine).
  Woburn (Cistercian).
  Dunstable (Augustinian, Black Friars).
  Bedford (Grey Friars).
HUNTINGDONSHIRE:
  St. Neots (Benedictine).
  Ramsey   ,,
  Saltrey (Cistercian).
  Huntingdon (Augustinian).
  Stoneley   ,,

CAMBRIDGESHIRE:
  Ely (Benedictine).
  Thorney   ,,
  Chatteris   ,,
  Cambridge (Gilbertines).
  Fordham   ,,
NORFOLK:
  Horsham (Benedictine).
  Norwich   ,,
  Wymondham   ,,
  Thetford (Benedictine, Cluniac, Augustinian).
  Bromholm (Cluniac).
  Castle Acre ,,
  Beeston (Augustinian).
  Coxford   ,,
  Flitcham   ,,
  Hickling   ,,
  Pentney   ,,
  Walsingham (Augustinian, Grey Friars).
  Westacre (Augustinian).
  Weybridge   ,,
  Crabhouse   ,,
  West Dereham (Præmonstratensian).
  Langley (Præmonstratensian).
  Lynn (Austin Friars, Black Friars, White Friars).
SUFFOLK:
  Bury St. Edmunds (Benedictine).
  Eye (Benedictine).
  Hoxne   ,,
  Bungay   ,,
  Ridlingfield (Benedictine).
  Wangford (Cluniac).
  Blythburgh (Augustinian).
  Butley   ,,
  Herringfleet ,,
  Ipswich   ,,
  Ixworth   ,,
  Leatheringham ,,
  Woodbridge   ,,
  Campsey   ,,
  Dunwich (Grey Friars).
ESSEX:
  Colchester (Benedictine, Augustinian, Crossed Friars).
  Hatfield (Benedictine).
  S. Walden   ,,
  Barking   ,,
  Hedingham   ,,

ESSEX (continued):
  Coggeshall (Cistercian).
  Stratford   ,,
  Tiltey   ,,
  Prittlewell (Cluniac).
  St. Osyth (Augustinian).
  L. Dunmow   ,,
  Leighs   ,,
  Waltham   ,,
  Beeleigh (Præmonstratensian).
  Chelmsford (Black Friars).
  Maldon (White Friars).

OXFORDSHIRE:
  Ensham (Benedictine).
  Oxford (Benedictine, Black Friars, Grey Friars, Austin Friars).
  Godstow (Benedictine).
  Studley   ,,
  Thame (Cistercian).
  Bicester (Augustinian).
  Dorchester   ,,
  Osney   ,,
  Goring   ,,

BUCKINGHAMSHIRE:
  Missenden (Augustinian).
  Noctele   ,,
  Aylesbury (Grey Friars).

BERKS:
  Abingdon (Benedictine).
  Henley   ,,
  Reading   ,,

MIDDLESEX:
  London (5 Benedictine, 1 Carthusian, 2 Augustinian, Austin Friars, Black Friars, Grey Friars, White Friars, Crossed Friars).

HERTS:
  St. Albans (Benedictine).
  Hertford   ,,
  Cheshunt   ,,
  Sopwell   ,,
  Royston (Augustinian).
  Wymondley   ,,
  Hitchin (Gilbertines, White Friars.
  King's Langley (Black Friars).

SURREY:
  Chertsey (Benedictine).
  Sheene (Carthusian).

SURREY (continued):
  Waverley (Cistercian).
  Bermondsey (Cluniac).
  Aldbury (Augustinian).
  Merton   ,,
  Reigate   ,,
  Southwark   ,,
  Tandridge   ,,

KENT:
  Canterbury (Benedictine, Augustinian).
  Dover (Benedictine).
  Faversham (Benedictine).
  Folkstone   ,,
  Rochester   ,,
  Sheppey   ,,
  Bexley (Cistercian).
  Monk Horton (Cluniac).
  Combwell (Augustinian).
  Westwood   ,,
  Dartford   ,,
  Mottenden (Trinitarian Friary).

SUSSEX:
  Battle (Benedictine).
  Boxgrove   ,,
  Eastbourne   ,,
  Rusper   ,,
  Robertsbridge (Cistercian).
  Lewes (Cluniac).
  Tortington (Augustinian).
  Michelham   ,,
  Hastings   ,,

HANTS:
  Winchester (Benedictine).
  Hyde   ,,
  Romsey   ,,
  Beaulieu (Cistercian).
  Netley   ,,
  Quarr   ,,
  Mottisfont (Augustinian).
  Selborne   ,,
  Southampton   ,,
  Porchester   ,,
  Twyneham   ,,
  Wintney (Cistercian).

WILTS:
  Malmsbury (Benedictine).
  Wilton   ,,
  Bradenstoke (Augustinian).
  Laycock   ,,
  Marlborough (Gilbertines).
  Purton   ,,

APPENDIX I.

DORSETSHIRE:
  Abbotsbury (Benedictine).
  Sherborne   ,,
  Shaftesbury   ,,
SOMERSETSHIRE:
  Bath (Benedictine).
  Dunster   ,,
  Glastonbury ,,
  Witham (Carthusian).
  Hinton   ,,
  Cleeve (Cistercian).
  Bruton (Augustinian).
  Keynsham   ,,
  Taunton   ,,
  Buckland   ,,
DEVONSHIRE:
  Exeter (Benedictine).
  Tavistock   ,,
  Totnes   ,,
  Buckland (Cistercian).
  Barnstaple (Cluniac).
  Plympton (Augustinian).
CORNWALL:
  Bodmin (Augustinian).
  St. Germans   ,,
  Launceston   ,,
GLOUCESTERSHIRE:
  Gloucester   (Benedictine, Augustinian).
  Tewkesbury (Benedictine).
  Winchcomb   ,,
  Hayles (Cistercian).
  Bristol (Augustinian).
  Cirencester   ,,
MONMOUTHSHIRE:
  Llanthony (Augustinian).
  Tintern (Cistercian).
  Usk (Benedictine).
  Monmouth   ,,
HEREFORDSHIRE:
  Hereford (Benedictine).
  Leominster   ,,
  Dore (Cistercian).
  Wigmore (Augustinian).
WORCESTERSHIRE:
  Evesham (Benedictine).
  Malvern   ,,

WORCESTERSHIRE (*continued*):
  Pershore (Benedictine).
  Worcester   ,,
  Bordesley (Cistercian).
WARWICKSHIRE:
  Coventry (Cistercian, Augustinian, Carthusian, White Friars).
  Henwood (Benedictine).
  Oldbury   ,,
  Polesworth   ,,
  Wroxhall   ,,
  Kenilworth (Augustinian).
  Maxstoke   ,,
  Warwick (Black Friars).
SHROPSHIRE:
  Bromfield (Benedictine).
  Shrewsbury   ,,
  Buildwas (Cistercian).
  Wenlock (Cluniac),
  Cherbury (Augustinian).
  Lilleshall   ,,
  Wombridge   ,,
RADNOR:
  Cym-Eir (Cistercian), in the vale of Clywedog.
BRECKNOCK:
  Brecknock (Benedictine).
GLAMORGAN:
  Neath (Cistercian).
CAERMARTHEN:
  Caermarthen (Augustinian).
PEMBROKE:
  St. Dogmel (Benedictine).
  Pembroke   ,,
  Haverfordwest (Augustinian).
CARDIGAN:
  Cardigan (Benedictine).
  Strata Florida (Cistercian).
MERIONETH:
  Cymmer Abbey (Cistercian).
CARNARVON:
  Bardsey (Benedictine).
  Beddgelert (Augustinian).
DENBIGH:
  Valle Crusis (Cistercian).

APPENDIX II.

DATES RELATIVE TO THE TRANSLATIONS AND USE OF THE BIBLE IN ENGLAND.

A.D.
- 1382. WYCLIFFE'S and HEREFORD'S MS. Bible.
- 1388. Same version revised by PURVEY.
- 1525. First printed English New Testament—TINDALE'S.
- 1535. First complete printed English Bible, COVERDALE'S.
- 1536. Cromwell orders the whole Bible, both in Latin and also in English, to be placed 'in the choir of every parish church,' 'for every man that will to look and read therein.'
- 1537. 'MATTHEW'S BIBLE' (John Rogers'), printed 'with the King's most gracious license.'
- 1538. Cromwell's order in anticipation of the publication of the 'Great Bible,' for 'one book of the whole Bible of the largest volume in English to be set up in the churches.'
- 1539. TAVERNER'S BIBLE.
- 1539. 'THE GREAT BIBLE,' or CROMWELL'S BIBLE, prepared under the editorship of Coverdale.
- 1540. Same version with Prologue by Cranmer, and therefore called CRANMER'S BIBLE.
- 1540. A proclamation ordering a copy of the Bible, 'of the largest volume,' to be provided by the curate and parishioners of every parish, under a penalty of 40s. per month.
- 1541. A Brief published enforcing the same.
- 1543. Reading of the Scriptures restricted, and use of Tindale's translation forbidden.
- 1547. The Protector Somerset's injunction directing that the whole Bible in English of the largest volume should be set up in every church.
- 1553. Mary's proclamation forbidding any 'from henceforth to preach, or by way of reading in churches and other public or private places, except in schools of the university, to interpret or teach any Scripture.'
- 1555. A proclamation calling in all service-books issued in reign of Edward VI., and of 'all books and writings teaching against the doctrine of the pope and his Church.'

1557. The GENEVA TESTAMENT.
1559. Re-issue of the Injunction of Edward VI.'s reign, that the whole Bible in English of the largest volume should be set up in every church.
1560. The GENEVA BIBLE.
1568. The BISHOPS' BIBLE.
1572. Same version revised.

APPENDIX III.

REFORMATION FORMULARIES OF FAITH.

A.D.
1536. Ten Articles devised by the King's Highness Majesty to establish Christian Quietness and Unity.
1537. *The Institution of a Christian Man*, containing the exposition of the Apostles' Creed, the Seven Sacraments, Ten Commandments, the Pater Noster, Ave Maria, Justification and Purgatory. [Called the Bishops' Book.]
1539. Six Articles, enforcing transubstantiation, declaring communion in both kinds unnecessary, marriage of priests unlawful, monastic vows of celibacy binding, and the necessity of masses and of auricular confession.
1543. *The Necessary Doctrine and Erudition for any Christian Man.* [A Romanist revision of the Bishops' Book, and in contradistinction called the King's Book.]
1544. The Litany published in English.
1547. First Book of Homilies published.
1548. The Communion Service published in England.
1549. The Book of Common Prayer.
1552. First Revised Book of Common Prayer.
1553. The Forty-two Articles (Cranmer).
1558. Second Revised Book of Common Prayer.
1562. The Thirty-eight Articles.
1562. Second Book of Homilies.
1571. The Thirty-nine Articles.

APPENDIX IV.

WORKS FOR REFERENCE ON THE HISTORY OF RELIGIOUS REFORM IN ENGLAND:

I.—MONASTIC ENGLAND.

The standard works of reference for detailed information of the history of the English monasteries from their first institution to the dissolution in the sixteenth century are :—

Dugdale's *Monasticon Anglicanum*. (Ed. by Caley, Ellis, and Bandinel.)

Stevens' *History of Ancient Abbeys, Monasteries, Hospitals, Cathedrals and Collegiate Churches*.

Tanner's *Notitia Monastica*.

For the history of the settlement of the Friars in England, see *Monumenta Franciscana*. (Ed. by J. S. Brewer for the Rolls Series). A good general outline of this history will be found in Milman's *Latin Christianity*, Book, ix., chapters ix., x., Neander's *Church History*, vol. vii. (Bohn's Stand. Lib.), Mrs. Oliphant's *Life of St. Francis of Assisi*, and Jessopp's *Coming of the Friars*.

For the condition of the social and religious life of the country reference may be made to *Letters of Bishop Grosseteste* (Ed. for the Rolls Series by H. R. Luard), and the *Life of St. Hugo* (Ed. by J. F. Dimock, for the same series). In Mr. Froude's *Short Studies on Great Subjects* there is a graphic sketch of Hugo, and there are other valuable papers bearing on the subject of monastic life and influence in England. William Langland's *Vision concerning Piers the Plowman* and Chaucer's *Canterbury Tales* and *Early English Homilies* (Ed. by Richard Morris for Early English Text Society), throw great light on the social condition of the times.

II.—THE WYCLIFFIAN REFORMATION.

(i.) *On the General History*.

W. Stubbs, *Constitutional History of England*.
J. R. Green, *History of the English People*.

(ii.) *Wycliffe's Life and Work*.

Contemporaneous references to Wycliffe appear in the writings of the chroniclers : Henry of Knighton, a canon of the abbey near Leicester; Walsingham, a monk of St. Albans; an anonymous chronicler, a monk of the same abbey, who wrote a *Chronicon Angliæ*, which extends from 1328 to 1388, edited by E. M. Thompson; and of Adam of Usk, a chronicler of events from 1377 to 1404, also edited by E. M. Thompson.

The *Fasciculi Zizaniorum* [*i.e.*, Little Bundles of Tares], ascribed to Thomas Netter, of Saffron Walden, and edited with a valuable introduction and notes by W. Shirley, for the Rolls Series, is of especial value as illustrative of the theological controversies of the times. Contemporary satire and popular sentiment are illustrated in *Political Poems and Songs*, edited by T. Wright. For the condition of the English peasantry and the circumstances that led to their revolt, see Thorold Rogers' *Six Centuries of Wages*.

For the study of Wycliffe's writings see list of his works on pp. 75—77. Mr. R. L. Poole's *Illustrations of the History of Mediæval Thought* contains an interesting chapter on Wycliffe's Doctrine of Lordship.

The influence of Wycliffe's teachings upon the Reformation movement in Bohemia is elaborately discussed in J. Loserth's *Wiclif and Hus*, translated by M. J. Evans.

Lechler's *John Wycliffe and his English Precursors*, translated and revised by P. Lorimer, is the standard authority for the biography of Wycliffe, with which should be read Montagu Burrows' *Wyclif's Place in History*.

(iii.) *On the Lollards.*

For interesting information, more especially with regard to the Lollards, see Pecock's *Repressor of over-much Blaming of the Clergy*, and its admirable introduction by C. Babington.

Foxe's *Acts and Monuments*.
Milman's *History of Latin Christianity*, Book xiii., chap. vii.
Summers, W. H., *The Lollards of Bucks*.

III.—On the Reformation Movement of the Sixteenth Century.

Blunt, J. H.—*Reformation of the Church of England*, 1514-47.
Burnet, Gilbert.—*History of the Reformation of the Church of England*. (Ed. by N. Pocock.)
Calendar of Letters and Papers of Reign of Henry VIII. (Ed. by J. S. Brewer and J. Gairdner.)
Cardwell, E.—*Documentary Annals of the Reformed Church of England*.
Cardwell, E.—*Synodalia*.
Collier, Jeremy.—*Ecclesiastical History of Great Britain*.
Foxe.—*Acts and Monuments* (Ed. by Pratt and Stoughton.)
Froude, J. A.—*History of England*. From Fall of Wolsey to Defeat of Spanish Armada.
Fuller, Thomas.—*Church History of Great Britain*.
Green, J. R.—*History of the English People*.
Hallam.—*Constitutional History of England*.
Heylyn, Peter.—*Ecclesia Restaurata*. (Ed. by J. C. Robertson.
Strype.—*Ecclesiastical Memorials*.
Stubbs.—*Lectures on Mediæval and Modern History*.
Tytler.—*England under Edward VI. and Mary*.
Zurich Letters. (Parker Society.)
Maitland, S. R.—*Essays on Subjects connected with the Reformation*.

On the Romanist Side.

Dodd, Charles.—*Church History of England*. (Ed. by M. A. Tierney.)

Lingard, John.—*History of England.*
Morris, John.—*Troubles of our Catholic Forefathers.*
Sanders.—*Rise and Growth of the Anglican Schism,* with Continuation by Rishton.

IV.—ON MORE SPECIAL SUBJECTS.

(i.) *Formularies of Faith and Liturgies.*

Cardwell, E.—*The Two Liturgies of King Edward Compared.*
Cardwell, E.—*History of Conferences on the Book of Common Prayer.*
Formularies of Faith put forth in the Reign of Henry VIII. (Oxford, 1825.)
Homilies appointed to be read in Churches.
Liturgies of Edward VI. (Parker Society.)
Private Prayers, put forth by Authority during the reign of Elizabeth. (Parker Society.)
Hardwick.—*History of the Articles of Religion.*
Maskell.—*Monumenta Ritualia Ecclesiæ Anglicanæ.*

(ii.) *History of the English Bible.*

Westcott.—*General View of History of English Bible.*
Edgar.—*Bibles of England.*

(iii.) *Biographies.*

Demaus.—*William Tindale,* the revised edition by R. Lovett, containing most interesting specimen fac-similes of the different editions of Tindale's Testaments and other books.
Demaus.—*Hugh Latimer.*
Hook.—*Lives of the Archbishops of Canterbury.*
McCrie.—*Life of John Knox.*
Seebohm.—*Oxford Reformers* (second edition).
Strype.—*Life of Archbishop Cranmer.*

(iv.) *Theology*

Works of the writers referred to; especially Luther's *Commentary on the Epistle to the Galatians,* Tindale's *Obedience of a Christian Man,* Latimer's *Sermons,* and Jewel's *Apology.*

INDEX.

Abbey lands restored, 252.
Act of Supremacy, 266.
Act of Uniformity, first, 184; second, 187; Elizabeth's, 267. [280.
Admonitions of Elizabeth,
Advertisements of Elizabeth, 282.
Albertus Magnus, 26.
Albigenses, the, 22; in England, 45.
Alexander of Hales, 26.
Allen, William, 293.
Altars, removal of, 186.
Alva, Duke of, 225. [140.
Annates, Acts concerning,
Anne, Queen, favours the Lollards, 78.
Anselm, 10.
Apology, Jewel's, 276. [140.
Appeals to Rome prohibited,
Area of persecution, 256.
Articles of Faith, the Forty-two, 187. [288.
Articles, the Thirty-nine,
Arundel, Archbishop, severity of, 81; at Oxford, 82.
Aske, Robert, revolt under, 146.
Askew, Anne, 153.
Assize of Clarendon, the, 44.
Augustine of Hippo, 17.
Augustinians, the, 17; their abbeys, 17.
Austin Friars, the, 27.
Babylonian Captivity of the Church, Luther's, 108.
Bacon, Roger, 26.
Badby, John, death of, 80.
Bagenall, Sir R., protest of, 227.
Bagley, Thomas, 86. [264.
Baine, Bishop, severity of,
Bale, John, his Brief Comedy, 173.
Ball, John, 49.
Barlow, Bishop, 275.
Barnardone, Francis, of Assisi, 21.
Barnes, prior, and Latimer, 125; before Wolsey, 126.
Baxter, Margery, 86.
Becket, Thomas, his character, 31; shrine of, 154.
Becon's Humble Supplication, 252.
Bedingfield, Sir Henry, 263.
Benedictines, the, 8; their rule, 9; eminent, 10.
Bentham, Thomas, 246.

Bernard of Clairvaux, 14.
Bernhes, Augustine, 246.
Berno of Clugny attempts reform, 11.
Bible, Wycliffe's, 72; ordered to be placed in every church, 164.
Biblical interpretation, 285.
Bilney, Thomas, 110; influence of, 120; troubles of, 126.
Bishops, Act for appointment of, 181.
Bishops against monasteries, 32.
Bishops' Bible, the, 278.
Black Book, the, 144.
Black Canons, the, 17.
Black Death, the, 47.
Black Friars, the, 23.
Blackfriars, council at, condemns Wycliffe, 71.
Black Monks, 10.
Blood of Hales, the, 153.
Bocher, Joan, 192.
Bolton Priory, 17.
Bonhommes, the, 18.
Bonner, treatment of, 192; his character, 230; sent to prison, 273.
Book of Martyrs, Foxe's, 277.
Boughton, Joan, 94. [218.
Bourne at St. Paul's Cross,
Bradford, John, preaching of, 211; trial of, 231.
Bradwardine, Thos., 30.
Breeches Bible, the, 249.
Brief Comedy of John Bale, 173.
Bristol, the plague in, 47.
Bruges, conference at, 67.
Bruno founds La Grand Chartreuse, 12.
Bucer, Martin, 203.
Calais, loss of, 253.
Campian, Edmund, 293.
Cambridge Reformers, the, 119. [255.
Canterbury martyrs, 236.
Canterbury Tales, The, 57-60.
Capital, conflict of, 49.
Cardigan, taper at, 153.
Carew, Sir Peter, revolt of, 223.
Carmelites, the, 26.
Carranza, Bartolomeo, 225; queen's confessor, 230.
Carthusians, the, 12; their rule, 12.
Cartwright, Thomas, 281.

Castro, Alphonso de, 226.
Catechism, Cranmer's first, 198; his second, 205; Nowell's, 290.
Catharists, the, 44.
Catholic rebellion, the, 291.
Catholic uprisings, 146.
Cecil, Sir William, 264.
Chaucer, Geoffrey, on the Friars, 28, 157; satires of, 57-60.
Cheke, Sir J., recantation of, 244.
Chichely, Archbishop, 85.
Church ales, 34.
Churches, destruction of, 33; abuses of, 34; visitation of, 177; destruction in, 178.
Circuitor, the, of Lewes, 11.
Cistercians, the, 13; rule of, 13; their abbeys, 14; character of, 15; influence of, 15. [90.
Claydon, John, his book,
Clement VII., 68.
Clergy, conflict with Friars, 27; character of, 33; submission of, 139; complaints against, 139; habits of, 178; allowed to marry, 183; and the Reformation, 271.
Clifford, Sir Lewis, 81.
Cluniac monks, 10; their rule, 11; their monasteries, 11. [82 85.
Cobham, Lord, history of,
Cole, Dr., and Cranmer, 243.
Colchester, martyrdoms at, 236.
Colet, John, at Oxford, 101; lectures of, 102; his influence, 102; at St. Paul's, 103; a Reformer, 103; founds St. Paul's School, 104; on Church reform, 107; charged with heresy, 108.
Colin Clout, Skelton's, 106.
Colleges, endowments of, appropriated, 181.
Commentary on the Galatians, Luther's, 168. [109.
Complutensian Polyglot, the,
Communion to be in both kinds, 188.
Communion Service in English, 198; changes in, 204, 270.

300

INDEX.

Conference of Romanists and Reformers at Westminster, 271.
Confessio Amantis, the, 60.
Confutation of the Apology, Harding's, 277.
Congé d'élire, the, 266.
Convocation, debates in, 221, 271, 281.
Council at Oxford, 44; at London and Winchelsea, 45; at Blackfriars, 71; at Oxford, 82; of Trent, 187.
Courtenay, Bishop, opposes Wycliffe, 67, 71.
Coverdale, his Bible, 134, 161; consecrates Parker, 275.
Cranmer, Thomas, promotion of, 131; marriage of, 131; on king's marriage, 131; character of, 132; Bible of, 164; his first catechism, 198; his connection with Prayer-Book, 202; his second catechism, 205; his *Reformatio Legum*, 206; trial of, 237; recantations of, 241; confession of, 245; death of, 245.
Cromwell, Thomas, 137; his Bible, 163; fall of, 164.
Crusades, the, 18.
Crutched Friars, the, 27.
Cursor Mundi, the, 72.
Day, Bishop, disobedience of, 187; deprivation of, 192.
Defence of the Apology, Jewel's, 277.
Despenser, Bishop, opposes Lollards, 80.
De Heretico Comburendo, statute of, 79.
Devil's mouse-trap, the, 35.
Disputation of Purgatory, Fryth's, 167.
Doctrines of Reformation, 281; eclecticism of, 284; authority of the Scriptures, 284; biblical interpretation, 285; justification by faith, 285; predestination, election, 287; the sacraments, 287; the future life, 288. [21.
Dominic Guzman of Osma,
Dominicans, the, character of, 22; land in England, 23; settlements of, 23; eminent, 26. [trine of, 66.
Dominion, Wycliffe's doctrine, the, and the Reformation, 172.
Duns Scotus, 26. [rule, 9.
Dunstan, Archbishop, his Eclecticism of Reformation, 284. [tribute, 65.
Edward III. refuses pope's

Edward VI., his youth, 177; his grammar schools, 183; closing years, 190; his death, 193; and Ridley, 210.
Election, 287.
Egmont, Count, 225.
Elizabeth, her early life, 263; her appearance and character, 263; crowned, 265; her Injunctions, 278; admonitions, 280; Advertisements, 282; and the Articles, 289; interrupts Nowell, 290; vigour of her rule, 291; excommunicated, 292.
Erasmus, his *Praise of Folly*, 104; Greek Testament, 108; his object in publishing it, 110.
Every Man, the drama, 173.
Examination of William Thorpe, 91.
Exeter, siege of, 185.
Exiled Protestants, 247.
Famine, 252.
Feckenham, last Abbot of Westminster, 265.
Ferrar, Bishop, 236.
Fisher, Bishop, death of, 142; his writings, 172.
First Blast against Women, Knox's, 250. [gars, 166.
Fish's *Supplication of Beggars*,
Fitzralph, Archbishop, 29.
Foliot, 43.
Forty-two Articles, the, 187.
Foule, Thomas, 246.
Foxe's *Book of Martyrs*, 277.
Francis Barnardone, of Assisi, 21.
Franciscans, the, character of, 22; tertiaries, 23; land in England 23; settlement of, 24; at Abingdon, 24; mission of, 24; increase of, 25; eminent, 26.
Frankfort troubles, the, 247.
Friars, institution of, 21; founders, 21; characters of, 22; land in England, 23; increase of, 25; eminent at the universities, 26; fresh orders, 26; privileges of, 27; conflict with clergy, 27; degeneracy, 27; abuses of, 28; their preaching, 29; pedlars, 29; opponents of, 29; conversions of, 45; denounced by Wycliffe, 70; at Wycliffe's sick-bed, 70.
Fryth, John, arrest of, 133; death of, 134; his *Disputation of Purgatory*, 167.
Future life, the, 288.

Gardiner, treatment of, 192; made chancellor, 218; *True Obedience*, 229; his character, 229; death of, 229. [cliffe, 67.
Gaunt, John of, and Wy-
Geneva Bible, the, 249. [43.
German weavers, arrest of,
Gilbertines, the, 17.
Gilby, Anthony, 249.
Gilpin, Bernard, sermon of, 191; his preaching, 213.
Goodman, Christopher, book by, 251.
Gower, John, 60.
Grammar schools of Edward VI., 183.
Great Abjuration, the, 95.
Great Bible, the, 163.
Great Schism, the, 68.
Greek Testament of Erasmus, 108.
Gregory XI., death of, 68.
Grey, Lady Jane, 217.
Grey Friars, the, 24.
Grosseteste, Robert, his character and labours, 37–39.
Guilds, social, 182.
Guzman, Dominic, 21.
Harding, Stephen, founds Cistercian order, 13.
Harding's *Confutation of the Apology*, 277.
Harley, Bishop, 240.
Harlots, the, 45.
Heath, Bishop, disobedience of, 187; deprivation of, 192, 273.
Henry II., conflict with clergy, 31; flogging of, 43.
Henry III. orders arrest of all apostatizing Friars, 45.
Henry V. at Badby's martyrdom, 81; and Cobham, 83.
Henry VIII. marries Anne Boleyn, 131; question of his divorce, 132; character of, 136; his *Necessary Doctrine*, 151; excommunicated, 155; his Seven Sacraments, 168.
Hereford, Nicholas, excommunicated, 72; work on the Bible, 73.
High Commission Court appointed, 266.
Hodgkin, Bishop, 275.
Homilies, old, 35.
Homilies, Book of, 197; second, 200.
Hooper, Bishop, opposes Prayer-Book, 202; his preaching, 209; trial of, 231; death of, 233.
Hugo, Bishop of Lincoln, a Carthusian, 12; his character, 37. [con's, 252.
Humble Supplication, Be-

INDEX.

Humphrey, Laurence, 281.
Hunter, William, 236. [280.
Hymn-Book, Reformation,
Indulgences, Act against, 138.
Injunctions, the, 177; concerning the clergy, 178; Divine service, 179; the poor, 179. [278.
Injunctions of Elizabeth, *Institution of a Christian Man*, the, 150.
Islington, arrest of a congregation at, 254.
'Jesus ship,' the, 247.
Jewel, John, recantation of, 241; *Apology* of, 276; his *Defence*, 277; on the Articles, 290.
Joye, George, his New Testament, 157; translates *Primer*, 195.
Justification by faith, 285.
Ket, Robert, 185. [260.
King, Bishop, clemency of, *King of Breeme, The*, 91.
Kitchin, Bishop, conforms, 272.
Knight, Stephen, 236.
Knights Hospitallers, 18.
Knights Templars, 19; their round churches, 20.
Knox, John, preaching of, 212; and Tunstall, 212; his *First Blast against Women*, 250.
Labour, conflict of, 49.
La Grande Chartreuse, 12.
Lancaster, Duke of, and Wycliffe, 67.
Lanfranc, 10.
Langham, Archbishop, 49.
Langland, William, history of, 52 ; his *Vision of Piers the Plowman*, 52–56.
Lantern, The, 90.
Lasco, John à, 204. [48.
Last Age of the Church, The,
Latimer preaches before Bishop West, 125 ; Prior Barnes, 125 ; before Wolsey, 126; fame of, 129 ; letter to the king, 130; weakness of, 130; convocation sermon, 148; pleads for Malvern Abbey, 156 ; on his father, 185 ; his preaching, 208; sent to the Tower, 218; trial of, 238; death of, 239.
Lawrence of Beauvais, in England, 24.
Lawrence, Martin, 236.
Ledbury, execution of, 50.
Leg, ruffianism of, 50.
Lever, Thomas, preaching of, 212.
Lewes martyrs, 237.
Lewes Priory, 11.

Lily, Wm., master of St. Paul's School, 104.
Litany published in English, 197.
Lollards, the, 78 ; creed of, 78 ; suppression of, 79 ; first martyrs, 80 ; decrease of, 81 ; revolt of, 84; clerical, 85 ; recantations, 86; literature of, 87; prayer of, 90 ; Pecock on, 93 ; renewed persecution, 94 ; the Great Abjuration, 95 ; in Henry VIII.'s reign, 96 ; extent of, 96 ; connected with Reformation, 96 ; laws against restored, 228.
London, plague in, 47 ; state of, under Mary, 224.
Longland, Bishop, on heretics, 96.
Luther's *Babylonian Captivity*, 168 ; on *Galatians*, 168 ; on the sacraments, 287.
Lutterworth, Wycliffe at, 67.
Map, Walter, poems of, 33.
Martyr, Peter, 203.
Mary, popularity of, 217 ; crowned, 220 ; marriage of, 222, 224 ; her entry into London, 226 ; last years of, 252 ; death of, 255 ; Protestant sufferings in her reign, 255. [Friars, 25.
Matthew of Paris on the
Matthew's Bible, 161.
Military orders, the, 18.
Minorites, the, 22.
Miracle plays, 34.
Monasteries, causes of their destruction, 3; fashion of founding, 6 ; Benedictine, 8; Cluniac, 11 ; Carthusian, 12 ; Cistercian, 14; bishops against, 32 ; and benefices, 32; heresy in, 45 ; suppression of, 117, 143, 153.
Monks, good work of, 4; deterioration of, 5.
More, Sir T., his *Utopia*, 113 ; death of, 143; his *Supplication of Beggars* 167 ; his reply to Tindale, 170.
Necessary Doctrine, King Henry VIII.'s, 151. [157.
New Testament of Tindale,
Norbert founds White Canons, 17.
Northumberland, Duke of, made protector, 186 ; recantation of, 219.
Nowell, catechism of, 290; and Elizabeth, 290.
Oath of Supremacy refused, 272.

Obedience of a Christian Man, Tindale's, 169.
Occleve, Thomas, 61.
Oglethorp, Bishop, 265.
Oldcastle, Sir John, history of, 82–85.
Orders in England, 10.
Oxford in Wycliffe's time, 65; Wycliffe at, 73 ; Reform at, 101 ; Colet at, 102 ; the Reformers at, 118.
Papacy, the, power of, 43.
Parable of the Wicked Mammon, Tindale's, 169. [275.
Parker made archbishop,
Parliament, petitions for limitations on prosecuting heresy, 82 ; the Reformation, 137 ; of Edward VI., 180 ; Mary's reactionary, 220 ; petitions against Mary's marriage, 223 ; Bagenall's protest in, 227 ; Elizabeth's, 265.
Peasant Revolt, the, 50 ; Wycliffe at, 70.
Peasantry, condition of, 7.
Peckham, Archbishop, register of, 35.
Pecock, bishop, his position, 93 ; recantation of, 94.
Peres the Ploughman's Crede, 91.
Philip of Spain, marriage of, 224; comes to London, 225 ; at war with the papacy, 253. [of, 52–56.
Piers the Plowman, Vision
Pigott, William, 236. [146.
Pilgrimage of Grace, the,
Plague, the great, 47 ; mortality, 47 ; effects of, 48.
Ploughman's Prayer, The, 89.
Ploughman's Tale, The, 92.
Pole, Reginald, his writings, 145, 172; made archbishop, 236 ; death of, 255.
Politic Power of Poynet, 251.
Pollanus, 204.
Poll-tax, the, 50.
Poor Caitiff, The, 89.
Poor Priests, the, 69 ; suppression of, 71.
Poynet's Catechism, 205 ; *Politic Power*, 251.
Practice of Prelates, Tindale's, 171. [17.
Præmonstratensians, the,
Praise of Folly, The, 104 ; effect of, 105.
Prayer-Book, revised, issue of, 187; first reformed, 199 ; peculiarities of, 200 ; excellences of, 201 ; Cranmer's connection with, 202; unfavourable reception of, 202 ; the second, 203 ; its changes, 204 ; abo-

lished, 221; Elizabeth's and Edward VI.'s compared, 267; favourably received, 271.
Preachers, mediæval, 35.
Preaching Brothers, the, 22.
Preaching, Reformation, 207.
Predestination, 287.[*The*, 48.
Pricke of the Conscience,
Primers, pre-Reformation, 195; reformed, 195. [295.
Private Prayer, Book of,
Protector, the, a Protestant, 177; unpopularity and death of, 186.
Protestant persecutions, 293.
Publinica or Paulicians, the, 44. [283.
Puritans, first use of name,
Purvey, John, his revision of the Bible, 73, 87; recantation of, 81.
Readers, order of, 276.
Reconciliation of England to Rome, 226; never satisfied, 228. [the, 226.
Reconciliation Parliament, *Reformatio Legum*, Cranmer's, 206. [the, 137-143.
Reformation Parliament,
Regular Canons, the, 17.
Rents, rise in, 184.
Repyndon, Philip, excommunicated, 72; a persecutor, 81.
Revolts, east and west, 185.
Richard of Hampole, poem of, 48.
Ridley, learning of, 210; preaching of, 210; sent to the Tower, 218; trial of, 238; death of, 239.
Roger of Worcester, 43.
Rogers, John, Bible of, 161; preaching of, 211; trial of, 231; death of, 232.
Rood of Boxley, 153.
Rough, John, 213, 246.
Round churches, 20. [141.
Royal supremacy, Act of,
Sacraments, the, 287.
St. Giles's Fields, Lord Cobham at, 84.
St. Michael's, Bishop's Stortford, extracts from registers of, 187, 221.
St. Paul's in Pre-Reformation times, 34; Wycliffe in, 67; Barnes's penance in, 125.
St. Paul's Cross, preaching at, 208; Ridley and Rogers at, 211; Bourne at, 218.
St. Saviour's, Southwark, trial in, 231.

St. Thomas', Exeter, body of vicar of, exposed, 185.
Salisbury, Bishop of, his pliancy, 261.
Salisbury, Earl of, 81.
Sampson, Thomas, 281
Samson, Thomas, 249.
Saunders, Lawrence, trial of, 231; his death, 232.
Sawtre, Wm., death of, 80.
Scambles, Edward, 246.
Scorey, recantation of, 241; consecrates Parker, 275.
Scriptures, the, authority of, 284.
Seminary priests, the, 293.
Serfs, emancipation of, 48.
Service-books, Pre-Reformation, 196.
Seven Sacraments, Henry VIII.'s, 168.
Shepherd's Calendar, *The*, 91.
Shrines, destruction of, 154.
Six Articles, Act of, 152; repeal of, 180.
Skelton's *Colin Clout*, 166.
Skilley, John, 86.
Smithfield, the place of martyrdom, 81.
Somerset House, 181.
Soto, Pedro de, 228.
Speculum Meditantes, Gower's, 60. [190.
Spoliation, a visitation of,
Suffolk, Earl of, revolt of, 223. [Fish's, 166.
Supplication of Beggars,
Supplication of Souls, More's, 167.
Tables used instead of stone altars, 186.
Taverner's Bible, 162.
Taylor, Rowland, preaching of, 213; trial of, 231; death of, 234.
Taylor, William, 85.
Ten Articles, the, 149.
Tertiaries, the, 23.
Teutonic Knights, 20. [289.
Thirty-nine Articles, the,
Thomas Aquinas, 26.
Thorpe, Wm., 91.
Tindale, William, history of, 122; death of, 134; his New Testament, 157; his *Obedience of a Christian man*, 169; his *Parable of the Wicked Mammon*, 169; his influence as a Reformer, 171; his *Practice of Prelates*, 171.
Treason Act, the, 142.
Trialogus, Wycliffe's, 69.
True Obedience, Gardiner's, 229.
Tunstall, buys Tindale's Testaments, 158; depri-

vation of, 192; and Knox 212.
Tyler, revolt of, 50.
Tylsworth, Wm., 95.
Unity of the Church, Pole's, 115.
Urban V. demands arrears of tribute, 65.
Urban VI., 68. [113.
Utopia of Sir T. More,
Van Parre, 193.
Vestments, 279, 282.
Villa Garcia, John de, 243.
Visitation of the churches, 177; one of spoliation, 190.
Vox Clamantis, Gower's, 60.
Waldenses, the, in Kent, 45.
Walsingham Abbey, 17.
Wars of the Roses, 93.
Welbeck Abbey, 17.
Westminster Abbey, Feast of Reconciliation in, 227.
White Canons, the, 17.
White Friars, the, 26.
White House, the, at Cambridge, 120.
White Monks, 15.
White, William, 85.
Whittingham's New Testament, 249. [*Benefices*, 88.
Why Poor Priests have no Wicket, The, 88.
William of Occam, 26.
William of Shoreham translates the psalms, 72.
William of Wykeham, a judge of Wycliffe, 67.
Wolsey, Cardinal, as a Reformer, 114; suppresses monasteries, 117; fall of, 117; his policy towards heretics, 121.
Wyatt, Sir Thos., revolt of, 223.
Wycliffe, John, as a Reformer, 62; his influence, 62; a patriot, 65; doctrine of lordship, 66; a royal commissioner at Bruges, 67; first attack on, at St. Paul's, 67; at Lambeth, 68; attacks transubstantiation in *Trialogus*, 69; denounces Friars, 70; condemned, at Blackfriars,' 71; translates Bible, 72; influence of, 73; last public appearance at Oxford, 73; last years, 74; his doctrine, 74; list of his works, 75; his followers, 78; *The Wicket*, 88; *Why Poor Priests have no Benefices*, 88; *Tracts for Priests*, 88.
Zwingli on the Sacraments, 287.

www.ingramcontent.com/pod-product-compliance
Lightning Source LLC
Chambersburg PA
CBHW030737230426
43667CB00007B/752